# BRITISH COLUMBIA

For Anne and Mark Thompson.
Anne prints beautiful books and makes interesting images;
I hope that she'll like this book and these images.
And Mark always has a grin and a hug for his dad. — JHT

# BRITISH COLUMBIA

## Land of Promises

By Patricia E. Roy and John Herd Thompson

*The*

*Illustrated*

*History*

*of*

*Canada*

OXFORD
UNIVERSITY PRESS

## OXFORD
UNIVERSITY PRESS

70 Wynford Drive, Don Mills, Ontario M3C 1J9
www.oup.com/ca

Oxford University Press is a department of the University of Oxford.
It furthers the University's objective of excellence in research, scholarship,
and education by publishing worldwide in

*Oxford   New York*
*Auckland   Cape Town   Dar es Salaam   Hong Kong   Karachi   Kuala Lumpur*
*Madrid   Melbourne   Mexico City   Nairobi   New Delhi   Taipei   Toronto*

With offices in
*Argentina   Austria   Brazil   Chile   Czech Republic   France   Greece*
*Guatemala   Hungary   Italy   Japan   Poland   Portugal   Singapore*
*South Korea   Switzerland   Thailand   Turkey   Ukraine   Vietnam*

Oxford is a trade mark of Oxford University Press
in the UK and in certain other countries

Published in Canada
by Oxford University Press

**Library and Archives Canada Cataloguing in Publication**

Roy, Patricia, 1939–
    British Columbia : land of promises / by Patricia E. Roy and John Herd Thompson.

(Illustrated history of Canada)
Includes bibliographical references and index.
ISBN 0-19-541048-3

    1. British Columbia—History. I. Thompson, John Herd, 1946- II.

Title. III. Series.

FC3811.R688 2005          971.1          C2004-906895-4

Cover and text design: Brett Miller
Cover image: Edward Roper, 'A Prairie Schooner on the Cariboo Road', oil on paper mounted on board, *c.* 1887.
Library and Archives Canada, Acc. No R9266-549, Peter Winkworth Collection of Canadiana.

This book is printed on permanent (acid-free) paper ∞.
Printed in Canada

# TABLE OF CONTENTS

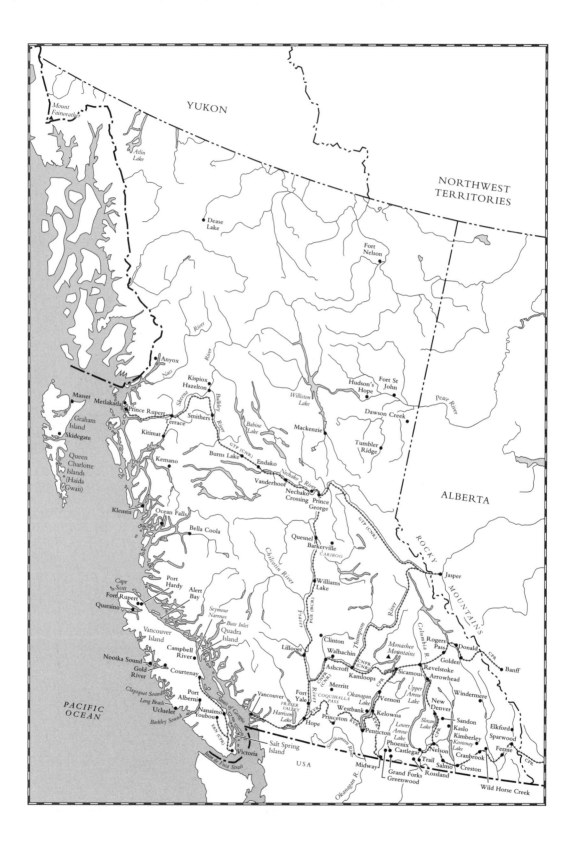

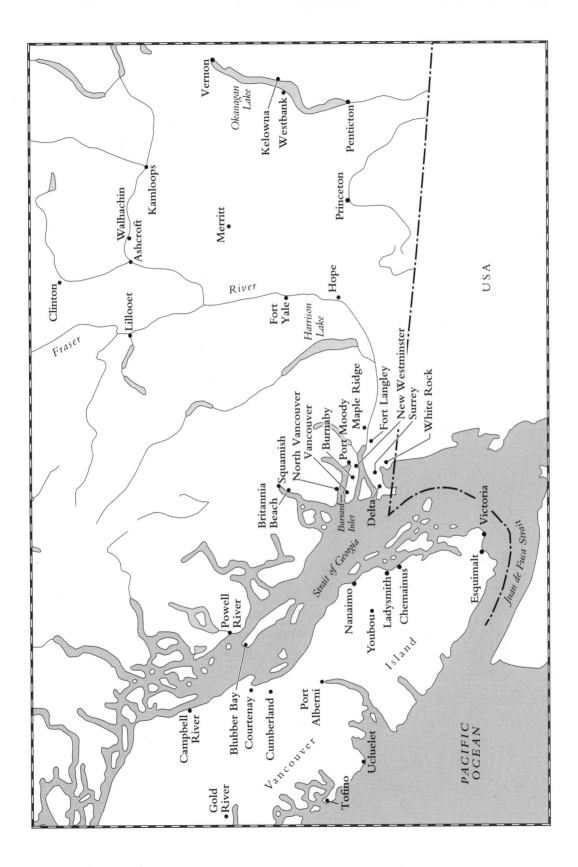

# MAPS

# ABBREVIATIONS

BCA: British Columbia Archives, Victoria, BC

*BCSP*: Province of British Columbia Sessional Papers

CPA: Canadian Press Picture Archive, Toronto, ON

D&M: Douglas and McIntyre

Glenbow: Glenbow–Alberta Institute, Calgary, AB

McCord: The McCord Museum of Canadian History, Montreal, QC

M&S: McClelland and Stewart

MQUP: McGill–Queen's University Press

NAC: National Archives of Canada, Ottawa, ON

NFB: National Film Board Still Photography Division

ROM: Royal Ontario Museum, Toronto, ON

Stark: Stark Museum of Art, Orange, TX

SFU: Simon Fraser University Library Editorial Cartoons Collection, Burnaby, BC

UBCP: University of British Columbia Press

UTP: University of Toronto Press

VPL: Vancouver Public Library, Special Collections, Vancouver, BC

# INTRODUCTION

❧

# Portraying a Province

This volume is the fifth in a series of six regional histories that together make up the Oxford *Illustrated History of Canada*.[1] The premise of the series—that six regional volumes might add up to one national story—reveals an assumption that many Canadians share. When Oxford University Press convened six historians in 1994 to plan the volumes, none of us questioned this assumption, and none of us noted how uniquely Canadian our new project was. What other country's historians would conceive of creating a comprehensive narrative of their nation state by chopping it up into its subnational components? Of course other countries have had multi-volume histories written about them. But those works are shaped by chronology. Were Oxford to commission a multi-volume Illustrated History of Britain, Mexico, or the United States, the editors would assign the volumes to the authors by time periods, and each volume would consider the nation state as a whole during the period assigned. In the case of the US, for example, a series of regional histories of New England, the Mid-Atlantic States, the South, the Midwest, the Great Plains, and the Pacific West is entirely conceivable. But Oxford University Press would never pretend it was a 'national' history of the country as a whole; nor would its title be *The Illustrated History of the United States*, but rather *The Illustrated History of America's Regions*.

Like the series in which it appears, this volume suggests how implicitly contemporary historians of Canada accept as legitimate the 'limited identity' of region—to use the term coined by Ramsay Cook and popularized by J.M.S. Careless.[2] Thus we must make clear at the outset that neither of us considers British Columbia (or any of Canada's regions) to be 'essential' or 'ontological'. Scholars such as Patricia Limerick, an authority on the American West, argue persuasively that regions and the regional identities that go with them are 'constructed' or 'invented', and are 'much more the creation of human thought and behaviour than they are products of nature'.[3] British Columbia is more than an intellectual construct, of course; as our cover image suggests, a 'sea of mountains' has disconnected it physically, and in some ways psychologically, from the rest of Canada. The diverse peoples who have lived in British Columbia belonged to many other 'imagined communities': the British Empire, North America, Canada, their region within the province, or their locality within that region.[4] These multiple geographic identities are not mutually exclusive. British Columbians can think and act as British Columbians. Yet, despite a long tradition of 'regional alienation', in critical situations they have been Canadians first and British Columbians second.

Furthermore, region is not by any means the only 'limited identity' that British Columbians have lived: among the others are race and ethnicity, gender, class, and generation. Assisted by the torrent of social history on these subjects over the past two decades, we've done our best to represent these identities and to suggest how they intersect with each other and with regional identity. Readers will note, however, that the chapter organization follows the contours of the chronology of 'great events': the creation of the colony, the completion of the transcontinental railway, the two world wars, the pivotal election of 1972. We offer no apology for making a central theme of what social historians sometimes dismiss as 'high politics'. In the history of British Columbia, the struggle for power is no secondary phenomenon: it has been a very real contest over the development of resources and the distribution of wealth.

We hope that this book will complement the standard history of the province, Jean Barman's *The West Beyond the West*,[5] but we would not presume to supplant it. We would naturally be delighted (as would our publisher) if our colleagues were to adopt this book for their history classes; to that end, we've included a bibliographic essay and an abundance of notes. We hope also to lure the elusive bookshop browser. Still, this is emphatically not another salvo in the 'barrage of photo-books, illustrated histories, coffee-table volumes, jack-daws, and pictorial compilations devoted to . . . British Columbia'[6] that the photo archivist Joan M. Schwartz was

already regretting a quarter-century ago.[7] With a handful of significant exceptions, such books run the gamut from the shallow to the truly dreadful. All too often the images they offer are 'selected with haste and indifference', 'tenuously related to the text', and published with 'inadequate captions'—unattributed, undated, or both. Sometimes an image is purported to show something quite different from its actual subject. In one case Doukhobor women in an obvious Saskatchewan setting were relocated to the Kootenays. In another, an editor unfamiliar with BC history correctly identified two ships in a single photograph: one was the legendary *Beaver*, the workhorse of the Hudson's Bay Company's coastal fleet in the nineteenth century; the other, one of the Canadian Pacific Railway's trans-Pacific *Empress* liners. Such an image might have made a very neat illustration for a discussion of changing trade patterns and technology. The problem was that the *Beaver* went aground at Vancouver's First Narrows three years before the first *Empress* entered the harbour. In short, the symbolic photograph was the product of a photographer's imaginative retouching.

Like popular historians, academic historians tend to use images as 'illustrations' rather than as sources in their own right. (And the title of the present series, The Illustrated History of Canada, perhaps contributes more to the problem than to a solution.) A scholar who digs hard and deep for documents may spend only a few minutes selecting images. At the Vancouver Public Library, only about 80,000 of the 250,000 images in the collections are catalogued; archivists at the National Archives of Canada estimate that the card catalogue contains only about 2 per cent of the two million images in the collection. Yet historians rarely pull on the white gloves and study nega-

'A trans-Pacific steamer passes the *Beaver*', Burrard Inlet, by Harry T. Devine. Two kinds of evidence, documentary and visual, suggest that this photograph is a fake. First, we know that the HBC's *Beaver* ran aground in 1888—three years before the first Empress liner sailed from Vancouver. Second, the water around the *Beaver* looks quite different from the water elsewhere in the image, and its mast and smokestack appear to have been superimposed on the background. VPL, 3600.

tives at a light table. Like the compilers of picture books, academic historians often choose images for their aesthetic appeal rather than the historical evidence they may convey—the equivalent of choosing to cite a written document simply because it was written with elegant penmanship on fine vellum! Historians who painstakingly document their manuscript sources will routinely present an image with only a terse caption and a general credit to the repository. The reference number—indispensable to anyone who wants to follow the trail of the image—appears only rarely, and the name of the creator and a discussion of the circumstances of the image's creation more rarely still. Imagine the opprobrium that would be heaped on an historian who cited a manuscript source as simply a 'letter in the National Archives of Canada'.[8]

Yet it should be possible for text-oriented historians to use images just as effectively as they do written sources. They need to search just as diligently for images as they do for written documents, and then ask the same questions of each image that they would ask of any document: not just what it tells us, but who created it, for what purpose, when, and under what circumstances. To ask these questions of an image requires some knowledge of the theory and history of image-making, but there is no dearth of studies available to serve as guides; several useful works are cited in the notes to this volume, and our discussions of the images reproduced here offer numerous examples of ways in which images can be interrogated.

In the case of this book, virtually all the pictures were created by men, and virtually all those men were of European background, especially British.[9] The images created by the dominant British-Canadian males became the dominant images. Members of elites, in British Columbia as elsewhere, rarely made pictures themselves. Instead, people of means, corporations, and governments employed others to do so. Some people sketched, painted, and photographed as part of their jobs, whether in the military, the civil service, or the private sector; others were small businessmen who hired out their image-making services and from time to time might see their work circulate internationally in the form of postcards. The idea of art for art's sake rarely entered the equation.[10] Nor did the prospect of documenting reality for the benefit of future historians.[11] The ethnic, class, and gender perspectives of these artists and photographers were often reflected in their work. Images of British Columbia's ethnic and racial diversity abound— Native people were especially popular subjects—

but the men, women, and children of the exotic 'other' are depicted almost exclusively through the eyes of British-Canadian painters and photographers. Gender representation poses a similar problem. The striking absence of Euro-Canadian women in images until quite recently can be explained by the fact that BC's population was overwhelmingly male in the early days; in fact, males predominated until the mid-twentieth century. Thus many pictures depict only men, and when men and women do appear together, often the men are engaged in some activity while the women stand by and watch. This pattern may not have had much to do with 'real life', but it did reflect socially defined gender roles: male photographers privileged men's public sphere over women's private one.

Artists and photographers seldom explored working-class subject matter. The NAC catalogue drawer that contains 'Industries-Mineral-Coal' has a dozen photos of coal mines for every one of coal miners. Technology had something to do with this, of course: it was not easy to get adequate light inside a mine. Similarly, the almost complete absence of working-class women from the photographic record can be explained in part by the difficulty of lighting interiors. Photos of working-class men, for their part, tend to depict what Bryan Palmer describes as 'a class frozen at work, at play, or on parade', contorted by the camera into 'inevitable passivity'.[12] Yet rather than reject these imperfect, biased images of race, ethnicity, gender, and class, historians must search for the meaning in the biases themselves, just as they would with elite-created written sources.

The images reproduced here fall into three broad categories: maps, documentary art, and photographs. Changes in technique, technology, and taste mean that particular periods produced particular types of images, and that some periods yield many more images than others. Virtually all eighteenth-century European marine expeditions to the Northwest Pacific coast had scientific dimensions and made room for artists, who created a large corpus of drawings and paintings. Fur traders, however, travelled in canoes, not ships, and cared more about profits than pictures. Thus we have very few images of the European–Aboriginal encounters in the interior. Until the 1850s, every image made of the Northwest Pacific coast took the form of documentary art; thereafter, many are photographs. Both the numbers and the quality of photographs increased rapidly as the technology evolved from the cumbersome and costly wet-plate collodion process to dry-plate and eventually to film used in small cameras that made photography available to the masses. Despite this democratization, most of the photos held in archives are the work of professional photographers. Archival sources tend to dry up around 1970. As a result, most of the images in our final chapter were created by either news photographers or editorial cartoonists (for whom the strange twists of BC politics have provided a wealth of material).

At first glance, documentary art may appear to be less reliable than photography as historical evidence. An example of unreliable artwork accompanied the published version of one of Premier W.A.C. Bennett's budget speeches. It showed a picture of beautifully manicured landscape and brightly coloured flowers around a brand-new building of the University of Victoria, even though at the time the 'garden' was actually a swamp. But photographs do not necessarily tell greater truths than sketches or paint-

'The Bowman—Nootka'. Determined to document the 'vanishing Indian', the American Edward S. Curtis (1868–1952) published more than 2,000 photographs of Aboriginal people from groups including the Kwakwaka'wakw, Nuu-chah-nulth, and Haida. Curtis himself staged scenes like this one in order to appeal to the market for romantic nostalgia. Apparently his subjects often laughed at the costumes and poses he invented for them. Yet Curtis believed that his work had value as historical documentation. See Daniel Francis, *Copying People: Photographing British Columbia First Nations, 1860–1940* (Saskatoon and Calgary: Fifth House, 1996), 49. NAC, C-20823.

ings. Precisely because they seem to provide incontrovertible proof, photographs can distort far more effectively than either documentary art or the written word. The first edition of *The Art of Retouching* appeared in 1880, and computer software makes it easy for the rankest amateur to doctor photos; a chapter in *Photoshop For Dummies* is titled 'Making a Mockery of Reality'. Similarly, hundreds of celebrated 'candid' photographs have in fact been staged.[13] The best BC examples are the carefully posed photos of Aboriginal men and women created in the early twentieth century by Edward S. Curtis. Charitably, these images could be described as 're-enactments'; uncharitably, they are simply fakes. 'Photographs may not lie,' the American photographer Lewis Hine liked to say, but 'liars may photograph.' Beyond the obvious point, Hine's aphorism also has a deeper, subtler, meaning. However honest photographers may be, they remove their subjects from context and manipulate meaning through their choices of viewpoint, lighting, and composition.[14]

Choosing a title for this volume was not easy. One possibility we considered was 'Empires on the Pacific'. The theme of empire would have been appropriate for the century before Confederation, when five empires—Spanish, French, Russian, American, and British—competed for control of northwest North America. The maps, paintings, drawings, and eventually photographs created by the servants of those empires were weapons in the competition as surely as the ships' guns and the diplomats' words. Native people cooperated and contested with the European intruders, and the great 'sea otter' chiefs—Maquinna of the Nuu-chah-nulth, Legaic of the Tsimshian, and Cuneah of the Haida—built fur-trade empires of their own. The word 'empire' recurs throughout historical accounts of the Hudson's Bay Company, and when the HBC's influence waned, Vancouver Island and British Columbia became 'outposts of Empire'. After Confederation, government and railway propaganda wooed immigrants and investors to BC

with variations on the theme of imperial destiny following a star that was moving inexorably westward. The idea of empire continued to resonate well into the twentieth century. As BC Premier T.D. Pattullo boasted to Prime Minister R.B. Bennett in the midst of the Great Depression: 'we are an empire in ourselves and our hills and valleys are stored with potential wealth that makes us one of the greatest assets of our Dominion.'[15] By mid-century, however, the connotations attached to the word had changed dramatically, and the empires most relevant to BC were the ones under construction by giant corporations.

Another possible theme for our title was the province's motto, 'Splendor Sine Occasu' (Splendour without diminishment). But we soon realized that, from the beginning, what has drawn so many people to the province is not 'splendour' in itself but the promise of it—the promise of wealth, the promise of a better life. We also realized that in many respects the province's splendour has been severely diminished. For many people—First Nations, native-born, or newcomer—British Columbia has been a land of promises unfulfilled.[16] While British Columbians have often enjoyed prosperity, their long dependence on primary industries and international markets has made them painfully vulnerable to economic downturns. We cannot know what the distant ancestors of today's First Nations expected to find in the land that became British Columbia. But there is no doubt about later arrivals. The Canadian and European fur traders, the 'Argonauts' of the 1850s and 1860s, the prospectors and miners of the 1890s—all expected to find their fortunes. A few even came in the hope of establishing utopias: the Danes at Cape Scott, the Finns at Sointula, the Doukhobors in the West Kootenay and Boundary districts, the 'hippies' who found havens in the Kootenays and the coastal islands.

British Columbia dashed many of those expectations. At the turn of the twentieth century, the adventure writer Matthew Baillie-Grohman commented that, for British investors, BC had 'the name of being the land of unfulfilled promises'.[17] The settlers who took up lands wholly unsuited for agriculture, or the jobless men who came looking for work in the 1930s and found themselves forced into government camps, would have agreed with him. Although wages in BC have always been among the highest in Canada, in many cases there has been a good reason: difficult and dangerous working conditions, or frequent bouts of unemployment. Early in the twentieth century, R.P. Pettipiece, a migrant from Ontario who was active in the labour movement, observed that the province was 'full of discontented people who, like myself, came here to get away from existing circumstances . . . it is of no use.'[18]

Yet some have found exactly what they sought in British Columbia, and even among those who have not, some have undoubtedly found compensations that they could never have imagined. The proof is in the numbers of people who continue to make their way to the province, from across Canada and around the world. British Columbia continues to hold out the promise of a better life.

We offer our thanks to the many people who have helped us create this book. Photo archivists at the National Archives of Canada, the BC Archives, the Canadian Press Photo archives, the Glenbow–Alberta Institute, and the Vancouver Public Library have been particularly helpful. Historians seeking image sources are now blessed with wonderful web-based resources. We are grateful to the many unacknowledged workers who have digitized the hundreds of thousands of images that appear on the websites of the archival repositories that we have drawn upon. Although we have done original research on the subjects in which we specialize, a book like this must be built on the work of dozens of other scholars. We ask these historians, political scientists, anthropologists, sociologists, geographers, and literary scholars to accept our endnotes as thank-you notes for their books and articles. Paige Raibmon helped two non-specialists in Aboriginal history make sense of the most rapidly expanding sub-field in BC historical writing. Jan Ewald listened carefully to John's half-baked ideas and often offered fully baked alternatives. Duke University helped with modest grants to support our work. Heather McAsh, Chris Wilkins, and Andrew Zabrovsky worked effectively as research assistants. Aqila Coulthurst's software skills made long-ago newspaper pages legible. If there are problems with the book, they are not the fault of any of these people, or of our editors—the ever patient Laura Macleod and Sally Livingston.

Collaboration through the long process of writing was aided immeasurably by the modern miracles of e-mail and the 'track changes' feature of MS-Word. John Thompson collected most of the images, prepared the captions for most of them, and wrote the first drafts of the introduction and Chapters 1, 2, and 6; Patricia Roy wrote the first drafts of Chapters 3, 4, and 5 and the Suggestions for Further Reading. But neither of us can claim even a paragraph as uniquely our own.

Patricia E. Roy and John Herd Thompson

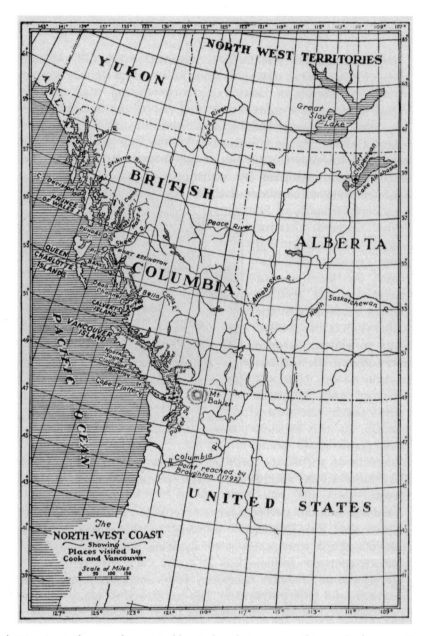

'The North-West Coast, Showing Places visited by Cook and Vancouver'. This was the first map that BC school-children encountered in Arthur Anstey's *The Romance of British Columbia* (Toronto: Gage and Co., 1927), which was an approved supplementary text for Grade 7 and 8 Social Studies from 1927 to 1937. Today no textbook would begin as this one does, with 'the arrival of the first white man to visit British Columbia, the great navigator, Captain James Cook'. Even so, it has one advantage over most of its modern counterparts. Whereas modern maps of BC generally show only the area contained within current political boundaries, this one sets the province in the broader context of northwestern North America as a whole.

The four corners of British Columbia— Mount Fairweather in the northeast, the Peace River Valley in the northwest, Moyie Lake in the southeast, and Long Beach in the southwest, on Vancouver Island—suggest the province's remarkably diverse physical geography. *Above*: Mount Fairweather, May 1999, photo by Fred Touche. *Below*: The Peace River Valley, fall 2003, photo by Abhay Minha. *Overleaf above*: Moyie Lake, October 1997, photo by Don Wilson, www.crowsnest-highway.ca. *Overleaf below*: Long Beach, summer 1978, photo by David Wasserman.

# CHAPTER ONE

# Contesting Empires: Prehistory to 1858

*W*here in historic time and geographic space does British Columbia begin? Different writers have chosen different starting points. Liz Bryan begins her story 'about four and a half billion years ago when a cloud of gas and primordial dust began to coalesce'. Geoffrey Molyneux leaps back twelve millennia in his opening chapter, '10,000 BC to 1871'. Margaret Ormsby began her classic history of the province more modestly, with the geography that eighteenth-century Europeans encountered as they sailed along the Pacific coastline or trekked overland across the Rockies. For her part, Jean Barman weaves the words of nineteenth- and twentieth-century witnesses into a poetic catalogue of ten geographic regions within the modern province, before looking back to introduce the Native peoples living in what is now British Columbia. But if their approaches seem very different, Barman, Bryan, Molyneux, and Ormsby all share one assumption: that historians can superimpose the tidy political map of the contemporary Canadian province of British Columbia on top of an untidy geography, and an equally untidy history. Whatever reservations historians may have about this assumption, they can never entirely escape it.[1]

A geopolitical entity named 'British Columbia' did not exist until 1858. The boundaries of the present-day province (like those of all the British colonies that became Canadian provinces) were defined in a manner that might be best described as piecemeal and haphazard. The plate that describes 'Territorial Evolution' in the *Historical Atlas of Canada* lists ten separate steps in this process of legal definition. Yet the boundaries are still disputed by the First Nations, who never accepted the 1927 agreement between the federal and provincial governments that defined the extent of their territories within the province.[2]

British and American diplomats drew British Columbia's boundaries with the United States to the south along the 49th parallel (in 1846) and to the north along the Alaska panhandle (in 1903). It was a neutral third party, however, that determined the ownership of the San Juan Islands (in the Gulf of Georgia between the US mainland and the southern tip of Vancouver Island). After a long dispute, Britain and the United States asked Kaiser Wilhelm of Germany to arbitrate, and in 1872 he gave the islands to the US. No physiographic differences mark the political frontiers dividing British-Canadian from

'Cutting on the 49th Parallel, on the right bank of the Mooyie (today Moyie) River, looking west, 1861'. This image, made by an unnamed sapper with the Royal Engineers, documents the work of the joint British–US North American Boundary Commission charged with marking the 49th parallel between the Rockies and Boundary Bay. Because the terrain is identical on both sides of the border, the negative has sometimes been printed in reverse. NAC, C-78979.

American territory. The landforms on either side of the border are identical. The terrain of the 'Boundary' district, for example, is equally rugged on both sides of the 49th parallel, and the desert through which the Okanagan River flows continues south from British Columbia to Sonora, Mexico.

The northeastern boundary with Alberta demonstrates how historical contingency determined the shape of modern British Columbia. At the 54th parallel of latitude, the line jogs abrupt-

ly away from the continental divide to follow the 120th meridian of longitude north to the 60th parallel. The original eastern boundary of 1858 had followed the Rocky Mountains north, but the British Colonial Office redrew it in 1861, in order to put gold-seekers in British Columbia under direct imperial control, rather than under the looser jurisdiction of the Hudson's Bay Company, which at that time owned 'Rupert's Land'. Thus the western plains of the Peace River Valley became a part of British Columbia rather than the Prairie West.[3] Of course neither international nor the internal Canadian boundaries initially meant anything to the Native peoples who had lived there for millennia before Europeans created 'British Columbia'.

Three broad themes can perhaps suggest the complexity of the physical geography contained within those lines: vastness, diversity, and isolation. With more than 950,000 square kilometres (365,946 square miles or 230 million acres) British Columbia is Canada's third largest province. It is roughly the size of France and Germany combined; Vancouver Island alone, at 31,000 sq. km, is only slightly smaller than the British Isles. Only one American state—Alaska (1,530,700 sq. km or 591,004 sq. miles)—is larger than British Columbia. Yet if the province's modern boundaries reflected the total area integrated by the fur trade until the 1840s, the province would be vaster by half.

Within this vastness is a physical geography as diverse as that of any political unit on earth. The customary division of the province into 'coast' and 'interior' provides only the most elementary indication of the varied environments that it contains. The narrow coastal region, which also includes the Queen Charlottes and Vancouver Island, extends inland only until the

'New Westminster: Unveiling the Simon Fraser Memorial', September 1908. In the British-Canadian narrative, fur traders like Fraser were transformed into 'explorers' and became the province's founding fathers. Although the group responsible for the monument called themselves the Native Sons of British Columbia, the descendants of the Native people who made his journey possible were neither physically nor rhetorically present when the Union Jack was removed to reveal the statue. BCA, A-03324.

mountains begin, and in some places they seem to rise directly out of the sea. The coast's moderate temperatures and abundant precipitation created forests of fir and cedar. Inland, even on the Cariboo–Chilcotin plateau or in the Peace River district, British Columbians are rarely far from the mountains, which tend to run in a north–south direction in ranges separated by long, narrow valleys. The rugged topography means that only a small portion of the province can be adapted to agriculture. At this point, however, easy generalizations about 'coast' and 'interior' fall apart. No individual part of British Columbia is geographically unique in itself; the province's uniqueness comes from the astonishing variety of physical geographies contained within its boundaries. The extremes of temperature, precipitation, and elevation—from sea level to 4,663 metres—are among the greatest in North America.

Topography and distance combined to insulate the region against the European intrusions experienced by the rest of continent in the sixteenth and seventeenth centuries. Distance made the northwest coast—the first landfall for prehistoric migrants from Asia—the last part of North America to be probed by European navigators, and mountain barriers isolated it and the interior from the rest of what became the Canadian West, which was readily approached from Europe via Hudson Bay. Yet ocean routes could also connect British Columbia to the Pacific Rim, and travel from tidewater to the interior was possible, if difficult, following a network of rivers and lakes. Central to that network was the Fraser River, which begins in a glacier high in the Rockies and twists 1,400 kilometres (870 miles) to the Pacific through a watershed that covers a quarter million square kilometres (more than 96,000 sq. miles). Simon Fraser, the North West Company trader whose name the river now bears, found the landscape 'so wild' that he could not find the words to describe it except to say that he and his companions at times 'had to pass where no human being should venture'. Paths through the canyon 'furnished a safe and convenient passage to the Natives but we, who had not the advantages of their experience, were often in imminent danger.'[4] The river that terrified Fraser became a consolation prize for the British Empire when the boundary was set at the 49th parallel; the more southerly Columbia, the river that Fraser mistakenly thought he was travelling, offered an easier route to the interior.

Non-Aboriginal historians who attempt Aboriginal history, however good their intentions, find themselves in methodological terrain almost as treacherous as Fraser's canyon. They must avoid oversimplification, which often reinforces stereotypes. They must also take care to avoid the 'bookends' syndrome, in which Native people appear at the beginning of the book as the first inhabitants of the region but vanish after the fur-trade era, reappearing only for the Aboriginal resurgence of the later twentieth century. In addition, historians must recognize that the Native peoples, however much colonizers tried to control them, have always shaped their own destinies.[5]

Terminology is another problem. The ancient Tlingit and Ktunaxa of the regions where the BC–Alaska borders were eventually drawn never guessed that some of their descendants would be 'Native Americans' and others members of a 'BC First Nation'. The term 'First Nations' itself creates a misleading analogy between pre-contact Aboriginal societies and modern nation-states. Modern maps, even very good ones, can leave readers with the mistaken impression that Native groups occupied the same territories throughout the pre-contact period. According to the origin stories of the Haida, whose homeland is Haida Gwaii (the Queen Charlotte Islands) and the northern coast, they originated in the interior, on the Skeena River. Linguistic evidence suggests that the Tlingit and the Nuxalk of the Bella Coola Valley also migrated to the coast. As the archaeologist Roy Carlson explains, Aboriginal peoples 'were united through ties of kinship and intermarriage into sophisticated networks of multi-village or multi-band networks', bound together and differentiated from their neighbours by similarities of language and culture. The fundamental division was the one between the peoples of the

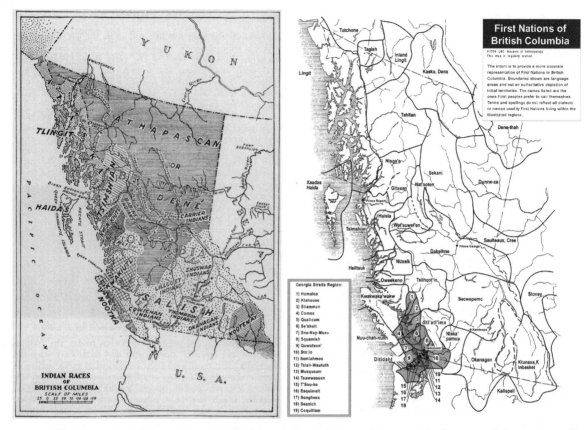

These two maps illustrate how the English vocabulary referring to Native peoples has expanded over seven decades. Names are not the only things that have changed. When the Anstey map was made in 1927, 14 Native groups were identified as distinct 'Indian Races'. The 1994 map shows more than forty 'First Nations'. 'Indian Races of British Columbia', from Anstey, *Romance of British Columbia*, 1927, 44; 'First Nations of British Columbia', 1994, reproduced courtesy of the UBC Museum of Anthropology, University of British Columbia.

Interior who supported themselves in a less-than-generous environment by living in semi-nomadic bands, and those of the more abundant coast, who lived in autonomous villages. The Aboriginal population of the future BC in the early eighteenth century was once estimated at less than 90,000, but recent scholarship has raised that number dramatically: the geographer Cole Harris argues convincingly that a reasonable estimate of the total would be well over 200,000, and that some 50,000 people lived in the area around the Strait of Georgia and up the Fraser Valley.[6]

Of all the Native peoples in North America, those of the Northwest Pacific coast were the most fascinating to Europeans. One reason was the timing of the first encounters in that region: at the height of 'the Enlightenment', when natural scientists were as keen to find, describe, and catalogue 'primitive' cultures as they were to study exotic flora and fauna. Another had to do with the social structures and material cultures of the Northwest coast, which seemed strikingly

'Petroglyphs in Petroglyph Park, near Nanaimo'. More than a thousand examples of 'rock art' from the prehistoric period have been identified in British Columbia; the images pictured here may have been carved two millennia ago, but most appear to date from just before or just after the arrival of Europeans. Petroglyphs were carved into the rock, while petrographs were painted on its surface, most often with red ochre. Neither form is easy to interpret. See Alan D. McMillan, *Since the Time of the Transformers: The Ancient Heritage of the Nuu-chah-nulth, Ditidaht, and Makah* (Vancouver: UBCP, 1999), 163–9. BC government photo. BCA, I-21971.

different from those of other North American Aboriginal groups. The abundant resources of the ocean, and the rivers that fed it, provided three essentials of the Northwest Coast economies: halibut, salmon, and oolichan (a 20–25 cm smelt). The Coast peoples used a variety of fishing tools and techniques, from weirs, nets, and traps (for spawning salmon) to spears and hook-and-line (for the larger fish) and two-metre-long rakes (to sweep up the oolichan). Air-dried salmon fillets represented a secure supply of year-round food, while the oolichan or 'candle fish' provided not only food but lamp-oil, which was also a valuable trade good: Tsimshian men carried oolichan oil (packed in leak-proof wooden containers) along 'grease trails' into the interi-

'Canoe with Indians at Port Rose, Queen Charlotte's Islands', drawing by Sigismund Bacstrom, March 1793. Most eighteenth-century depictions of canoe travel on the northwest coast show only men, but this one includes women and children as well. The notes at the right indicate colours for an eventual painting. The Dutch-born artist travelled as a surgeon on various trading ships between 1791 and 1795; when this drawing was made, he was serving aboard the American brig *Amelia*. He hoped to profit from his drawings, but as of 1801 had not made a single sale. See Douglas Cole, 'Sigismund Bacstrom's Northwest Coast Drawings and an Account of His Curious Career', *BC Studies* 46 (Summer 1980), 61–85. BCA, PDP-01332.

or to exchange it for obsidian blades, animal hides, and ochre. With reliable food supplies, the Coast peoples were able to live in permanent villages of perhaps 200 to 1,000 people. The other essential element of coastal economies was the forest. Abundant building materials made it possible to construct large and sophisticated plank houses; John Jewitt, an American seaman who spent three years (1803–5) as a captive in a Nootka village, described a 'King's House' that was 50 metres long and 15 metres wide. Giant cedars provided everything from the 15-metre ocean-going dugout canoes used by the Nootka and Makah for hunting whales to the fibres used to make clothing, baskets, and mats.

Economic abundance also allowed residents of the Northwest Coast to develop complex art forms. The easily worked wood of the red and yellow cedars was the basic medium for intricate masks as well as the elaborate totem poles that stood in front of the houses in coastal villages. The totems were part of an intricate social organization. The societies of the Northwest Coast were the most highly stratified of any north of central Mexico, with well-developed concepts of rank. The best comparison, the anthropologist Edward Sapir suggested, would be the class structure of medieval European feudalism, with 'royalty', nobles, commoners, and slaves. Status was inherited, not achieved (although heirs had to prove themselves worthy of their ancestors' legacy) and slaves were prisoners taken in war or bonded to their masters by debt. Most Coast societies were matrilineal, meaning not that women enjoyed any exalted status, but simply that descent was traced through the maternal line. Each 'house' in a village would be composed of the families of men related through their mothers. Everyone in a vil-

'The inside of a house, in Nootka Sound', engraving by William Sharpe after a drawing by John Webber, in *A New Authentic, and complete Collection of Voyages Round the world of Captain Cook* (1784). Webber (1752–93), the 24-year-old painter assigned to Cook's third Pacific voyage, is as famous as Sigismund Bacstrom is obscure. The British Admiralty paid him the considerable sum of £250 a year to supervise the preparation of his drawings for publication in Cook's *Voyages*, and he was elected a member of the Royal Society. Webber made the field sketches for this drawing when he landed with Cook at the Nuu-chah-nulth village of Yuquot in April 1778. The local people did not object so long as Webber worked out of doors, but demanded payment for permission to make this interior sketch. Webber paid with the brass buttons off his coat. Archaeological evidence suggests that Webber's representations of the pre-contact Nuu-chah-nulth houses are essentially accurate; see McMillan, *Since the Time of the Transformers*, 54. NAC, C-3676.

lage was part of a clan or phratry. Among the Tsimshian, for example, there were four: Blackfish, Eagle, Wolf, and Raven. People were born into both their clan and their place or 'name' within it. Village leaders came from whichever clan had the highest traditional rank. Rank carried privileges such as the right to exploit the best fishing grounds, to establish a weir at a specific place, or to consume particular parts of a large kill (a whale, for example). For a noble, rank could also mean the authority to commandeer the labour of his clansmen. But non-material privileges also mattered: certain seats at ceremonies, the use of certain titles, or certain symbols in art.[7]

Rank also brought responsibilities. A complex system of homage and reciprocity held Northwest

'Various articles at Nootka Sound', engraving of a John Webber drawing, from Captain James Cook, *A Voyage to the Pacific Ocean*, vol. 2 (1785). Webber and his shipmates disagreed on the purpose of these 'articles'—actually ceremonial masks. Some argued that they would be used as face shields during war, others that they were intended for entertainment. A similar drawing in the British Library is entitled 'Representation of Animals Used as Decoys', reflecting Webber's understanding. NAC, C-038616.

Coast societies together. An essential part of this system was the potlatch ceremony: a feast at which the hosts—usually a kin group rather than an individual—shared gifts as well as food with their guests. The subject of a voluminous anthropological literature, the potlatch has been variously described as a form of 'fighting with property', an embryonic welfare state, and one of 'the knots holding together the fabric' of Northwest Coast society. Above all, perhaps, it served to 'publiciz[e]

social status' and demonstrate clan prerogatives. A potlatch could mark a right of passage, establish the position of a younger heir as the designate a successor of a chief, confirm the status of an existing chief, or provide a face-saving opportunity to amend a slight.[8]

Aboriginal societies of the Interior lived very different lives from those of the Coast. Robin Fisher summarizes the fundamental differences when he points out that 'partly as a result of their

'Fiesta Celebrada en Nutka por su Xefe Macuina—Causa de Haber Dado so Hija Indicios de Entar en la Pubertad', from José Cardero, *Atlas para el viage de las goletas 'Sutil' y 'Mexicana' en 1792*. Members of a Spanish expedition, led by Juan Francisco de la Bodega y Quadra, that spent four months at Nootka Sound in 1792 observed this 'fiesta', a potlatch celebrating the coming of age of Apenas, daughter of the Nuu-chah-nulth chief Maquinna. The expedition's botanist, José Mariano Moziño, described the ceremony in his *Noticias de Nutka— An Account of Nootka Sound in 1792*, trans. and ed. Iris Higbie Wilson (Seattle: University of Washington Press, 1970). The occasion was marked with 'savage pomp': Maquinna greeted 'the nobles . . . come to offer their congratulations' with 'presents of otters, copper, shells, and as many precious items as he [could] afford'. Here Maquinna's brother Quatlazape is shown distributing gifts from the platform in the centre of the picture. Two Spaniards stand among the group watching to the right of the platform. The creator of this painting, published in 1802, is listed as 'unknown' in both the NAC and the BCA, but the sketch on which it is based was the work of Atanásio Echeverría, the artist assigned to Quadra's Nootka expedition. NAC, C-27698.

mobility, the social organization of the interior peoples was looser and . . . their ritual and material culture appeared less elaborate'. While the Interior peoples also differed among themselves in language and culture, anthropologists have identified two basic 'culture areas' (geographic regions within which the cultures of the various societies were similar): Subarctic and Interior Plateau. The migratory Subarctic peoples hunted moose and caribou, in addition to fishing, and their cultures in most ways resembled those of the peoples on the other side of the continental divide.[9] Farther south, in the Plateau region, a milder climate and the availability of salmon—dried and stored from the summer catch—made it possible to settle down for the winter in villages of perhaps 150

'Indian Pit-house, Nicola Valley', c. 1898, photographer unknown. Native people of the southern interior plateau spent the summers on the move but settled down for the winter in houses like this one. Unfortunately, there is no visual record of the early contact period in the interior equivalent to the one created on the coast by the artists who accompanied maritime expeditions. Although the interior peoples were among the last in North America to encounter Europeans, the latter were mostly fur traders and gold miners who created almost no images. BCA, G-00754.

people. Population estimates for the interior in the mid-eighteenth century range between 30,000 and 50,000.

Several conclusions about the Native peoples who encountered Europeans in the 1770s suggest themselves. First, those peoples were extraordinarily diverse—more different from each other than the Spanish from the French, or the Russians from the English. Pre-contact Native peoples were not static, frozen in an unchanging stone-age world: they adapted to changing circumstances just as all human societies have done (and continue to do).[10] Native peoples, especially those of the coast, had sophisticated cultures and relatively high standards of living. If they lacked some European technologies, they had

skills and knowledge on which Fraser—and every trader that followed him—depended. The arrival of Europeans was a trigger for change, but Native people influenced both its pace and its direction.

For eighteenth-century Europeans, the Northwest Pacific was the least accessible area of the globe. The 'backside of America' could be reached only after an arduous voyage, whether around Cape Horn, at the southern tip of the Americas, or by the much longer route south around Africa (the Cape of Good Hope) and then through the Indian Ocean to the Pacific. Mariners were constrained not only by distance and uncooperative winds, but also by the limits of navigational technology: until the mid-eighteenth century, no timepiece was sufficiently accurate to allow navigators to determine longitude with precision.

Four European kingdoms had pretensions to America's north Pacific coast—Russia, Spain, Britain, and France—and after the American Revolution, Britain's former colonists in the new United States joined the list of claimants. The new wave of exploration differed from its predecessors in one important respect. Imperial aggrandizement and profit remained the ultimate goals, and every voyage to the north Pacific still hoped to uncover the western entry to the elusive Northwest Passage across the top of the American continent. In the eighteenth century, however, expeditions to the Pacific had the additional objective of scientific discovery, and brought along scientists and artists charged with making a systematic catalogue of all the flora, fauna, and indigenous peoples they would encounter. The imperial governments that sponsored these expeditions set their discoveries in the context of the Enlightenment, as disinterested contributions to universal human knowledge, but each government was well aware that any new discovery would also strengthen its own geopolitical claims.[11]

Russia was the first into the field, dispatching two expeditions—sponsored by the Crown and captained by the Danish mariner Vitus Bering—from its Pacific port of Petropavlovsk in 1729 and 1741. Georg-Wilhelm Steller, the German naturalist on the second voyage, is remembered in the names of three species of birds as well as the four-tonne Steller's sea cow. But the sea otter pelts that Bering's men took back to sell in China made a more profound impact than Steller's science. By 1800 the trans-Pacific trade in furs was enough to persuade the

Russian Crown to grant a charter to the Russian-American Company (giving it a monopoly similar to that of the British Hudson's Bay Company) and to establish a colony of approximately 400 company employees on Kodiak Island in Alaska to service the otter hunt. Over that same 60-year period, the region's indigenous Aleuts declined from an estimated 20,000 to perhaps 2,000 as a result of the diseases that the Russians brought along with their trade goods.[12]

In the meantime the Spanish had become uneasy about the possibility of a Russian challenge to their territorial claims. Venturing north from their Mexican colony, they settled Alta California (the present-day state of California) in the 1760s to forestall this largely imagined threat. In the spring of 1774 the frigate *Santiago* sailed north under the command of Ensign Juan Pérez. The expedition turned back in July when it reached the Queen Charlottes. On the return voyage on 7–8 August the Spanish encountered Nuu-chah-nulth in canoes at the entrance to what later would be called Nootka Sound. Although the Nuu-chah-nulth were at first 'exceedingly Terrified' (according to accounts reported by later European visitors), 'the most daring took their canoes out to examine more closely the huge mass that had come out of the ocean.' They boarded the ship, 'inspected with wonder all the new and extraordinary objects that were presented before them', and traded otter skins for knives. To the frustration of his superiors, Pérez did not land to make a formal act of Spanish possession. In his log he blamed 'this fateful omission' on difficult winds, but perhaps the Spanish were less successful in overcoming their terror than the Nuu-chah-nulth had been. If so, the experience of a second Spanish expedition, the next year, suggests that the decision not to go ashore was a wise one after all. In July 1775 the crew of the schooner *Sonora*, commanded by Juan Francisco de la Bodega y Quadra, watched from the decks as Salish warriors killed every man in a heavily armed landing party of seven and then paddled out to attack the *Sonora* itself before they were driven off by Spanish gunfire. Bodega (known today in BC as Quadra) continued north along the coast to 57° 2' latitude, in the present-day Alaska panhandle. When he landed to take on water and claim the land for Spain, the local people he encountered—probably Tlingit—demanded payment for the water, and tore down the cross that the Spaniards erected to mark their country's claim.[13]

Local people were not the only ones who rejected Spain's pretensions on the Pacific rim. British Captain James Cook—'el famoso Capitan Kook' to his Spanish rivals—had an international reputation by the time he embarked on his third voyage to the Pacific, in 1776. In the spring of 1778 Cook and the weary crews of HMS *Resolution* and HMS *Discovery* sojourned at Nootka Sound to provision and refit their storm-battered ships before sailing north to continue the search for a Northwest Passage. The Nuu-chah-nulth villagers who met him there called the place Yuquot, and themselves Moachaht. 'Nootka' was the name attached to the place in Cook's published journals, and it endured until recently as the European name for the people. Cook's month at Nootka Sound was a short chapter in his extraordinary career, but it later became one of the founding moments in the Euro-Canadian narrative of British Columbia's history. The Nuu-chah-nulth showed none of the reticence that Pérez had reported four years earlier, and approached Cook's ships in canoes 'without shewing the least mark of fear or dis-

'Captain James Cook, RN', engraving, 1784, by J.K. Sherwin, from a 1776 portrait by Nathaniel Dance. This portrait was commissioned by Joseph Banks (1743–1820), the botanist who, as a young man, accompanied Cook's first voyage (1768) and later served as president of the Royal Society (1778–1820). It helped to make Cook an icon of the British Empire, 'a monument rather than a man', as Nicholas Thomas puts it in his *Cook: The Extraordinary Voyages of Captain James Cook* (New York: Walker and Co., 2003). Reproductions continue to be sold as tourist souvenirs throughout the Pacific region. The portrait is ubiquitous in histories of British Columbia, although the artist is almost never identified. NAC, C-17726.

trust'. Trading began almost immediately. The local people had no interest in the trinkets and beads they were offered, but demanded iron, brass, or copper, in return for which the British took furs, food, and art. The people of Yuquot

'A View of Habitations in Nootka Sound', engraving of a John Webber drawing from Captain James Cook, *A Voyage to the Pacific Ocean*, vol. 2 (1785). Cook had a strong sense of his historic mission, and he made certain that Webber accompanied him on any occasion that might require commemoration. Webber's original drawing was based on field sketches made during a landing at the Nuu-chah-nulth village of Yuquot on 22 April 1778. In the right foreground is the boat in which Cook and his party went ashore. NAC, C-6641.

had long experience with trade with their neighbours, and, in the words of one of Cook's officers, got 'as much as they could for everything they had; always asking for more'. During the month that Cook spent at Nootka, people from other villages along the coast came to trade. But the Yuquot villagers maintained a monopoly of direct access to the British, acting as middlemen and extracting profits from the others.[14]

The British expedition sailed north from Nootka on 26 April, but never found an opening to the Northwest Passage. On the return voyage

Cook was killed in a bloody confrontation with indigenous people in the Sandwich Islands (later Hawaii) and his sailors made their way to China, where they bartered the otter pelts for porcelain, silks, and spices a hundred times more valuable in Europe than the metal they had traded at Nootka. On their return to England, their stories launched a trans-Pacific trade conducted not only from Britain but from Boston in the newly independent United States, a trade that grew from a handful of ships in the mid-1780s to 21 in 1792. In less than twenty years the once

HMS *Resolution* and HMS *Discovery* at Nootka, March 1778; a copy of a painting by John Webber made for the NAC by Mabel B. Messer, 1930. Although Webber's work has been praised for its historical accuracy, this scene appears to have been intended specifically to convey Britain's power in the North Pacific. Cook's ships are out of proportion to the Nuu-chah-nulth's canoes, and the ensign flying at the stern of the *Resolution* is unrealistically large. The painting was created as two separate panels; hence the faint vertical line that bisects this reproduction. NAC, C-011201.

remote Northwest coast had been integrated into an international capitalist market.

The Spanish struggled to uphold their claim to the Northwest by force. In the spring of 1789 Esteban José Martínez led a small garrison to establish a fort at Nootka Sound. There he found a British trading post and the ship *Argonaut*; he seized the post, captured the ship, and imprisoned its captain and crew. After threats of war, Britain's superior naval power persuaded Spain to return the British traders' property and release the captives as part of the 'Nootka Conventions', a series of agreements (1790–4) in which Spain and Britain agreed that neither would claim exclusive sovereignty, and that other countries' ships could trade and use harbours freely on the Northwest coast. The Conventions were in effect a victory for the British and, indirectly, the Americans. The Spanish did not give up immediately, and until 1795 maintained a presence at Nootka, sending expeditions north for the purposes of geographic and scientific exploration. They also undertook missionary efforts among the Native people; in at least one case, the Spanish even paid local people to redeem child slaves, who were then sent to Mexico for religious instruction. Unlike the British, the Americans, and the Russians, however, they did not develop a trade in otter pelts, and without commercial profits they could not sustain their other activities in the region. Thus, the historian Alan Taylor concludes, 'By investing in children's souls instead of the sea otter trade, the Spanish ensured their own long-term irrelevance in the north Pacific.'[15]

In the 1790s, however, the Spanish were still active on the northwest coast, and it was in part to ensure that they kept the promises made in

'A Woman of Nootka Sound', by John Webber, and 'Mann und Frau aus dem Nootkasunde', from *Der Deutsche Jugenfreund Zeitschrift* (Karlsruhe, 1829). The unattributed drawing on the right appeared in 1829 as an illustration to an excerpt from Cook's *Voyages* published in a German young peoples' magazine. It was one of many 'engravings, etchings, woodcuts and aquatints . . . pirated from illustrations of Cook's narratives'. The original images were 'often altered and badly distorted'; however, the pirated versions made the peoples of the northwest coast the best-known Native North Americans in Europe. The pirate artist unknowingly repeats an error in Webber's image: only Nuu-chah-nulth chiefs wore the bulb-topped hats depicted here. See Rudiger Joppien, 'The Artistic Bequest of Captain Cook's Voyages—Popular Imagery in European Costume Books of the Late Eighteenth and Early Nineteenth Centuries', in Robin Fisher and Hugh Johnston, eds, *Captain James Cook and His Times* (Seattle: University of Washington Press, 1979), 187–210. BCA, PDP00233.

the first Nootka Convention that Captain George Vancouver set out with the officers and men of HMS *Discovery* and HMS *Chatham* on the last of the great eighteenth-century Pacific voyages. Vancouver's mission was diplomatic, but the expedition's most important achievements were geographic and scientific. Over the summers of 1791, 1792, and 1793 (the expedition wintered in Hawaii) the botanist Archibald Menzies collected plant specimens and made ethnographic notes on the local inhabitants, while Vancouver and his crews painstakingly surveyed the coastline between 30° and 60° north latitude, produc-

ing charts that would remain in use for a century. In the course of this activity Vancouver proved that the vast island later named for him was in fact an island, killing whatever hope remained of finding a Northwest Passage accessible to ocean-going ships.[16]

For Native people and European newcomers alike, the fur trade shaped the subsequent half-century. A decade after the maritime trade began, employees of the Montreal-based North West Company crossed the Rockies and established the tentative beginnings of a land-based fur trade that would eventually stretch the length of the

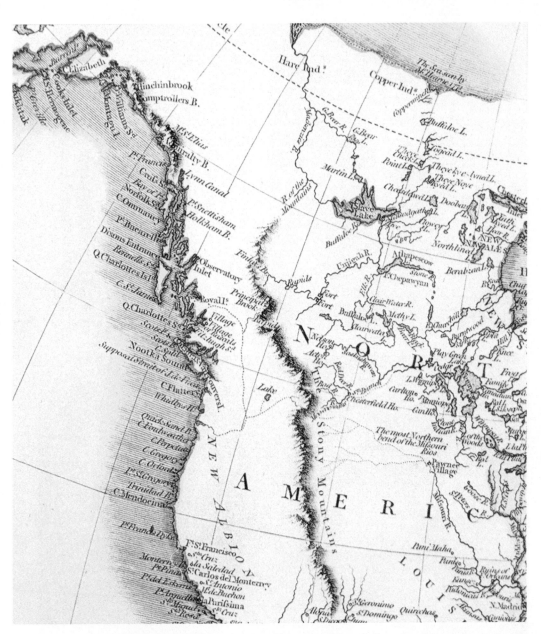

'A New Map of North America from the Latest Authorities', 1803. Although this map of 'North America' covers only part of the continent, the detail on this map is a testament to the work accomplished in the late eighteenth century by expeditions such as that of Captain George Vancouver. The virtually blank area between the coast and the Rocky Mountains—here labelled the 'Stony Mountains'—suggests how little knowledge Europeans had of the area, despite Mackenzie's overland dash to the Pacific ten years earlier. BCARS, CM B1037.

Alexander Mackenzie, portrait by Ren Emile Quentin (1860–1914). This dreadful portrait by an undistinguished BC artist has been misrepresented as dating from the period of Mackenzie's 1793 journey overland to the Pacific. In fact it was painted to mark the centennial of that event, in 1893. During the intervening century Mackenzie had become a national hero. Canadians were especially proud that (as the plaque erected at Bella Coola in 1934 by the Historic Sites and Monuments Board reminds visitors) his transcontinental journey 'preceded by more than ten years that of Lewis and Clark'. Mackenzie's pose is a clumsy copy of the one in Nathaniel Dance's iconic portrait of Captain Cook (see p. 21). BCA, PDP02244.

'Clal-lum Woman Weaving a Blanket', oil on canvas, by Paul Kane. The Clal-lum are a Salishan people of the area around the Strait of Juan de Fuca. Explicitly imitative of the American painter George Catlin, Kane did more than any other image-maker to define the 'vanishing' Native peoples of what became the Canadian West. Having toured the HBC's territories between 1846 and 1848 as the official guest of Governor Sir George Simpson, Kane titled his account of the tour *Wanderings of an Artist among the Indians of North America* (1858), but he was hardly a 'wanderer': Simpson had commanded that he receive the 'kind attentions and hospitalities . . . of the Company's posts', and ordered that he be carried 'from post to post in the Company's craft—free of charge'. ROM, E/912.1.93.

'Drying salmon at the Dalles, Columbia River', by Paul Kane, watercolour on paper. Kane visited the HBC's Columbia district a year after the Oregon Treaty made it part of the United States, but before the company had completely withdrawn. Courtesy Stark Foundation, Orange, Texas. Stark 31.78/50 wwc50.

'Fort Victoria, with an Indian Village', by Paul Kane, watercolour, 1847. As the company's guest, Kane painted most of HBC forts in which he stayed. He always included the adjacent Native village in the scene, however. ROM 946.15.212.

'The Rocky Mountains', by H.J. Warre, watercolour, pencil, and charcoal on tinted paper, 1848. In 1845 the British Army sent Lt Henry James Warre (1819–98) overland from Canada to survey the HBC territory south of the 49th parallel with a view to defending it in the event of war with the US. Travelling with HBC brigades in the disguise of a gentleman hunter, Warre concluded that Oregon territory could not be defended, but his report arrived too late to influence the diplomatic outcome. Although Warre had no formal training as an artist, it was through his paintings that many people in Britain and British North America formed their first impressions of the Rocky Mountains. NAC, C-1618.

Pacific Slope from Alaska to the Oregon Country. In October 1792 Alexander Mackenzie and a party from Fort Chipewyan on Lake Athabasca headed west to winter quarters on the Peace River. The next spring Native guides led Mackenzie and his men across the continental divide to the Fraser watershed. Advised by Sekani and Secwepemc informants not to try descending the Fraser, the Nor'Westers instead travelled due west to the Bella Coola River, and reached the Pacific on 21 July 1793.[17] The next morning he inscribed his name, along with the date, and the fact that he had arrived 'from Canada' by land, on the rock where he had spent the night. Mackenzie's journey to the Pacific was eventually to acquire enormous symbolic value, but the route he took was not useful for trade purposes. Over the next 15 years, other North West Company partners, most famously Simon Fraser and David Thompson, worked to find and establish river networks for the company's trade.

The new territory across the mountains had enormous fur potential, but the techniques developed for the Canadian Shield, east of the mountains, were not easily translated to the cordillera, where the direction of the rivers was more north-and-south than east-and-west, and there were no birch trees to provide the bark for repairs to canoes torn by rocks and rough water. The Native peoples with whom the Nor'Westers traded in the cordillera and especially nearer the coast were not only much more numerous than the groups they knew from the Shield and the Plains, but different in many ways. As one trader wrote back, 'the eye can fix on no one object, which is not directly the reverse, of what it has been accustomed to, on the east side of the Mountains'[18]

Distance alone posed new challenges: the cordillera was 5,000 kilometres from the NWC's Montreal headquarters. The Nor'Westers' solution was to divide the Pacific Slope into two districts. The area north of Fort Kamloops, established in 1812 where the two branches of the Thompson River came together, received its trade goods from the east and sent its furs back to Montreal by the same route. Simon Fraser, one of many ethnic Scots among the North West partners, named the northern area New Caledonia ('New Scotland'). In the area south of the Thompson, by contrast, the Columbia River provided an east–west axis anchored at its mouth by the NWC's Fort George. Trade goods were shipped north from the Columbia and furs shipped south to it, passing through Fort George for shipment to market in Canton, China. The North West Company partners envisioned an integrated regional resource economy under their control that would ship not only fur but also fish and timber to markets down the coast and across the Pacific. But this grand promise was never to be fulfilled; in fact, the Nor'Westers never made a profit from their fur business west of the mountains.

Fur-trade profits did, however, transform the Native societies that sold pelts to the Nor'Westers and other British and American maritime traders. Historians vigorously debate the extent of that transformation, and the nature of the Native–European relationships created by the fur trade. In the 1970s, a scholarly consensus emerged that the trade was best understood as an economic partnership that provided significant benefits to both parties. The most influential statement of this 'partners in furs' interpretation is Robin Fisher's *Contact and Conflict: Indian–European Relations in British Columbia, 1774–1890*, published in 1977. In Fisher's view, the Native participants were sharp traders who drove

'Macuina', 1791, charcoal sketch by Tomás de Suría (1761–183?), one of two artists on Alejandro Malaspina's 1791 Spanish expedition to Nootka. The Nuu-chah-nulth chief Maquinna built a sea-otter trading empire that made him one of the most powerful men on the northwest coast. BCA, A-02678.

hard bargains, and played competing traders off against one another. They would 'comparison shop', and—once they had some experience and standards to judge by—insisted on high-quality goods. European traders depended on the local indigenous people not only for furs but for everything from geographic information to food and shelter. Northwest coast chiefs like Maquinna of the Nuu-chah-nulth and Legaic of

the Tsimshian built up trading empires by controlling commerce between Europeans and other Native groups. Traders married local women 'after the custom of the country', occasionally in political alliances, as when one of Legaic's daughter's married an HBC surgeon. Many of these marriages became life-long unions. Fisher points to evidence that the fur trade stimulated an artistic 'golden age', increases in both the size and the numbers of totem poles, and larger, more frequent potlatches. In short, although the fur trade undoubtedly introduced new elements to Aboriginal cultures, most of those elements were chosen by the people themselves and were not necessarily destructive. According to this scenario, it was only after the 1850s, when European settlers began to supplant fur traders, that the dispossession of Native peoples began.[19]

More recent scholarship, synthesized by the geographer Cole Harris, offers a much less benign picture of the Native–newcomer interaction brought about by the fur trade. These scholars do not deny that it promoted a certain artistic flowering, nor do they question the idea of Native 'agency' in general. But whereas Fisher seldom mentions the incidence of violence between traders and Native peoples, they call attention to it. Harris suggests that traders responded to any Native threat with 'quick violent retaliation', whenever possible carried out in public in order to demonstrate the Europeans' power. The land-based trade had a quasi-military structure, and most of the fur-trading posts were heavily armed and fortified. Bands of traders on the move were referred to as 'brigades', and the military analogy was appropriate: not only were they well armed, but 'with any indication of Native threat, they moved in close formation, portaged under cover of arms, and camped in tight squares with sentries posted'. The maritime trade was equally violent, according to recent historians, one of whom goes so far as to describe 'a culture of terror' on both sides. Maritime traders took Native hostages to force their people to trade, bombarded villages with ships' cannon, and fired on canoes. The *Columbia*, captained by the Boston trader John Kendrick, did all of these things in June 1791, when Haida who had boarded the ship to trade seized the keys to the arms locker; the *Columbia's* log recorded that 60 Haida were killed.[20] Local people picked off individual traders when they landed, and attacked ships that ran aground, although the superior weaponry of the traders usually prevented attackers from capturing a ship. Twice, however, the Nuu-chah-nulth overwhelmed and destroyed insufficiently guarded vessels and killed all or most of their crews: the *Boston* in 1803, and the *Tonquin* in 1811.

By introducing new rivalries, as well as firearms, the fur trade also seems to have increased the scope and intensity of inter-Aboriginal warfare. In the prehistoric period different Native groups had occasionally gone to war for slaves or food. After the fur trade began, such wars became both more frequent and more vicious. The archaeologist George MacDonald cites documentary evidence and excavations of fortifications from the late eighteenth and early nineteenth centuries to argue that warfare became endemic as a result of the fur trade's 'destabilization of traditional boundaries'.[21]

The most dramatic new interpretation concerns the size of pre-contact populations and the role played by European diseases in reducing them. Alien germs were the most deadly of all the ecological invaders that accompanied Europeans everywhere in the Americas. Diseases such as

'John Jewitt, Captive of Chief Maquina [sic] at Nootka, 1803', C.W. Jeffreys, 1945. The scenes from Canadian history drawn by Charles William Jeffreys (1869–1951) are frequently reproduced and often largely imaginary. This illustration, from *The Picture Gallery of Canadian History* (Toronto: Ryerson Press, 1945), is a useful historical document nonetheless, because it neatly encapsulates British Columbia's longest-running 'white victim' story—a genre devoted to justifying the dispossession of Native peoples by Europeans. Jewitt and his shipmate John Thompson were the only crew members left alive after Nuu-chah-nulth destroyed the trading vessel *Boston* in 1803. Because they had useful skills, as a blacksmith and gunsmith respectively, they served Maquinna as slaves until 1805, when the captain of an American ship redeemed them. In 1807 Jewitt published the first edition of *A Journal Kept at Nootka Sound: A Narrative of the Adventures and Sufferings of John R. Jewitt*. Two centuries later, his captivity narrative is still for sale in BC bookstores, albeit with the more lurid title *White Slaves of Maquinna* (Surrey, BC: Heritage House, 2000) ed. Art Downs; we recommend instead the edition annotated by Hillary Stewart (Seattle: University of Washington Press, 1987). NAC, C-073425.

smallpox, measles, malaria, whooping cough, typhus, and typhoid fever had never before existed in North America, and therefore the Native populations had never developed immunological defences against them. When a 'virgin soil epidemic' struck, virtually every member of a group would fall ill at the same time. Such diseases carried off not only the very young and old, but also the men and women in the prime of life who were normally responsible for all the most vital functions, from providing food and defending the village to procreating. Smallpox first appeared in the Pacific Northwest at the end of the continent-wide 'Pox Americana' of 1775–82. When George Vancouver found deserted villages, he wondered about the absence of Native people around Puget Sound and the Strait of Georgia and concluded that smallpox had been 'very fatal amongst them'. One of his officers reported meeting Salish 'much pitted with the Small Pox', and a crewman claimed that he 'frequently met with human bones during [his] rambles'. Smallpox returned to parts of the Northwest in 1836 and in 1853, and a widespread epidemic wreaked havoc on the new colony of British Columbia in 1862–3. The effects of the diseases introduced during the fur-trade period, according to Robert Boyd, were 'both devastating and revolutionary', affecting 'virtually every aspect of Native culture, from subsistence patterns to oral literature'.[22]

The merger of the North West Company into the Hudson's Bay Company in 1821 reduced violence and stabilized the fur trade. The British government granted the expanded HBC a 'license of exclusive trade' west of the Rocky Mountains in the hope that it would be an effective agent of British imperialism on the Pacific Northwest. In its western interior base of Rupert's Land the HBC had at least a theoretical monopoly, but in New

Caledonia, the Columbia district, and on the Northwest Pacific coast it had to compete not only with the Russian–American Fur Company, but also with both maritime and overland US traders. When Britain and the US settled on the 49th parallel as the boundary from Lake Superior west to the Rocky Mountains in 1818, they agreed that from the Rockies to the Pacific traders of both countries could operate freely for another ten years.

The HBC's new governor, George (after 1841 Sir George) Simpson maintained the Columbia and New Caledonia districts, but integrated the Pacific Slope into the company's Western Division. Dr John McLoughlin, one of several NWC traders kept on by the new company, took charge of the division. In 1824 the company established Fort Vancouver, on the north side of the Columbia River near its juncture with the Willamette, as the division headquarters. The British fur traders hoped that the Columbia—the river that their brigades used to travel into the interior—would become the permanent boundary between US and British territory. But Simpson developed a contingency plan. Without ever seeing it, he formed the erroneous impression that the Fraser was 'a fine large bold stream . . . not barred by dangerous Rapids or falls'. He decided that the turbulent river should be developed as another route into New Caledonia, and to that end the company built Fort Langley on the south shore of the lower Fraser in 1827. The next year, Simpson travelled the Fraser himself and realized his mistake, concluding that the passage down meant 'certain Death, in nine attempts out of Ten'. That ended any prospect of making Fort Langley a commercial centre for the interior. Still, the area did have a salmon fishery so rich that Chief Factor James McMillan claimed

'Interior of Fort Langley Gard (sic) looking s(outh) showing "the Hall", 15 Dec. 1858', by Edward Mallandaine. This drawing of the BC's first capital suggests the Spartan nature of a fur-trade fort. Edward Mallandaine (1827–1905) was an architect who later practised in Victoria and in 1860 published the city's first directory. BCA, PDP03395.

it could feed everyone in Rupert's Land, as well as excellent agricultural potential. Accordingly, the company retained the post and in 1832 began exporting salted salmon to Hawaii.[23]

Under Simpson the Hudson's Bay Company ruthlessly pushed aside its competitors. 'I entertain sanguine hopes,' he wrote in 1830, 'that before the expiration of 5 years there will not be an American on the coast.'[24] Acquiring ships to battle the American maritime traders for the coast and to provision its own posts on the major rivers (the Fraser, Nass, Skeena, and Bella Coola), in 1839 the company reached a diplomatic agreement with the Russians according to which the HBC would not only do all the trading itself—buying pelts and then selling 5,000 of them to the Russian–American Company every year—but would supply provisions to Russian posts in the Alaska panhandle. This agreement further undermined the US maritime traders, who had previously supplied the Russian posts.

In addition the HBC devised a brutal way of relieving the competitive pressure exerted by the American 'mountain men' who travelled overland to trade and trap in the Snake River Valley, 'a rich preserve of beaver' in the Columbia basin. Simpson ordered McLaughlin to hire 'the very scum of the earth' to turn the valley into a 'fur desert' that would serve as a buffer zone between its own territory and the Americans. Former Nor'Wester Peter Skene Ogden led expeditions into the valley to carry out Simpson's order to trap every animal 'as fast as possible'. Between 1824 and 1830, Ogden and his men took 20,000 beaver pelts out of the Snake River watershed.[25] If the HBC won the commercial battle with its American business rivals, however, Britain lost the political struggle for control of the Columbia basin.

The British claim to the territory was stronger than the American. But it was outweighed by the HBC's fear that any substantial agricultural settlement would damage its trade.

In the 1820s the company did launch a modest agricultural settlement to grow food for its brigades and a surplus to trade with the Russian–American Fur Company, but its subsidiary, the 'Puget's Sound Agricultural Company', was strictly an ancillary to the fur trade; it never became a foundation for a colony.

The United States won the territory from the Columbia River north to the forty-ninth parallel because during the 1840s American settlers flooded the Oregon country, attracted by the writings of missionaries and publicists who promised that Oregon would be the perfect place to raise every conceivable crop, as well as 'fat and healthy babies'. American migrants who read their tracts poured across the 3,000-kilometre trail from Missouri to the Willamette River Valley, taking up land from which epidemic disease had eradicated almost all the Aboriginal inhabitants. On 4 July 1843 a provisional government of settlers demanded that the US government claim Oregon. John L. O'Sullivan, the editor of *The New York Morning News,* dismissed British claims to the Northwest as 'cobweb tissues'; rather, he told Americans that it was their 'manifest destiny to overspread and possess the whole of the continent which Providence has given us for the great experiment of liberty.'[26] When the Democrat James Knox Polk won the presidency in 1844—with a bare plurality—he made this bellicose doctrine into official US public policy. Polk's slogan '54°40' or fight' was just bluster, but the British government, with a worldwide empire to manage, was not prepared to go to war for the sake of the Pacific Northwest. In 1846 the boundary was set at the 49th parallel on the mainland, with a southward dip to accommodate Vancouver Island.

If the HBC had hoped that the Columbia would become the boundary between British and US territory, it nonetheless made alternative plans. Three years before the Oregon Treaty, the company established Fort Victoria at the southern tip of Vancouver Island. Thus in 1849 it simply closed Fort Vancouver and made Fort Victoria its western headquarters. That same year, Vancouver Island formally became a British colony with Fort Victoria as its capital. The British government hoped that the HBC could serve as an effective agent for British interests on the northwest coast of America. The company agreed to pay the Crown a nominal seven shillings a year to lease the Island for ten years and promised to make progress towards settling it within five years, but senior management did not take this responsibility seriously. For them the real purpose of Fort Victoria and the Vancouver Island 'colony' was to safeguard the company's 'license of exclusive trade' in the furs of New Caledonia. From 1849 to 1851, Chief Factor James Douglas was the absolute ruler of the Europeans in New Caledonia—all but a handful of whom were HBC employees—and de facto governor of Vancouver Island. After a brief and dismal experiment with a governor—a young barrister named Richard Blanshard—the British Colonial Office officially recognized the company's real authority by appointing Douglas governor.[27]

Over the next decade, Fort Victoria and Vancouver Island evolved from what Margaret Ormsby called an 'outpost of Empire' to a 'colony on the seaboard'. Before the fort was constructed, there had been ten or twelve Coast Salish villages along the beaches in both directions. Thereafter, six or seven hundred local Salish people congregated across the harbour in what became known as Songhees Village (named after one of the bands). The Royal Navy charted the harbours of the coast and provided a comforting presence to the European community. Her Majesty's sailors also provided a ready market for Fort Victoria's provisioners, as did American whaling ships and Russian fur trading posts. Accordingly, the HBC—always keeping an eye open for profitable opportunities—expanded its farming operations around the fort, and, as at Red River, many retired HBC traders set up their own farms nearby. Although the HBC steamer *Beaver* plied the coast northward from Fort Victoria, its job had more to do with keeping American traders away than with trading for furs. Instead, Native traders paddled to the Fort to trade and sometimes to work for wages. The company imported English miners to dig coal at Nanaimo, and a privately owned sawmill near Fort Victoria exported its products to San Francisco.

Even so, the tiny colony fell far short of the British government's hopes. To be fair to the HBC, there were many obstacles to successful settlement besides the company's own reluctance to encourage it, beginning with the arduous three- to six-month voyage around Cape Horn. Many potential agricultural settlers were also deterred by the price that the HBC charged for its land: £1 an acre, at a time when parcels of 640 acres could be had in Oregon for free. But the British government and the HBC management shared the view that if Britain's new colony on the North Pacific was to be an effective barrier against US expansion, its inhabitants had to have the financial means to uphold the standards of the mother country. Representative government was introduced in 1856, but the first Assembly was, in Governor Douglas's words, 'little better than a parody'. The House had seven members, chosen by 43 voters—the only men in the colony who met the 20-acre property qualification.[28] Less than two years later, the tiny outpost of empire would be transformed into the commercial centre of a gold mining boom.

# CHAPTER TWO

# A New Colony, A New Province: 1858–1885

*T*he discovery of gold at John Sutter's California sawmill in 1848 launched a wave of rushes that, over the next half-century, moved through many of the western states before finally coming to an end in Yukon and Alaska. Native people had known of the gold in the streams and rivers of New Caledonia but did not broadcast the fact. The Haida drove off would-be miners who descended on the Queen Charlotte Islands in 1852. Nevertheless, to safeguard British sovereignty, the Royal Navy's HMS *Thetis* paid a visit, and the Colonial Office extended Governor Douglas's authority over the Islands.[1] Douglas hoped that First Nations people would take on the role of suppliers to the Hudson's Bay Company, becoming partners in gold just as they had been in furs.

The deposits on the Queen Charlottes were limited, but Douglas knew there was more gold in New Caledonia. Fearing that it would be difficult to control a rush on the mainland with the scant military forces at hand, the governor did his best to keep discoveries secret. In 1857, however, a British parliamentary committee investigating the HBC in its capacity as an agent of empire learned that the company had bought gold from Native people on the Thompson River. In February 1858, the company sent 800 ounces of the precious mineral to the assay office at San Francisco. The secret was out.

The news was greeted with particular interest in California, where yields of placer gold in the streambeds of the new state had declined by almost half, and more and more prospectors were recognizing that they were not going to make fortunes there. Within weeks miners were heading north. At noon on Sunday 25 April 1858 the side-wheeler *Commodore* arrived at Victoria and more than 400 passengers disembarked, instantly doubling the town's population. Alfred P. Waddington, a grocer recently arrived from England himself, characterized this motley crew as 'an indescribable array of Polish Jews, Italian fishermen, French cooks, jobbers, speculators of every kind, land agents, hangers-on at auctions, bummers, bankrupts, and brokers of every description'. Although most miners only passed through Victoria on their way to the Fraser, by the end of 1858 its population increased tenfold, to roughly 5,000. In June of that year it counted 223 new buildings under construction; an English visitor exaggerated only slightly when he remarked that there were 'more drinking saloons and bowling alleys than dwelling houses'.[2]

In May and June 1858 an estimated 10,000 miners moved up the Fraser, some travelling up the river itself, others overland, by the Whatcom Trail (which crossed the border from the United States just west of Fort Langley), and others still following the fur brigade route along the Columbia River and up the Okanagan. By the fall an estimated 25,000 men were panning for gold along the banks of the Fraser and its tributaries. At the height of the rush in 1861, there may have been as many as 50,000 miners in a region that only three years earlier had been exclusively fur country. Probably 40,000 of them were 'forty-niners' from California, and although they represented a range of nationalities, virtually all were gold-rush veterans. Not many of them came from Britain's eastern North American colonies, since the first reports of the gold discoveries in 'British Oregon' did not reach Canadian newspapers until the end of May 1858. A correspondent from San Francisco told the Toronto *Globe* that 'California as a state is convinced . . . of the richness of Frazer River', and that 'every mining camp is losing a portion of its population . . . some even one-half.' A number of the early arrivals were Chinese, travelling up from California, but in time others began coming directly from China. It has been estimated that at its peak in 1862, Barkerville's Chinatown had 3,000 residents. Although the Chinese were never welcomed by the whites, their presence was generally tolerated because they were willing to work over ground that other miners had abandoned, and because those who ran restaurants, laundries, and market gardens provided indispensable services and did not compete with

European operations. A Canadian visitor to the goldfields observed that only the 'Celestial' laundryman had 'the courage to undertake the "lively" operation of washing a Cariboo shirt'—a miner's shirt infested with swarms of lice.[3]

As in California, what the 'Argonauts' were after was alluvial gold: nuggets and 'dust' washed down from a mountain lode to rest in the banks and sandbars of streams and rivers. The simplest method was 'panning'. A miner dug into the streambed with a pick and shovel and used the river's water to separate the relatively heavy gold from the lighter sand and gravel. The miner would fill a metal pan—not unlike a large pie plate, about 10 cm deep and perhaps 40 cm wide at the rim—with gravel and water and then carefully swirl it around while allowing the gravel to spill until only the gold glinted in the bottom. An average pan might yield 10 cents worth of gold, but the possibility of a $50 pan kept the rush alive. 'Sluicing', a slightly more sophisticated technique, required only a little more capital and expertise. A miner would construct a box known as 'rocker' or a 'long tom', fill it with sand, and direct river water through it. Wire mesh screened out the nuggets, and a layer of felt in the bottom of the box caught the gold dust.

The sudden influx of thousands of men into a region without any of the governmental or social institutions that provide social stability made violence unavoidable. A British surveyor reported that 'so much young blood & no female population' sometimes resulted in 'fierce scenes' in which 'the bowie knife & revolver which every man wears are in constant requisition.' The stereotype of the Canadian west as a model of peace and order, compared to the 'wild' American version, does not fit gold-rush British Columbia. As Adele Perry points out, however

Washing gold with a 'rocker'. The dipper this miner is using to pour water through the rocker was made from an empty tin can. Chinese placer miners continued to work the alluvial deposits along the Fraser long after their European counterparts had given up. The NAC tentatively attributes this image to Richard Maynard (1832–1907), a boot-maker who learned photography from his wife, Hannah Hatherly Maynard (1834–1918); the Maynard Studio operated in Victoria from 1864 until 1912. Although we know that Maynard followed the Fraser and the Cariboo Road to Barkerville in 1868, the NAC has dated this photo 'ca. 1875'. NAC, C-125990.

much an earlier generation of historians praised the colony's first chief justice, Matthew Baillie Begbie, for making the British Columbian frontier uniquely peaceful, 'it was hard to ignore the barroom and back-alley brawls.' Recent scholarship makes the differences between the US and Canadian wests seem much smaller than either country's mythology would suggest.[4]

In both wests, the bloodiest conflicts erupt-

ed not among the miners themselves, but when miners in well-armed groups ran into Native resistance. Mining disrupted the salmon fisheries on the Fraser and Thompson rivers that sustained the Stó:lō and Nlaka'pamux. HBC traders had bought fish from Native suppliers, but miners simply took whatever cached food they happened to find. 'We do just about as we please without regard to the Indians,' one miner admitted in 1858, 'but there will be hell to pay after a while.' Writing about the summer of 1858, Daniel Marshall describes what he calls the 'Fraser River War', in which as many as two dozen miners died; some, according to their comrades, were found decapitated floating in the Fraser. 'Scarcely a day passes but some person loses their lives & boats,' wrote a miner from Fort Yale in August. But vengeful miners killed many more Native people. When Governor Douglas forcefully imposed colonial government on the mainland in 1858, the miners made no effort to fight back; one reason, Marshall suggests, was 'the overwhelming threat of war with Native peoples'.[5]

As a fur trader, Douglas had witnessed the influx of American settlers into Oregon that had trumped Britain's claim to the area. He also knew that gold and Americans together had turned a Mexican colony into the state of California. Both he and his superiors in the Colonial Office were well aware that these patterns could easily be repeated. New Caledonia was not simply the prize in a physical contest between two empires; it was also the site of an ideological confrontation between two imperial myths, the American myth of a 'manifest destiny' to build Thomas Jefferson's 'empire of liberty' and the British-Canadian counter-myth of order and stability, of a manifest duty to thwart US expansionism. In a letter to the Colonial Secretary in December 1857, Douglas referred to fears that the looming gold rush would make New Caledonia 'the scene of lawless misrule'. The danger that the colony would be overrun was real enough, to judge by a ditty reportedly popular among Americans who coveted the territory north of the 49th parallel: 'Soon our banner will be streaming / Soon the Eagle will be screaming / And the Lion, see, it cowers /

Hurrah Boys! The river's ours!' Douglas's view was firmly established when Viscount W.F. Milton and Dr W.B. Cheadle repeated his argument in their immensely successful book *The North West Passage By Land*, which went through eight editions within ten years of its first publication in 1865. Confronted by 'the most desperate and lawless of the Californian rowdies,' they wrote, 'Governor Douglas, without the aid of a single soldier or regular police-force, preserved an order and security which contrasted most forcibly with the state of things in San Francisco and Sacramento under similar circumstances.' Milton and Cheadle exaggerated the weakness of Douglas's position, as he did himself in some of his dispatches to London. Two Royal Navy ships with companies of Royal Marines aboard were in Esquimalt before the 'desperate and lawless' American miners arrived, and a third arrived in July 1858, bringing more Marines and 65 Royal Engineers. A fourth, the 84-gun *Ganges*, arrived in mid-October, with 700 sailors and Marines.[6]

In the name of preserving British constitutional authority, Douglas had already usurped it, confident that the Imperial government would sanction his actions after the fact. In December 1857, even before the gold rush really began, Douglas required every gold seeker to obtain a mining licence. The 10-shilling licence fee (later raised to 21 shillings) provided both revenue for his government and a degree of control over access to the interior. The fee itself was merely a token, since on a good day a miner could earn at least twice that amount. But Douglas also imposed a 10 per cent customs duty on imported goods. The Royal Navy helped with the enforcement of these decrees, intercepting vessels that bypassed Victoria on the way to the Fraser, and in August 1858 the British Parliament conferred legality on Douglas's actions, ending the HBC's reign on the mainland and making New Caledonia a separate colony. Apparently Queen Victoria herself suggested the name for her latest acquisition: because 'the citizens of the United States call their country also Columbia, at least in poetry, "British Columbia" might be . . . the best.' Historians G.P.V. and Helen Akrigg, writing 120 years later, described the Queen's choice in language that would have come easily to James Douglas: 'BRITISH COLUMBIA! It preserved the name of the empire lost to the Americans, and at the same time it served as a reminder that a portion of it had been saved, to grow and mature in another tradition.'[7]

Correspondence between London and Victoria moved only as quickly as the ships that carried it, and until 1855 the shortest route was the one around Cape Horn. In that year the opening of a railway across the Isthmus of Panama allowed for speedier transmission of the mail. Even so, it was not until a rainy 19 November 1858 that Douglas read the proclamation creating the mainland colony of British Columbia. The location chosen for the event was Fort Langley, which might have become the capital had Colonel Richard Moody, commander of the 175 Royal Engineers stationed in the new colony, not decided that its proximity to the US border made it vulnerable to American attack. Instead, the capital would be located in a more easily defensible position on the north side of the Fraser and a few kilometres to the west, at a place that in 1859 would be given the impressive name of New Westminster.

History has been kind to James Douglas. Historians praise him for taking the same sort of high-handed unilateral action that they condemn in the governors of other British North American colonies. Most historians are nationalists, and for them Douglas's behaviour is justified by the urgency of the need to 'save' British Columbia from the United States. But many of the colonists Douglas governed were less sympathetic. Among them was a newspaper editor, born William Smith in Windsor, Nova Scotia, who in 1854 adopted the unforgettable name Amor De Cosmos. Having earned a substantial living photographing mining claims in California, in June 1858 he moved to Victoria, where he worked briefly as a building contractor. The first editorial he wrote for his newspaper, the *British Colonist*, published on 11 December 1858, attacked Douglas for the apparent conflict of interest in his serving as governor of both Vancouver Island and British Columbia while remaining a senior HBC officer with a financial interest in the future of New Caledonia. De Cosmos would be a constant critic of Douglas and the 'Family-Company-Compact'—his term for the influential group that in his view ran the colony of Vancouver Island.[8]

Transportation was an obvious priority for the new mainland colony, and government played an active role in providing it. Lowering transportation costs, and employing miners as construction workers when high water or frozen ground kept them from the riverbanks, visibly demonstrated the value of government. In 1860 the Royal Engineers teamed up with private contractors to build a wagon road to link with steamers at Harrison Lake to carry freight north to Lillooet. In 1862, when it became clear that the rush was moving on to the Cariboo region, construction began on a road connecting Yale to Barkerville, 600 kilometres to the north. With the completion of the Cariboo Road, the prices of goods plummeted from their gold-rush peaks: a shovel that had cost $14 fell to $1.50, and a pair

'Pack animals "cooling off",' Barkerville, 1868, by Frederick Dally. Pack horses and mules continued to play an important role in transport well into the twentieth century; there are 30 photos of pack animals in the BCA, half of which post-date 1900. This image was published in an album about life in the Cariboo sold by the photographer. Having arrived in Victoria from England in 1862 and established a drygoods store, Dally set up a studio in Barkerville in 1867, but it burned down—with most of the rest of the town—in September 1868. Two years later, for reasons that are unclear, he abandoned photography and left the colony to study dentistry in Philadelphia. See Carol J. Williams, *Framing the West: Race, Gender, and the Photographic Frontier in the Pacific Northwest* (New York: Oxford University Press, 2003), 66–7. Glenbow NA-674-46.

of gum boots from $40 to $9. But the destinations of the gold miners shifted faster than the roads could be completed. By 1865 the new hot spot was a tributary of the Kootenay River known as Wild Horse Creek; but before the Hope–Similkameen Trail was finished, the fever moved on to the Big Bend of the Columbia.[9]

The costs of road-building were considerable, and among them was conflict with First Nations. In May 1864 Tsilhqot'in killed 17 white construction workers employed by the Bute Inlet Wagon Road Company to push through a road from the head of the Inlet east to the Cariboo. Resistance to the road was not the only reason for the attack:

'Attack on Indian village in Clayoquot Sound by Boats of HMS Sutlej and HMS Devastation, Sept. 1864', by J.R. Mackey. In August 1864 at Clayoquot Sound, on the west coast of Vancouver Island, the trading sloop *Kingfisher* was pillaged and burned and all hands aboard were lost. The Native villagers insisted that the traders had provoked the attack, but Governor Arthur Edward Kennedy demanded that 'the perpetrators of this diabolical crime' be punished as 'a warning example to other tribes'. Admiral Joseph Denman sailed to Clayoquot Sound on his flagship, the screw-frigate HMS *Sutlej*, accompanied by the sloop *Devastation*. When the villages refused to surrender the attackers, Denman ordered full-scale reprisals, including the use of the incendiary rockets shown here. Denman reported that his men had destroyed nine villages, along with 64 canoes, and killed 'at least fifteen Indians'. Governor Kennedy offered official thanks to the Admiral for this stern reprimand to the 'piratical and bloodthirsty attitudes of the coast Indians, which have been left too long unpunished'; see Barry Gough, *Gunboat Frontier: British Maritime Authority and the Northwest Coast Indians, 1846-90* (Vancouver: UBCP, 1984), 114–21. BCA, PDP00084.

apparently one of the road crew had written down a number of the local people's names and threatened to infect them with smallpox as punishment for an alleged theft. Outraged journalists demanded retribution for the 'treacherous massacre', but took care to emphasize the contrast between proper British justice and the 'Lynch Law' of the United States: thus editorialists point-

'Esquimalt Harbour Vancouver Island (B.C. c. 1870).' No doubt these Royal Engineers were delighted to take a break from their pick-and-shovel work to pose for the anonymous photographer. The important subjects of the photo, however, were the four Royal Navy ships behind them: HMS *Boxer, Sparrowhawk, Charybdis,* and *Zealous.* The Royal Navy began calling at Esquimalt harbour during the Oregon crisis of the 1840s and continued through the 1850s, when Russian vessels posed a potential threat during the Crimean War. Finally in 1862 it formally established its north Pacific base in Esquimalt. There it remained until 1906, when the federal government took over the responsibility for managing the base—even though Canada did not yet have its own navy. NAC, C-28530.

ed out that all members of the punitive expedition were sworn constables, and that the killers would not be punished indiscriminately as they would have been by those 'who hold the American doctrine of "manifest destiny" in its most fatal form'. In the end, five Tsilhqot'in men were tried, convicted, and hanged for the 'massacre,' no doubt oblivious to the fine distinctions between US 'lynch law' and the proper British justice that had condemned and executed them.[10]

From the mid-1860s onward, government 'Indian policy' was based on the assumption that Aboriginal people were on an unalterable course towards extinction, and that those who survived

'Graves of coast Indians, BC, c. 1870', by Frederick Dally. Given the hundreds of drawings, paintings, and photographs made of Aboriginal graves in the nineteenth century, there must have been a significant market for such images; perhaps they appealed to colonizers seeking confirmation of their belief that Native people were doomed to disappear in the face of inevitable progress. This photo of five men—one of them armed with a shotgun—lounging among the monuments like hunters posing with their trophies, is not typical. Most such images were composed to convey respect and sadness. NAC, C-10338.

would be gradually assimilated. Abundant evidence supported that assumption. A smallpox epidemic that reached Victoria in April 1862, probably brought by a passenger on a steamer from San Francisco, not only devastated the local Native population but spread to a nearby encampment of 'northern Indians'—Haida, Tsimshian, Tlingit—who had gone to Victoria to trade. The local authorities responded by burning their huts, forcing them to return to their villages. Thus they carried the disease north along the coast, and from there it travelled inland with trade along the rivers, leaving almost no Native group unscarred. In July 1862 a Royal Engineers lieutenant reported that, on the coast, Nuxalk were 'dying and rotting away by the score, & it is no uncommon occurrence to come across dead bodies lying in the bush'. By mid-October a prospector 500 kilometres inland on the North Thompson informed the Victoria *Colonist*, 'There were no Indians on the river, as they nearly all died of smallpox this year.' The accepted death toll for the epidemic is 20,000 people—a third of the colony's Native population at mid-century. Those who survived the epidemics were still susceptible to the debilitating effects of venereal disease (which also reduces fertility) and more gradual killers such as tuberculosis. Inevitably, disease never worked alone, but combined with economic dislocation to devastate Native communities. When Indian Reserve Commissioner Gilbert Sproat visited the lower Fraser canyon—an area that had been spared the worst effects of smallpox—in 1878, he found only about 1,100 of the 7,500 Native people who had been counted by the HBC in 1830.[11]

James Douglas gave at least limited recognition to the need for treaties to extinguish Aboriginal title, and to the First Nations' right to compensation in the form of reserves when title was relinquished. He created the first reserve in 1852, across Victoria harbour from the European settlement: 'a patch of land set aside for Natives in their own former territory', as Cole Harris has put it. Over the next half-century, the newcomers confined the First Nations to the tiny fraction of the province's land mass allocated for reserves, and assigned the rest to themselves for develop-

'An Indian prayer meeting with Roman Catholic clergy', [c. 1870]. This title was the caption that Frederick Dally used in his published album. But the original albumen print in the BCA (E-04419) bears two inscriptions in Dally's own hand: 'Indians Shamming to be at prayer for the sake of photography, Fraser River', and 'At the priests' request all the Indians kneel down and assume an attitude of devotion. Amen.' J. Robert Davison has praised 'Dally's candour' in 'Turning a Blind Eye: The Historian's Use of Photographs', *BC Studies* 52 (Winter 1981–2), 18–19. But in this case, at least, the photographer was candid only in his private comments; in public he maintained the illusion that his photo was a straightforward record of an unstaged event. NAC, C-24289.

ment. Douglas's reserve allocations seem generous only in the light of his successors' behaviour. The personification of the post-Douglas policy, and the villain in historians' eyes, was Joseph Trutch, who in 1864 became chief commissioner of lands and works for British Columbia, and after 1866 for the united colony. Trutch unilaterally reduced the size of reserves already granted, allotting ten acres (4 ha) to each 'family' (assumed to consist of four people). Thus BC reserves were conspicuously smaller than those in Canada's Prairie West or the western US, where 80 to 160 acres (32–64 ha) per family was the norm.[12]

Gold mining continued to move north and east in the course of the 1860s, and as it did it became more capital-intensive. This pattern, typical of industrial capitalism, was repeated across the North American west. The gold in the Cariboo lay deep in dirt and rock. Here the individual miner with his simple pan—the image celebrated by gold-rush enthusiasts—was replaced by gangs of men who tunnelled into creek banks, dug out the 'pay dirt', and used increasingly complicated sluices to extract the gold from it. Hydraulic mining required even greater investment. William Hind, one of a party who travelled overland from Canada in 1862, found the Cariboo to be 'difficult to come at, difficult to get along in and very partial in its favours'. Canadians who had made their way to the Cariboo with dreams of becoming independent miners were lucky if they could find wage work: 'Of all the Overlanders who have come here, those who are mechanics and axemen have done the best.'[13]

It soon became clear that gold mining was not a stable basis for an economy; as Douglas told the Colonial Office, 'The miner leaves no traces but those of desolation behind.' Coal mines around Nanaimo were able to serve local needs, fuel steamships, and export very modest quantities to San Francisco. But distance, together with American tariffs, made it difficult to find export markets for the colonies' forest and agricultural products. Saw-milling capacity was not enough even for local needs: lumber had to be imported from Puget Sound. Attempts to attract farmer-settlers met with very limited success; agricultural production was not always enough to fill even local demand. And the technology that would make salmon canning possible had not yet arrived in British Columbia.

The 1866 bankruptcy of the still incomplete Collins Overland Telegraph—an ambitious project to provide telegraph service from North America to Europe via a line running north through British Columbia and across the Bering Strait—symbolized the colonies' economic misfortunes. The success of the trans-Atlantic cable, which went into service in 1866, made the company worthless—although Native people found a variety of uses for the wire that it left behind. The European population of the two colonies, which had reached more than 50,000, dropped to perhaps 10,000 by the mid-1860s.[14] Many people left altogether; others moved from the Cariboo to Vancouver Island. The most visible of these internal migrants were the Chinese who entered domestic service, mainly in Victoria. While many Victoria residents were glad to have Chinese servants do their cooking, laundry, and other chores, some white workingmen complained that their presence discouraged the immigration of white women.

When Douglas retired in 1864, the British government appointed separate governors for British Columbia and Vancouver Island. But the costs of administering and creating infrastructure for two separate colonies, on top of the huge debt incurred for road-building on the mainland, led the British government to change its mind. Accordingly, the Colonial Office prevailed on British Columbia's governor, Frederick Seymour, to undertake discussions towards a marriage of convenience. Neither colony wanted a wedding, and rivalry between their capital cities, New Westminster and Victoria, made the prospect of union all the more disagreeable. The tariff was the first issue. Victoria was a free port, but the mainland charged a modest tariff on goods entering from anywhere other than Vancouver Island. New Westminster merchants complained that Cariboo residents were ordering duty-free goods directly from Victoria, while Islanders feared that,

'The Canadian Claim, Cariboo District, BC, 1865', by C(harles) Gentile. The Canadian Company was an association of 'free' (independent) gold miners who responded to the need for increasing investment by pooling their labour and capital. The woman in this photo (probably the wife of the man she stands next to) and the man holding the child in his arms suggest that these miners saw themselves as independent proprietors rather than 'wage slaves'. The photographer (born Carlo Gintile, 1830?–93) arrived in Victoria from San Francisco in 1863 to start a fancy goods store and launched a photography business. This photo was made when he accompanied Governor Seymour to the Cariboo in 1865. The fact that he moved back to California the next year suggests the instability of the photo business in the nineteenth-century west. NAC, C-88923.

with union, Victoria would lose its tariff advantage. In the course of discussions the Islanders also became concerned that they would lose their Legislative Assembly, since the Colonial Office held that the mainland, with its shifting population, was not yet ready for full representative government. The terms of the union seemed to favour British Columbia. Not only its name but its form of government—a Legislative Council partly elected and partly appointed—and its tariff were applied to the whole colony, and Seymour was named its new governor. On 19

'Morning Star Claim, Barkerville, c. 1868', by Frederick Dally. Hydraulic mining used jets of water under pressure to loosen gravel and wash it into a flume—the wooden trough at the front centre of the photo. John Keast Lord, naturalist to the North American Boundary Commission, explained the process: 'traverse strips of wood called *riffles*—gold traps in other words—seize on the fine-dust gold.' Lord restricted his report to a simple inventory of the colony's wildlife; he offered no comment on the environmental damage caused by hydraulic mining and its deleterious effects on animal life. See *The Naturalist in Vancouver Island and British Columbia* (London: Richard Bentley, 1866), 228–9. BCA, A-04782.

November 1866, the eighth anniversary of the creation of the colony of British Columbia, the union of the two colonies was proclaimed in both New Westminster and Victoria. No excitement or celebration attended this forced marriage, and the question of which city would be chosen for the capital remained unresolved for another year and a half. Finally, although Seymour favoured

'Victoria Pioneer Rifle Corps, also known at the time as Sir James Douglas' Coloured Regiment', c.1860s, photographer undetermined. This photograph regularly appears in popular histories of British Columbia, probably
as evidence of the colony's superiority over the US with regard to persons of colour. The caption in George
Woodcock's *Picture History of British Columbia* (Edmonton: Hurtig, 1980), 39, reads: 'To show their apprecia-
tion of the freedom they sought under the British flag, the blacks formed their own volunteer militia unit.' For
a thoughtful discussion of the discrimination that African-American migrants to the colony actually faced, see
Adele Perry, *On the Edge of Empire: Gender, Race, and the Making of British Columbia, 1849–1871* (Toronto: UTP,
2001), 40, 68, 84, 132, 181. BCA, C-06124.

'the manly, respectable, loyal and enterprising
community established on the banks of the
Fraser',[15] he reluctantly yielded to the Legislative
Council when, on 2 April 1868, it voted 14 to 5
to establish the capital permanently at Victoria.
That decision did nothing to ease the antagonism
between the island and the mainland.

Meanwhile, the united province of Canada
(the future Quebec and Ontario) had negotiated
a union with its counterparts in Nova Scotia and

New Brunswick. The British Colonial Office,
which favoured confederation, also looked forward to a time when British Columbia would fulfill the vision of a dominion extending from sea
unto sea. As a part of Canada, British Columbia
would have greater commercial and strategic
value to the British world system, and British tax-
payers would be relieved of some of the costs of
administering a colony. Union with the other
British North American colonies would also

reduce the possibility—however slight it might have been in reality—of annexation to the United States. The colony's trade was largely north–south, and with a transcontinental railroad under construction in the US, there was considerable logic to the idea of closer political integration along the same economic axis. The California legislature certainly thought so: it resolved in February 1868 to use all 'fair and honorable means' to detach British Columbia from its 'Kingly Empire' and attach it to the American union. But California's enthusiasm for annexation diminished as the placer gold that attracted American miners ran out. The American consul in Victoria assured Washington that the British Columbians were 'restless and dissatisfied', and hence eager for annexation, but only 48 signed an 1869 petition asking President Grant for annexation, and only three of them were British subjects.[16]

The real push to annex British Columbia came from Canada. As early as 1858, George Brown, the Reform leader of Canada West and proprietor of the Toronto *Globe*, had urged his readers to join the Fraser gold rush and predicted that the presence in the west of immigrants from Canada would have 'a favourable effect in breaking up the quarantine which the Hudson's Bay Company have preserved over the territory'. Unaware of the geography of western British North America, Brown claimed that it was 'perfectly possible for a person entering a canoe at Toronto to float it, without any other aid than the labour of two men, into the Pacific Ocean'. Henry Youle Hind, leader of a Canadian expedition into that HBC territory in 1858–9, waxed rhapsodic about British Columbia: 'Such an extent of country, and having such resources of gold, silver, and other metals, and a large quanti-

ty of agricultural land, is *an empire* . . . the gold field of British Columbia is practically illimitable, and its wealth inexhaustible.'[17] During the 1864 discussions of the proposed federation of British North America, Brown persuaded the delegates to provide for the eventual entry of British Columbia and Vancouver Island, and the British government agreed. The legislation that created the dominion, the British North America Act, included a clause (Section 146) providing for the new federation to admit British Columbia if the BC legislature so requested.

It took four years for British Columbians to accept the invitation. Not many of them had any enthusiasm for union with Canada. Moreover, Governor Seymour and his appointees, who dominated the hybrid Legislative Council, actively opposed the idea, as did some of the elected members of the Council. The most prominent among the latter was Dr John Sebastian Helmcken, a Victoria surgeon, former Hudson's Bay employee, and son-in-law of James Douglas. He believed that confederation was premature, given British Columbia's small population and its limited communication with Canada (as he later put it, 'with Canada we had nothing to do') and feared that the loss of the colony's own tariff revenues would reduce its income. The appointed members of the Council, who were colonial civil servants, feared they would lose their jobs as well as the British connection, and they had no love for Canada. As a piece of doggerel written by a former colonial surveyor, J.D. Pemberton, put it: 'True loyalty's to Motherland / and not to Ca-na-da. / The love we bear is second-hand / to any step-mama.' Attorney-General Henry Crease explained the situation to a friend in October 1869: 'we are threatened with Confederation, i.e. to be a distant dependency of a poor and hungry province of the Empire instead of a self-dependent Colony of the Empire directly connected with the parent state'. He told his brother-in-law, 'No one here trusts the Canadian Govt's word. . . . Canadians are called North American Chinamen.'[18] The latter comment was an allusion to the suspicion that Canadians came to the colony only to make their fortunes, planning all along to return home once they had done so.

In fact the prominent Canadians in the colony had come to stay. Amor De Cosmos, now an elected member of the Council and one of the few Islanders to support union with British Columbia, had been a fervent advocate of confederation since the early 1860s, and had even travelled to Canada to lobby Canadian politicians for support. After failing to convince Seymour and the Council to pursue union, De Cosmos took his campaign to the people of the colony through the Confederation League, established in May 1868. At the League's convention at Yale in September 1868 De Cosmos linked the idea of joining Canada to a proposal with much more public support in the colony: responsible government. Another elected member, John Robson, an Upper Canadian who published the *British Columbian* in New Westminster, also supported Confederation and responsible government.[19]

But Governor Seymour had no interest in either. He rebuffed the Confederation League's petition, and in his dispatches to the Colonial Office he misrepresented the extent of support both for union with Canada and for responsible government. In an effort to stack the Legislative Council with anti-confederates, Seymour expanded the franchise for the election of October 1868 to include every white male in the colony, regardless of ethnic background, apparently assuming that those who were not British

'Our party at Lilloeet [*sic*]', 1865, by Charles Gentile. When Governor Seymour (seated second from the left with his pet terrier in his lap) and his entourage toured the goldfields, they took Gentile along to create a photographic record. This photo came to the NAC as part of the collection of Seymour's Colonial Secretary, Arthur Nonus Birch, the young gentleman standing on the right of the photo, whom Gilbert Sproat described as 'tallish, lean, flexible-limbed, . . . good-looking, well-mannered and immaculately British'; quoted in Margaret A. Ormsby, *British Columbia: A History* (Toronto: Macmillan, 1958), 200. NAC, C-88938.

subjects would have little interest in union with Canada. Although pro-confederates won every district on the mainland, their opponents took the Island, and even De Cosmos lost his Victoria seat to Dr Helmcken.

Disappointed with these results, Canadian

'Street scene, showing sign for L.A. Blanc's Photographic Gallery, Barkerville', c. 1870, by Louis A. Blanc. Blanc (active 1865–72) was a Washington watchmaker and jeweller who became a photographer in Victoria in 1865 and moved on to Barkerville in 1868. The 28 Blanc photos in the BCA suggest how an independent photographer earned a living: 20 of them are portraits and three are photos of businesses, likely made for sale to their proprietors. This image is one side of a stereographic photo, made with a dual-lens camera that produced two almost identical images. Viewing them through a device called a stereopticon created the impression of three dimensions. NAC, PA-143462.

Prime Minister John A. Macdonald suggested that the Colonial Office replace Seymour with Anthony Musgrave, the governor who had worked hard but unsuccessfully to persuade Newfoundlanders to join Confederation. The suggestion was more timely than Macdonald could have imagined. Seymour contracted dysentery while investigating a disturbance between the Nass and Tsimshian peoples of the north coast. When his condition became serious, the ship he was travelling on dropped anchor at Bella Coola, where he died on 10 June 1869.[20]

News of Seymour's death reached Victoria on 13 June, when the ship returned, and the Executive Council informed the Colonial Office of his death the next day. The speed with which the Colonial Office responded was a sign of how the world had shrunk with the introduction of the transcontinental telegraph and the Atlantic cable. On receiving the news, the Colonial Office immediately informed Queen Victoria: 'It is important to fill his place as soon as possible with the best man, for on the future Governor will much depend whether British Columbia will join the Canadian Dominion, or become American- ized'. Within twenty-four hours of hearing that Seymour had died, British Columbians learned that they would soon have a new governor.[21]

Musgrave, who arrived with instructions to promote union, understood the diplomatic skills required of a governor who would have to placate all factions in the colony. Instead of simply joining forces with the pro-Canada group and ramming the confederation proposal through, Musgrave toured the colony to build a personal following. His most important convert was Dr Helmcken. When the Legislative Council debated the Terms of Union (at Musgrave's request), Helmcken offered qualified support if suitable terms could be negotiated. Musgrave then appointed Helmcken, along with Joseph Trutch (the commissioner of lands and works), and Dr R.W.W. Carrall (a native of Ontario and elected Legislative Council member for the Cariboo) as British Columbia's three-member team to negotiate with Canada; of the three, only Carrall had supported union from the start. The Victoria *Daily British Colonist*—then under the control of John Robson and David Higgins, staunch advocates of responsible government—appointed a 'special correspondent' to accompany the delegates and report on the negotiations. Henry Seelye's primary task, however, was to lobby for the inclusion of responsible government among the Terms—against the wishes of the Legislative Council, which had asked for the indefinite continuation of the existing form of government.

Canada readily agreed to the introduction of responsible government as soon as British Columbians wished it. The only significant controversy concerned financial terms. The British Columbians said they needed an annual allowance of $75,000 plus a per capita subsidy that would yield $96,000 based on the standard subsidy of 80 cents a head and a population that they claimed to number 120,000. The Canadians may not have known much about British Columbia,

'Firemen's Arch, William's Creek Fire Brigade Welcoming Governor Musgrave, Barkerville', by L.A. Blanc. A hotbed of pro-Confederation sentiment, Barkerville offered the colony's new governor a warm welcome when he visited in October 1869. Membership in organizations such as the local band or volunteer fire brigade was an expression both of civic pride and of personal respectability. The arch—made of the firemen's ladders, festooned with buckets—carries a banner reading 'GOD SAVE THE QUEEN'. BCA, A-03762.

but they knew that figure was a gross exaggeration. British Columbia entered Confederation too late to be counted in the 1871 census, but estimates suggest that its population at the time consisted of 25,661 'Native Indians' and only 8,576 European and 1,548 Asian residents, for a total of 36,247. Although the federal government included the Native peoples in its calculation for the purpose of the subsidy and promised to cover the cost of administering 'Indian Affairs', the British Columbians claimed the subsidy was too small and threatened to end the negotiations. By this time the negotiators had received promises from Canada not only to assume responsibility for the colonial debt, but to build a marine hospital and a penitentiary and to provide federal services such as lighthouses and telegraphic and postal services. But that was not all. Having asked for a coach road to Fort Garry and the spending of at least a million dollars a year on surveys for a railway that was to be completed 'at the earliest possible date', the British Columbians were astonished when the Canadians promised to begin construction of the railway within two years of the province's joining Canada—and to complete it within ten. Nevertheless, the subsidy issue threatened to be a deal-breaker until Sir George Étienne Cartier, who led the Dominion negotiators, had the 'brilliant idea' of giving British Columbia a subsidy in return for the lands it would surrender for the railway. The Legislative Council readily endorsed the agreement.[22]

A fulsome editorial in the *British Colonist* welcomed Her Majesty's proclamation on 20 July 1871:

> *Today British Columbia and Canada joined hearts and hands across the Rocky Mountains. . . . At 12 o'clock last night there were manifestations of great rejoicing in the city. Bells were rung, guns fired, blue lights and Roman candles burned, and crackers snapped. And people met on the streets and shook hands with and congratulated each other and cheered and cheered. . . . They were celebrating the Birth of Liberty.*

Selections from that editorial were to become a standard feature of future Dominion (later Canada) Day celebrations.[23]

The addition of British Columbia to Canada was part of an overall development strategy—implicit in the concept of Confederation—for the entire West. But Ottawa treated BC quite differently than it did the other parts of the West. British Columbia entered Confederation largely on its own terms, through peaceful negotiations. In the former Rupert's Land, by contrast, it took Louis Riel and the Red River resistance to create the 'postage stamp' province of Manitoba with self-government and representation in the Dominion parliament, and the rest of the North-West Territories only slowly acquired representative institutions. Moreover, British Columbia controlled its public lands and natural resources, whereas neither Manitoba nor the North-West Territories gained that power until 1930. Thus the Prairie West in effect remained a 'colony' of Ottawa, while British Columbia, despite its tiny population, became a 'white settler' province with institutions of self-government and control of its own natural resources. Constitutionally, it was a province equal to the four original members of the Canadian federation.

The first years after Confederation suggest that those who questioned BC's readiness for responsible government and provincial status may have been correct. Although the franchise qualifications were relatively generous (all literate 'natural-born' British subjects, male, aged 21 or more, who fulfilled minimal property and residence requirements), not many British Columbians met them. In the 1871 election only 3,804 men voted. Federally, some British Columbians allied themselves with the Liberals and Conservatives, but there were no political parties in the provincial legislature; premiers relied on their personal followings to maintain power. In the fourteen years between Confederation and the arrival of the railway in 1885, the province had seven different governments, two of which were led by the same man—George A. Walkem, an Irish immigrant and lawyer who has been described as 'British Columbia's first modern politician'.[24] One premier (Andrew C. Elliott) was defeated in a general election; two resigned for other posts (Amor De Cosmos to retain his federal office and Walkem to accept a judgeship); three resigned after losing votes of confidence, and William Smithe, one of the more successful, died in office in 1887.

The early legislatures were preoccupied with basic housekeeping: establishing procedures for the conduct of their own business and the administration of justice, devising a municipal act, replacing the tradition of the open vote with a secret ballot, and disfranchising the Chinese and Aboriginal people lest they vote as a bloc in some sparsely settled constituencies. The legislature also established a non-sectarian system of public schools. Under the new School Act, tuition was to be free except in high schools, which did not yet exist. To provide for children in the interior who lived far from any school, Superintendent John Jessop recommended establishing a public boarding school. The Cache Creek Boarding School opened in 1874, and although one principal, at least, had trouble keeping the girls and boys from visiting one another's dormitories, it remained in operation until 1890, when increased settlement made it feasible to establish more day schools.[25]

One of the more controversial issues debated by the first provincial legislature was the tariff. The Terms of Union provided that until the railway was finished, British Columbia could decide whether or not to adopt Canadian tariffs. The tariff was a live issue in the 1871 provincial election. John Robson, who had taken over the editorship of the Victoria *British Colonist* and was running in Nanaimo, favoured the lower Canadian tariff, but Amor De Cosmos, who was now editor of the *Victoria Standard* and running in a rural area near Victoria, insisted that if the Canadian tariff were adopted it must protect farmers. The election results showed a rural–urban split, but John Foster McCreight was able to form a government because a majority of those elected wanted the immediate introduction of the Canadian tariff. Over the objections of members who represented rural areas, that was done. That decision did not settle the issue, and some members later switched positions, but the Canadian tariff remained.[26]

Continuing controversy illustrated the fluidity of political alliances and uncertainty about the province's relationship with Ottawa. Although British Columbians had not asked for the railway to be completed within a decade, once Ottawa had made the promise, they regarded it as a sacred trust. Thus on 20 July 1873 at Esquimalt—fixed by a federal Order in Council as the terminus—a symbolic sod was turned, and before long a few hundred metres of right of way had been cleared.[27] Actual construction, however, was delayed. One reason was the difficulty of finding a suitable route through the mountains. The second was a change of government in Ottawa following the 'Pacific Scandal' of 1873, when it was revealed that Prime Minister Macdonald and some of his colleagues had accepted campaign funds from Sir Hugh Allan— who at the time had been seeking the contract to build the transcontinental railway. The new

'On the Skeena River 3 miles above Hazelton, B.C. Rocher Deboule Mt. in distance, December 28th, 1872', by Charles Horetzky. The dog-drawn toboggan carries surveying equipment. This photograph was made in the course of extensive surveying to determine the route for the transcontinental railway promised to BC when it entered Confederation. That this location on the Skeena River turned out to be more than 1,000 kilometres north of the final route suggests how far afield the surveyors searched. As Andrew Birrell points out, the photographs that the CPR commissioned from Charles Horetzky (1838–1900) have been widely admired for their 'artistic qualities'; yet they were 'used solely for information'. Horetzky was among the first to master the new dry-plate process, which required only a camera, plates, and a tripod. By contrast, the load of gear required for the old wet-plate collodion process weighed down three packhorses. See Birrell, 'Survey Photography in British Columbia, 1858–1890', *BC Studies* 52 (Winter 1981–2), 49–53. NAC, C-81508.

Liberal Prime Minister, Alexander Mackenzie, had always been cautious about the railway, believing that construction should not begin until all the surveys were complete, and that it should proceed only as the nation's finances permitted. More ominous for British Columbia was the presence in Mackenzie's cabinet of Edward Blake, who had described the province as 'a sea of mountains'. Moreover, Mackenzie had the misfortune to come to office just as a severe economic depression hit North America. When he sought to be relieved of the promise to complete

the railway by 1881, the young province threatened to secede from the Dominion.

Within the province, the situation was complicated by conflict between Fraser Valley residents, who expected the railway to follow the
Fraser River to the coast and who were benefiting
from expenditures on surveying, and Islanders,
who were determined that the railway must terminate at the best harbour on the coast,
Esquimalt—in which case it would follow a more
northerly route across the Cariboo–Chilcotin
Plateau, bypassing the Fraser Valley altogether. It
was technically possible to build switchbacks to
take the line down from the plateau to sea level
and then bridge Seymour Narrows (between
Quadra Island and Vancouver Island, just north of
Campbell River). But in the end engineers advised
that a line through the Fraser valley would be less
expensive both to build and to operate.[28]

Meanwhile, provincial politics remained
unstable. Members elected to support one candidate often changed their minds and supported
another, moving back and forth between the government and the opposition. The last days of the
A.C. Elliott government, in the spring of 1878,
were so boisterous, and the legislative proceedings such a popular entertainment, that the
speaker threatened to close the galleries.[29] After
Elliott's government was defeated over redistrib-
ution of the legislative seats, Walkem returned as
premier. 'Fight Ottawa' had been one of his campaign slogans; he did so much to that end—
including increasing tolls on the Cariboo wagon
road, which the railway needed to transport supplies—that some mainlanders feared Ottawa
might not fulfill its railway promise after all. In
an effort to capitalize on the rising hostility of
white workingmen to what they considered
'unfair' competition from Chinese labourers,

Walkem's government briefly required the latter
to purchase licences, until the federal government disallowed the law. A law denying Chinese
workers employment on provincial public works
projects remained on the statute books, but it did
not prevent Andrew Onderdonk, who had the
federal contract to build the Canadian Pacific
Railway through the Fraser Canyon, from
importing at least 2,000 Chinese labourers in
1881 and 6,784 during the first half of 1882
alone, with many more to come. When forced to
choose between what Amor De Cosmos called
'two evils'—accepting Chinese workers or doing
without the railway—British Columbians reluctantly chose the former.

Walkem's 'fight Ottawa' policy made him a
thorn in the side of the prime minister, but in June
1882 the wily Macdonald solved the problem by
appointing Walkem to the bench. That complicated provincial politics.[30] Immediately on taking
office, Walkem's successor as premier, Robert
Beaven, called for a general election that proved to
be his undoing. His government was trounced.
Still, Beaven put off resigning as long as he could,
postponing the final meeting with the legislature
until the following January, when, at the first
opportunity, the opposition moved a want of confidence. William Smithe became premier.

Even before Walkem's departure from the
premiership, British Columbians had begun to
look more favourably on Ottawa. In the 1878
election Victorians provided John A. Macdonald
with a parliamentary seat after the voters of
Kingston, Ontario, rejected him. Even though he
had never seen British Columbia, let alone lived
there, they voted for him because they expected—rightly—that if re-elected his Conservative
government would start building the railway.
The beginning of construction in 1879 helped to

'La Part du Lion', *Le Canada* (Montreal), December 1879. By the late 1870s political cartoons were evolving from complicated, text-laden illustrations into pithy statements on public issues. In this variation on the theme of British Columbia as the 'spoilt child' of Confederation, 'Bas Canada' (Quebec) goes hungry while 'Colombie' gorges on the 'lion's share' of Dominion government spending.

ease BC's sense of regional alienation, as did Smithe's success in negotiating a Settlement Act (1884) whereby Ottawa agreed to build a graving (dry) dock that had been promised to Victoria as part of the confederation deal and to subsidize the construction of the Esquimalt and Nanaimo

Railway (E&N)—the consolation prize given to the Island after the CPR terminus was awarded to the mainland.

The grant to the E&N was an outstanding example of the government largesse to industry that has been described as 'The Great Potlatch'.[31]

'B.C. Legislative Assembly in front of the Legislative Buildings, 1882', by Richard Maynard. British Columbia MLAs pose in front of the nineteenth-century legislature, a complex of three buildings that, because of their pagoda-like roofs and exterior decoration, were popularly known as 'the Birdcages'. The dress of the legislators suggests their homogeneity. By 1882 Richard Maynard had become Victoria's photographer of choice for important occasions. BCA, A-02561.

The connections between business and politics were intimate, and sometimes the businessmen were politicians themselves. A prime example was Robert Dunsmuir, the head of the group that was granted the contract to build the E&N. A coal magnate and MLA for Nanaimo (1882–9), Dunsmuir received nearly a million hectares of provincial land on Vancouver Island, including timber and mineral rights, and a federal bonus of $750,000, in return for building a railway that happened to serve his own mines. Noted for their disdain of labour unions and their exploitation of Chinese labour, Dunsmuir and his son James were BC's own 'robber barons'. Robert, a skilled Scottish miner, arrived as an indentured worker to the Hudson's Bay Company coal mine at Fort Rupert, at the north end of Vancouver Island, in 1851, shortly before the HBC moved its coal mining operations to Nanaimo. In 1855 the Company gave him a free-miner's licence to work an abandoned shaft as a reward for not joining other miners in a strike, and when the HBC sold its collieries in 1862 he stayed on as manager. Then in 1869, while prospecting on his own, he discovered the rich Wellington seam and staked a claim, which he developed with capital invested by naval officers at Esquimalt. By 1877 the business was flourishing, but Dunsmuir decided to cut wages at the mine. When the workers responded with a strike, he brought in strike-breakers and, despite stout resistance by miners and their wives, managed (with the help of the militia) to evict some strikers from their company-owned homes. Four months after the strike began, the miners surrendered and Dunsmuir rehired most, but not all, of them.[32] When they struck again in 1883, Dunsmuir simply waited them out until they returned to work. The Wellington mine was particularly dangerous: explosions and fires cost the lives of 11 miners in 1879, 65 in 1881, 23 in 1884, and 75 in 1888.

Dunsmuir became the dominant collier on the Island through the purchase of other mines. When he died in 1889, he was probably the wealthiest man in British Columbia, but the mansion he had commissioned to display his wealth—the baronial Craigdarroch Castle, which still towers on Victoria's skyline—was not yet finished. There was perhaps more symbolism than intended in the fact that his hearse was pulled by miners rather than horses.[33]

San Francisco and the American railways provided important markets for Vancouver Island coal, but US tariffs effectively closed those markets to BC lumber. The lack of a US market discouraged investment in the industry. Nevertheless, mills were established at Burrard Inlet and at several points on Vancouver Island. In addition to supplying local markets, they shipped lumber around the Pacific Rim to places including the Australasian colonies, China, and Mexico, as well as several South American countries, and sent spars for sailing ships as far away as England. The construction of the CPR brought an extended boom: not only did the railway itself need wood for bridges, ties, and buildings, but when it was

*Facing above* 'Prospecting for Alluvial Gold in British Columbia, c. 1862–1870', by William G.R. Hind, oil on board. The lone prospector with his simple pan is the archetype of the gold rush. Yet of the 36 'panning' images available on the BCA website, only three date from the nineteenth century. Virtually all the rest were created after 1950 and show actors performing for tourists. William George Richardson Hind (1833–89) was an art teacher and illustrator from Toronto who travelled to the Cariboo goldfields with a party of approximately 150 men and one woman (known as the 'Overlanders of 1862') and stayed in the west for several years. His sketches and paintings were intended both for individual sale and for possible use by his older brother Henry Youle Hind, the leader of the 1857–8 scientific expedition to the western interior and an outspoken propagandist for the westward expansion of Canada; see Mary Jo Hughes, *Hindsight: William Hind in the Canadian West* (Winnipeg: Winnipeg Art Gallery, 2002). BCA, PDP-02612.

*Facing below.* 'British Columbia Miners, 1864', by William G.R. Hind, watercolour on card. Many pictures from the gold rush era show miners at their leisure, playing cards and drinking in rowdy taverns. This painting shows a more domestic scene. Although there is a bottle on the table at which two miners relax, one of their comrades is washing his hair in a bucket just outside the door. BCA PDP00014.

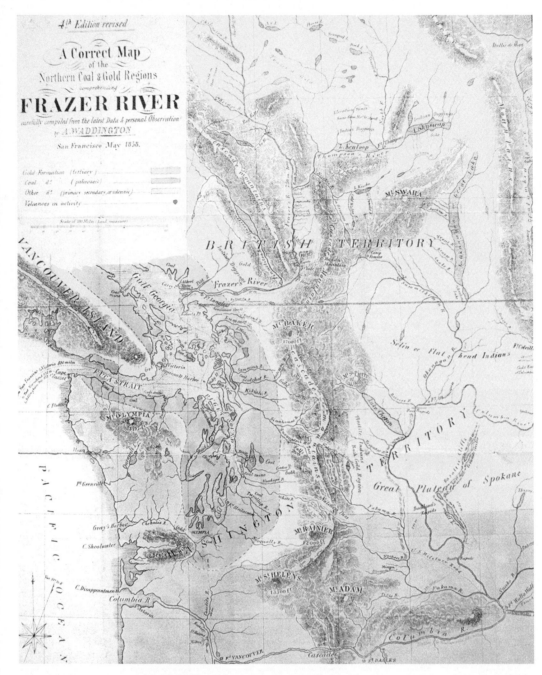

Alfred Waddington (1801–72) was an Englishman who arrived in Victoria from San Francisco early in 1858 to seek his fortune without soiling his hands in the gold fields. He published his promotional book *The Fraser Mines Vindicated* after only four months in the colony. This colourful map is evidence of his 'booster' mentality, exaggerating not only the colony's 'gold formations' but also its reserves of coal—the fuel indispensable to industrial development as well as ship and rail transportation in the nineteenth century. BCA, CM A79.

VIEW OF VICTORIA, VANCOUVER'S ISLAND, BRITISH AMERICA. 1858

finished, the newcomers it carried west needed lumber for construction. Even in those early years, mill owners were lobbying for access to the most desirable timberlands, as the provincial government, which retained control of forest lands, was experimenting with different leasing and licensing arrangements in an effort to provide fair access for both large and small operators, keep out speculators, and secure some revenue for itself.[34]

Until the turn of the twentieth century, however, British Columbia's most important export was canned salmon. BC's first salmon canneries were relatively small-scale operations established on the Fraser River in the late 1860s. Keith Ralston has recovered the career of one early cannery entrepreneur, an African-American tinsmith named John Sullivan Deas who found his way into the business because he knew how to make the cans in which the fish was packed. Deas and his partners bought tinplate from a British commission merchant, who later purchased their product and sold it in Britain. In the early days he competed with other small-scale canners to buy salmon from independent fishers, and in the mid-1870s his company packed the most salmon on the Fraser. By the late 1870s, however, the trend towards large-scale industrial capitalism in the fisheries was clear. In part it was dictated by the four-year migration cycle of the fish itself, which meant that a canner had to have enough capital to ride out the three lean years. But developments in canning technology only added to the financial burden. Despite his success in the early 1870s, Deas was no more able than any other small-scale canner to survive long. By the end of the 1880s all of them had sold out or failed, unwilling or unable to invest enough in modernizing their operations.[35]

More typical of an emerging regional entrepreneurial class was Edgar Crow Baker, who arrived in Victoria in 1874 as a retired Royal Navy officer. This background gave him the

---

*Facing above.* 'View of Victoria, Vancouver's Island, British America', 1858. To portray the sudden burst of activity in Victoria at the start of the gold rush, the anonymous maker of this coloured drawing showed 17 vessels bustling around the harbour. The 'British America' in the title suggests a US source. BCA, PDP01898.

*Facing below.* 'Construction of the Collins Overland Telegraph, 1865', by John Clayton White. A corporal in the Royal Engineers, White (1835–1907) documented the BC portion of the ill-fated telegraph project in a series of 25 paintings. Here the newly installed wire hangs overhead as pack horses laden with spools of wire struggle across a stream. The man standing in the foreground has apparently waded across in his bare feet; to the left, a colleague wears a hat equipped with a mosquito net. BCA, PDP02908.

*Overleaf above.* 'Strait of San Juan, BC, 1860s', by William G.R. Hind, watercolour, graphite, and gouache on paper. Note the boundary cairn at the top of the hill on the right of the painting, the two houses on the hill in the distance, and the steamer trailing smoke in the strait. Mary Jo Hughes argues convincingly that Hind included these details as 'carefully considered messages about the possession of the frontier by its new Canadian inhabitants' (*Hindsight*, 133-4). McCord, M473.

*Overleaf below.* 'Chinook Indians Gathering Shellfish, Vancouver Island, 1860s', by William G.R. Hind, watercolour, ink, and graphite on paper. Hind's title for this work is puzzling, since the Chinook people are native to the Columbia River area, not Vancouver Island. Perhaps he was referring to the Chinook jargon used in the fur trade. In any event, Hind rarely depicted Native subjects, and his apparent lack of interest in Aboriginal life marks a sharp contrast with Paul Kane. McCord, M607.

social standing necessary to establish political connections. Beginning as the manager of the Hastings Saw Mill Company, he learned the lumber business and speculated in Victoria real estate with sufficient success to build a modest fortune—aided not inconsiderably by his position on Victoria city council. In 1882 Baker won a seat in the federal parliament as a Conservative, and he managed to turn his small fortune into a larger one after inside information about where the transcontinental railway would terminate led him to buy land on Burrard Inlet. His political career was simply an extension of his business ventures, which also included investments in saw milling, mining, and railway companies; in 1895 he became the first president of the short-lived Victoria Stock Exchange. As his biographer G.W.S. Brooks points out, Victoria in the late nineteenth century may have followed British social customs, but in matters of business 'it followed the American tradition with no apparent conflict in ethics.'[36]

Soon after BC joined Canada, preparations were already underway for rapid exploitation of the province's resources after the railway arrived, and Native people paid the most obvious human cost. Because the provincial government wanted to encourage economic development and population growth, it was unwilling to acknowledge any Aboriginal land claims. As for the Dominion government, it was equally committed to capitalist development, and it had no desire to create additional conflict with the province for the sake of its Native people. Clause 13 of the Terms of Union provided that 'The charge of Indians, and the trusteeship and management of the lands reserved for their use and benefit, shall be assumed by the dominion, and a policy as liberal as that hitherto pursued by the British

Columbia Government shall be continued by the Dominion Government after the Union.' But of course 'a policy as liberal' as that of the BC government was even less liberal than the one applied elsewhere in the Canadian West. Although Ottawa was hardly generous in its treatment of Native people in Manitoba and the North-West Territories, it looked beneficent compared to British Columbia. [37]

In the Prairie West First Nations signed seven numbered treaties with the Crown between 1871 and 1877. Whatever the limitations of these treaties, they provided larger reserves, guarantees of cash grants, agricultural instruction or rations during the period of economic transition, and a basic legal framework within which Native signatories would be able to negotiate with the Dominion. Yet with a few exceptions—Treaty No. 8 (1899) in the northeast and the treaties that James Douglas negotiated on southern Vancouver Island—Native people in British Columbia were without treaties. Furthermore, Aboriginal people were largely denied the rights enjoyed by other British subjects living in the province, among them the political right—for men—to vote and the right as individuals to 'pre-empt' public land for the purpose of establishing their own homesteads.

Because the provincial government controlled British Columbia's lands, it dictated the size of the reserves that the federal Indian Affairs Branch was able to assign to First Nations. The provincial government obstructed Ottawa's efforts to establish reserves in BC until after the land most suitable for agriculture had been distributed to white settlers and the number of Native people in the province had decreased still further. In 1876, fearing Native violence if policy that so flagrantly favoured white settlers over Native peo-

'View of Totem Poles at Masset' c. 1890, by Robert W. Reford. Totem poles held a particular fascination for non-Native visitors to BC. In the 1920s, a group of totem poles at Kitwanga, between Hazelton and Terrace on the CNR, was said to be the second-most-photographed spot in Canada, after Niagara Falls. By then, Douglas Cole points out, 'as a result of private and museum acquisition, natural decay, and occasional wanton destruction, the . . . totem pole had become an endangered specimen'; see Cole, *Captured Heritage: The Scramble for Northwest Coast Artifacts* (Seattle: University of Washington Press, 1985), 270–9. Reford (1867–1951)—an amateur photographer from Montreal who lived in Victoria from 1889 until 1891—was among the first in Canada to use the Kodak rollfilm camera, which cost $25 and came loaded with 100 exposures; see Ralph Greenhill and Andrew Birrell, *Canadian Photography: 1839–1920* (Toronto: Coach House Press, 1979), 126. Given that a box camera and tripod appear in this photo, it was probably made with the Kodak. NAC, C-60823.

ples continued, the Alexander Mackenzie government insisted on the establishment of a joint Dominion–provincial commission on 'Indian Lands'. The joint appointee as Indian Reserve Commissioner, Gilbert Sproat, had arrived in British Columbia as a settler himself in 1860. Despite his background, he believed that Native peoples did hold title to their lands, and that the most effective way to extinguish that title was through the prompt provision of generous reserves. For four years Sproat fought a losing battle with the provincial government. He mapped reserves, but the province refused to recognize most of the reserves that he proposed, and instead granted or sold the land to white settlers who simply ran the Native occupants off. The Indian Lands Commission also created a grazing policy to enable Native peoples to support themselves by ranching. This policy too was rejected by the province.[38]

In 1880 the Macdonald government bowed to pressure from the province and dismissed

'Crosby and the Congregation of Fort Simpson Church, 1881', by Edward Dossetter. The Revd Thomas Crosby established this Methodist mission to the Tsimshian in 1873. Determined to extirpate Tsimshian traditions, Crosby crusaded against the potlatch and insisted that converts behave like Europeans. The large group that turned out for this photograph suggests that to some extent Crosby succeeded. Yet Susan Neylan argues persuasively that the people did not relinquish their traditions: rather, they 'added Christianity to their identities as Tsimshian'; see Neylan, *The Heavens Are Changing: Nineteenth-Century Protestant Missions and Tsimshian Christianity* (Montreal: MQUP, 2003). Edward Dossetter (active in BC 1881–90) was a commercial photographer who enjoyed the double patronage of the Dominion government and the Royal Navy; he made this photo when he accompanied Indian Superintendent Dr Israel Wood Powell on an inspection tour up the coast on HMS *Boxer* in 1881. BCA, B-03538.

Sproat, replacing him with Peter O'Reilly, a retired magistrate with ranching investments in the interior who happened to be Joseph Trutch's brother-in-law; far from preventing O'Reilly from accepting the job, apparently these conflicts of interest recommended him. He served as Indian Land Commissioner until 1898, and drew the map of British Columbia's reserves along the lines established by settler governments in the 1860s. Native communities were assigned tiny and scattered allotments, provided without any provincial recognition that Aboriginal peoples had a right to be compensated for the land that had been theirs before the Europeans took it

Potlatch, Alert Bay. Confusion surrounds this photograph. The BCA catalogue lists it as 'Untitled'—and yet 'Indian Potlatch, Alert Bay BC' is clearly written across the bottom of the print. Edward Malin is even more precise, describing the scene as 'An intensely dramatic moment in a Kwakiutl potlatch in Alert Bay during the first decade of the 20th century' and identifying the 'painted construction' in the background as 'a temporary totem'; see Malin, *Northwest Coast Indian Painting: House Fronts and Interior Screens* (Portland: Timber Press, 1999), 269. Malin attributes the photo to William H. Halliday, the Indian Agent at Alert Bay (the initials 'HH' appear in the lower right corner). But Halliday was a bitter enemy of the potlatch, and it seems unlikely that he would have been allowed even to observe such an important ceremony, much less to photograph it. There is another possibility, though. Halliday reported in 1907 that 'several of the young men have cameras and take fairly good pictures' (quoted in Williams, *Framing the West*, 171). Perhaps one of them snapped the picture and Halliday later obtained a copy of it. BCA, H-04231.

from them. In many cases the reserve lands were unsuitable for agriculture, and some groups lost land that they had already been cultivating. The most important reason for Native peoples' 'failure' to make the transition to agriculture was the failure of white British Columbians to provide

'Chinese workers excavate the Kootenay Canal, 1887.' This photo provides an excellent example of the difficulties of working with images. It has been mistakenly used to depict 'Chinese at work on CPR in Mountains'—an unsurprising error, given that that is the inscription on the copy in the NAC (reproduced here) and the copy in the Provincial Archives of Alberta. The BCA identifies the photo accurately, and it was used correctly in Mabel E. Jordan, 'The Kootenay Reclamation and Colonization Scheme and William Adolph Baillie-Grohman', *BC Historical Quarterly* XX (July–October 1956), facing p. 192. Jordan thanks Baillie-Grohman's son for the photograph, but no photographer is identified. The NAC attributes the image to Edmonton photographer Ernest Brown (1877–1951), whose name is printed on the photo, but Brown's dates rule him out. We know, however, that Brown purchased the photo library of C.W. Mathers, a photographer who preceded him in Edmonton and who worked with W.H. Boorne; either Mathers or Boorne likely made the photo. NAC, C-6686B.

farmland. When the Canadian Pacific Railway crossed the province, Native communities that lost land to the right-of-way were not compensated—unlike whites in the same circumstances. On the coast and along the salmon rivers, First Nations faced special problems with regard to fishing rights, since the rapidly proliferating salmon canneries appropriated the best fishing sites at the river mouths. Denied adequate space either to fish or to farm, many Native people found seasonal waged work as freight packers, or in sawmills or canneries; in the 1880s as many as 6,000 'Canadian Indians' made annual migrations south to Washington in search of work.[39]

In the light of Sproat's efforts on behalf of Native people in British Columbia, it is ironic that his only significant success as Indian Lands Commissioner was the prohibition of the potlatch. In 1879 he wrote to Prime Minister Macdonald explaining 'the giant evil' of this 'most pernicious custom' and why it was inimical to the individualistic commercial economy that Euro-Canadians were trying to establish. Potlatching, he claimed, led to 'numerous vices which eat out the heart of the people' and promoted 'habits inconsistent with all progress'. Native people would never be able to 'acquire property' or 'become industrious' until the gov-

Saloon (left) and NWMP detachment at Donald, BC, 1884–5, by A.J. Smyth. The photograph of the saloon
became iconic when it was used on the cover of James H. Gray's best-selling popular history of prostitution in
the Prairie West, *Red Lights on the Prairies* (Toronto: Macmillan, 1971)—even though Donald (northwest of
Golden, BC) is clearly in the mountains. It has been used repeatedly to portray a 'wild west' of 'whores' and
hard-drinking navvies, most recently in Terry Reksten's *Illustrated History of British Columbia* (Vancouver: D&M,
2001), 121, and in Craig Heron, *Booze: A Distilled History of Canada* (Toronto: Between the Lines, 2003), 107.
Yet the very next photograph in the Glenbow catalogue has never been reproduced to our knowledge. 'NWMP
detachment at Donald, BC', was taken by the same photographer, and probably on the same day. One man
appears in both photos—sitting to the left of the saloon door and standing in the doorway of the police station. The more charitable explanation is that the historians who have used the saloon photo have never examined the Glenbow catalogue. The less charitable one is that the NWMP photo conveys a message that propo-
nents of the 'wild west' image don't want to acknowledge: that law and order were often just around the
corner. Glenbow, NA-782-2 and NA-782-3.

ernment placed 'an iron hand upon [their] shoul-
ders' and eradicated the custom altogether. As a
further irony, it seems that colonialism itself may
have been responsible for some of the features
that Euro-Canadians found most troubling about
the potlatch. The 'aggressive, hostile, or boastful'
potlatch, for example, which one anthropologist
has described as 'fighting with property', could
be used to establish a new status hierarchy when
government uprooted the people of two villages
and relocated them on a single reserve. A month
after Sproat's letter, the Indian Affairs Branch
ordered its agents to forbid the practice, and in
1884 a single amendment to the Indian Act formally outlawed both the potlatch and a custom
called the 'Give Away' Dance, practised by some

Native groups on the plains. But the ban proved
impossible to enforce and the potlatch continued, as Doug Cole and Ira Chaikin put it, 'by
stealth, disguise, [and] surreptitiousness'.[40]

The impending completion of the Canadian
Pacific Railway obscured what little concern
there might have been about the dilemma of
Native people. Nor was there much concern
about the conditions of the Chinese contract
labourers who built the railway in the Fraser
Canyon. When one of them was blown to pieces
while setting an explosive, the Kamloops newspaper commented on white callousness: 'Of
course there will be no investigation—only
another Chinaman gone—that's all. Another of
the same sort fills the gap and the work goes on

as usual.' As contractor Andrew Onderdonk's crews pushed east up the Fraser and the Thompson Rivers, an estimated 1,500 of the Chinese workers on the job lost their lives, albeit more to disease than to accidents. Chinese contract labourers rarely resisted their bosses, and when they did they felt the full weight of the law. The CPR's own crews of white workers drove the line from east to west through the Rockies and into the Selkirk Mountains. In 1884 the federal North-West Mounted Police were charged with enforcing the law within a 10-mile (16 km) band on either side of the CPR right of way through British Columbia. In the winter of 1884–5, the navvies at the end of the track in the mountains put down their tools in protest against their hazardous working conditions and unpaid wages. The NWMP shot and wounded one leader of the strike and arrested several others. That show of force, along with a payday, persuaded the strikers to return to laying the track.[41] The provincial and Dominion governments, and the railway and resource entrepreneurs whom they represented, shared a common determination to see British Columbia fulfill their vision of its destiny as Canada's empire on the Pacific. Little would be allowed to stand in their way.

# CHAPTER THREE

# Promise and Disappointment: 1885–1914

On 7 November 1885, at an otherwise undistinguished place about half-way between Revelstoke and Sicamous called Craigellachie, Donald Smith—one of the principal investors in the Canadian Pacific Railway—drove the plain iron spike that completed its main line. The most significant hammer blow in the province's history made British Columbia a part of Canada economically as well as politically. A year earlier a provincial government pamphlet included an invitation 'to enter and participate in the work of developing her dormant resources, increase her budding industries, and make for themselves homes where they may enjoy the comforts and, in time, even the luxuries of life'. Many people accepted. In 1881 British Columbia had had only about 25,000 non-Aboriginal residents; by 1911 it would count almost 400,000 people in total, of whom only one in five had been born in the province. Yet for many—First Nations, native-born, or newcomer—Canada's Pacific province became a land of promises unfulfilled.[1]

The railway put an end to the province's physical isolation from the rest of Canada, but not its psychological separation. British Columbians still considered themselves to be 'very far west indeed',[2] even though the journey from Vancouver to Ontario or Quebec now took no more than five or six days. For first-class travellers, the trip to the Pacific could be a magnificent experience. The CPR advertised the scenic wonders of the Rockies to wealthy tourists and built resort hotels such as Glacier House, near Rogers Pass, expressly for them. Among the first tourists, in the summer of 1886, were Sir John A. and Lady Macdonald. During his visit the prime minister drove a last spike himself at Shawnigan Lake, marking the completion of the Esquimalt and Nanaimo Railway.

Victoria may have got only a minor railway, but it had still enjoyed a boom during the CPR's construction, when the contractors brought in almost all of their supplies through its port. As long as the province depended largely on water-borne trade, Victoria remained its commercial centre, especially for coastal industries as salmon canning and sealing, while nearby Esquimalt housed the North Pacific base of the Royal Navy—tangible evidence of the continuing British presence.

Victoria was also British Columbia's seat of government. After heated controversy reminis-

Wm. Taylor    Syd. Lobb    A.E. Hodgins    G.H. Duggan    Sheriff Redgrave    W. Robinson    D.D. Man    Dr. Sweat    Orman Crook

Ed. Laugham

## The Last Spike C.P.R
### Staged by Construction party that missed the Official Ceremony

Some historians have interpreted this image as a statement of working-class resistance to capital. But we do not know who made it, or exactly when or where, let alone what the subjects were thinking. The official ceremony was held at Craigellachie, where Donald Smith (later Lord Strathcona) drove the last spike on 7 November 1885. NAC, C-14115.

cent of the old 'Island versus Mainland' conflict, its status as the capital was anchored by the government's decision in 1893 to build permanent Parliament Buildings there. A young English architect, Francis Rattenbury, won the competi-

tion to design them. Built at the then breathtaking cost of almost one million dollars, the buildings were opened in 1898.[3]

Rail construction in the 1880s also brought some prosperity to the old colonial capital of

'Sir John and Lady Macdonald at Stave River, BC', 24 July 1886. The photographer who recorded the Macdonalds' trip, 'Professor' Oliver B. Buell (1844–1910), travelled in a private rail car provided by the general manager of the CPR, W.C. Van Horne. Buell later used the slides he made in a lecture entitled 'Across Canada', which promoted tourism on the CPR. After Prime Minister Macdonald saw this 'entertainment', he wrote a testimonial praising Buell's work as 'so accurate that I almost fancied that I was again at Stave River posing for my photograph'. See E.J. Hart, *Trains, Peaks & Tourists: The Golden Age of Canadian Travel* (Banff: EJH Literary Enterprises, 2000), 40. Glenbow, NA-4967-132.

New Westminster, since the railway builders bought some of their supplies from local merchants and farmers. Sandbars at the mouth of the Fraser River made it difficult for ocean-going ships to reach New Westminster, so it was never seriously considered as a terminus for the railway. Instead, the CPR satisfied its legal obligation to reach tidewater by naming Port Moody, at the head of Burrard Inlet, its Pacific terminus. In 1884, however, when general manager William Van Horne visited the site, he realized that it was unsuitable: the shallow harbour could be reached only through the treacherous Second Narrows, and the steep hills surrounding it could

'Sealing fleet at Victoria Hr., B.C., 1891', photographer unknown. Ships that hunted seals in Alaskan waters used Victoria as their home port for several decades beginning in the 1860s. Local businessmen provided financial backing for the sealers, and local merchants provisioned them. Concern about decreasing numbers of seals and increasing competition for American sealers led the US government to seize 25 Canadian vessels in the summer of 1892, touching off an international incident. This photograph, one of many made in the early 1890s, showed the economic importance of sealing and buttressed the British-Canadian position. Victoria-based sealers won $500,000 in compensation in 1893, when an international tribunal prohibited sealing within 60 miles (96 km) of the Pribiloff islands in the Behring Sea, where the seals raised their pups. The sealers then hunted in Russian and Japanese waters until 1911, when Britain (acting for Canada), the US, Russia, and Japan agreed to ban pelagic sealing north of 35° N latitude. NAC, C-86452.

not accommodate railway yards and warehouses. Anticipating a change in the CPR's plans, several Victoria residents had already bought up Crown land some 20 kilometres (13 miles) to the west. Formerly the home of the Musqueam and Squamish bands (now living on nearby reserves), this location offered both the sheltered deep water of Coal Harbour and potential anchorage on English Bay. Among the investors were the German-born Oppenheimer Brothers—whole- sale grocers who had come from California in the wake of the gold rush—and John Robson, the provincial secretary and founding editor of the *New Westminster British Columbian* (in the easy ethical atmosphere of British Columbia in the 1880s, the fact that Robson held public office did not disqualify him from land speculation). To enhance the value of their land by attracting the railway to it, the investors gave the CPR one-third of their holdings. The provincial government was

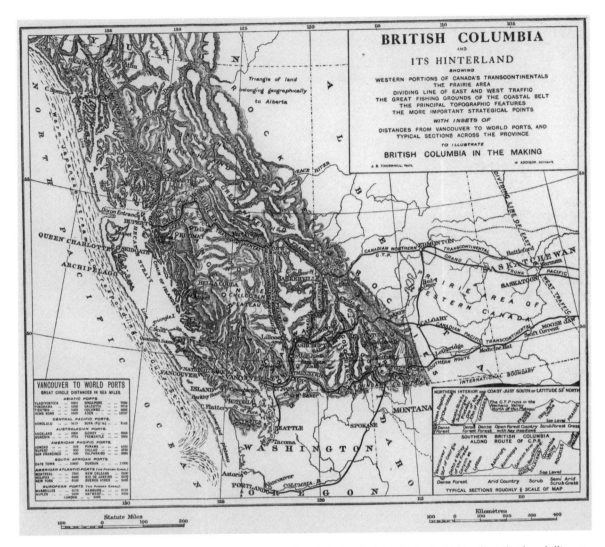

'British Columbia and Its Hinterland', from J.B. Thornhill, *British Columbia in the Making* (1913). Thornhill's was one of many promotional books published during the economic expansion of the years before 1914. Typical of the 'boosterism' behind such books, the map is somewhat premature: the Canadian Northern Pacific Railway, the Grand Trunk Pacific, and the Coast-Kootenay Railway were incomplete when it was published.

at least equally generous: it blessed the railway with another 6,000 acres (2,400 ha), setting aside only a few acres for schools and government buildings at the new townsite.

Late in 1884 the CPR announced it would extend the line to Coal Harbour, and on 6 April 1886 the provincial legislature incorporated the city of Vancouver—the name chosen by Van Horne despite the risk of confusion with Vancouver Island and Fort Vancouver on the Columbia River, because of Captain George Vancouver's renown as the discoverer of Britain's

'Arrival of first train from eastern Canada on eve of Queen Victoria's Golden Jubilee . . . at "the Bluff" foot of Howe Street, Vancouver, May 23, 1887'. The arrival of the first regularly scheduled CPR passenger train in Vancouver coincided almost exactly with the queen's 68th birthday, a month before her symbolically significant Golden Jubilee. Canadians took pride in the CPR and its important role in providing an 'All-Red Route' that linked the United Kingdom with British interests in Australasia and passed entirely through British territory. The BCA does not credit a photographer for this image, but the VPL attributes it to Harry Torkington Devine (1865–1938), an English immigrant recently arrived from Brandon, MB, who in 1887 had a photo studio on Cordova Street in Vancouver. BCA, G-01257.

possessions in the North Pacific. By June a few buildings had been erected, and although a clearing fire that blew out of control that month destroyed almost all them, killing an unknown number of people, the population grew quickly. By the time the first train arrived in May 1887 the new city boasted a number of modern brick buildings. The CPR built the luxurious Vancouver

'Paddlewheeler at Harrison Hot Springs, Fraser River BC, August 1890', by Robert Reford. River and lake steamers remained an important part of British Columbia's transportation infrastructure long after the arrival of the railway. NAC, PA-118170.

Hotel and a large station to accommodate passengers and service the deep-sea ships that were part of its integrated trans-Pacific transportation network. Initially, the CPR chartered vessels, but in 1891 it launched the first of its own 'Empress' liners. In addition to tourists and Asian immigrants, the Empresses carried the Royal Mail and valuable imports such as silk and tea.

The railway also brought a new economy to the areas near its main line. The old Hudson's Bay post of Fort Kamloops became a divisional point that employed a number of men in running and servicing the trains. Ranchers in the Cariboo expected to benefit when rail transport replaced the cattle drive as the main way of getting their stock to market (not only did the old system cost the cowboys' time, but it reduced the quality and weight of the beef). Alas, Alberta ranchers had lower production costs, and the railway allowed them to compete for coastal consumers. Local manufacturers suffered a similar disappointment. Instead of opening new out-of-province markets for them, the CPR made it easy for the larger eastern manufacturers who enjoyed significant economies of scale, to ship their wares to British Columbia.

The railway also allowed the forest industry to ship its products eastward, but there was little

'A "round-up" of the cattle ranges near Kamloops, B.C.', n.d., by S.J. Thompson. The precise location of this spring round-up is not identified, but it may have been on the property of the Douglas Lake Cattle Company, which in the 1890s was one of the largest ranches in Canada. Thompson (1864–1929) enjoyed the patronage of both the CPR and the Dominion government. This photograph was commissioned and published by the government to illustrate the potential of south central BC for investment in ranching. NAC, PA-51372.

demand until massive migration to the prairies after 1896 created a huge market for all kinds of building materials—even prefabricated homes, commercial buildings, and schools—produced by coastal manufacturers. By 1907, when coastal mills sold 435 million board feet (1,026,485 cubic metres) of lumber, 16 per cent was exported by sea; 40 per cent was sold in BC, and the remaining 44 per cent went to the Prairies.[4]

Exports to the US were limited by American tariffs, but by the 1880s the timber stands of Michigan, Wisconsin, and Minnesota were so depleted that American investors began to look to BC. They bought timber rights and established sawmills including one at Chemainus that in 1889 came under the control of the Weyerhauser company, then already on the way to becoming one of the largest lumber firms in the United States. In 1909 it was estimated that Americans owned 75 per cent of British Columbia's forest industry. Later, investors from Minneapolis and Seattle established two of the largest pulp and

'Making up a turn, logging party, BC.' The steam 'donkey' engine transformed logging in the 1890s. As the *Vancouver Daily World* (27 Nov. 1893) explained, 'With his steel cable and windlass and powerful engine, the steam logger can yank the huge giants over the ground when oxen could not be used at all'; see Gordon Hak, *Turning Trees into Dollars: The British Columbia Coastal Lumber Industry, 1858–1913* (Toronto: UTP, 2000), 12. But steam never entirely supplanted the workhorse in the woods. Comparison with another photo (BCA, A-04897) suggests that this is the Walter Gilley outfit, which operated just north of New Westminster between 1895 and 1900. Although the photographer is uncredited, the image is part of the William J. Topley collection in the NAC and may have been the work of W.J. Topley's brother, Horatio Nelson Topley, who photographed for the Geological Survey of Canada in BC in the mid-1890s. NAC, PA-11639.

paper mills, the Powell River Co. (1912) and the Ocean Falls Co. (1917) respectively. But in many cases the nationality of ownership changed over time. In 1890, for example, two Ottawa Valley lumbermen established a large mill just east of New Westminster. The mill closed during the slump of the early 1890s and reopened in 1904 when an American syndicate bought it. Four years later another syndicate including both Americans and Canadians bought it; two years

'Miss British Columbia: —"He's a most welcome citizen, but should pay more for his privileges in increased royalty"', *Saturday Sunset,* 5 Oct. 1907. Although an ethos of resource development at almost any price prevailed in BC during the first dozen years of the twentieth century, some voices demanded that the province receive higher resource rents, in particular for its timber. Cartoons invariably depicted the province as a woman. Usually she was helpless before the onslaught of capital and corrupt politicians. This 'Miss British Columbia', however, wears a patriotic Union Jack on her skirt, and her posture suggests that she is not about to defer to the axe-wielding 'capitalist'. *Saturday Sunset,* a weekly magazine modelled on *Toronto Saturday Night,* first appeared in Vancouver on 15 January 1907. At first it claimed to have no political affiliation, but by the time of its demise in 1915—probably a consequence of the general economic disruption of the time—it was published by the *Vancouver Sun* and had a Liberal bias.

after that, the Americans sold out to the railway entrepreneurs William Mackenzie and Donald

Mann, who formed the Canadian Western Lumber Company. In 1909 it was 'said to be the largest [mill] in the world' producing as much as 400,000 board feet (944 cubic metres) of lumber in a single ten-hour shift.[5]

Anxious to get the maximum revenue from the forests while at the same time conserving them for future use, the provincial government appointed a Royal Commission to investigate the forest industry. Its report shaped the new Forest Act in 1912, which changed the timber licensing system and established a provincial Forest Branch under the direction of H.R. MacMillan, a recent recipient of a Master's degree in the new science of forestry. In principle, this put British Columbia 'at the cutting edge of progress' in the conservation movement, but for the major operators the goal was simply to protect their own interests.[6]

Lumbering also developed in the southern interior. Although producers near the CPR sold some lumber to the Prairies, local mining operations represented the more important market, illustrating the symbiosis between different aspects of the economy. Prospectors, many of them from Spokane's 'Inland Empire' and Idaho's Coeur d'Alene, began searching for minerals in the Kootenay and Boundary districts in the 1860s after the gold rushes at Wild Horse Creek and the Big Bend faded. Because the rivers and lakes of the Kootenays run in a north–south direction, communication with the United States was relatively easy, but the mountains stood as formidable barriers to trade with the rest of Canada. In 1882 the arrival of American transcontinental railways just south of the border, and the possibility of access to the CPR's main line via steamboats on the Arrow Lakes, stimulated interest in the area's silver, lead, and zinc. That year, an American named Robert Sproule discovered what became the fabulously rich Bluebell silver–lead mine on Kootenay Lake, but another prospector, Thomas Hammill, took advantage of Sproule's temporary absence to register the claim. The ensuing legal case so unhinged Sproule that he murdered Hammill and was himself executed following a widely publicized trial.[7]

In 1888 G.M. Dawson of the Geological Survey of Canada reported that 'a large number of prospectors' had had 'most encouraging results' in the Kootenay District, finding gold at the Le Roi mine at Rossland, silver at Toad Mountain, and lead and zinc at what became the Sullivan Mine at Kimberley in the East Kootenay. Yet, as British Columbians well knew, demand was no less important than supply. Severe economic depression in the United States and political controversy over the use of silver as a base for its monetary system slowed development in the early 1890s. As the world economy improved in the latter part of the decade, British speculators became so enthusiastic about Kootenay mines that a magazine devoted entirely to the BC mining industry appeared in Britain. The speculative boom collapsed in financial scandal within a few years, but by then Canadian capitalists, led by the CPR, were investing in mines, smelters, and transportation. The Vancouver Stock Exchange, incorporated in 1907, traded speculative local issues, Coeur d'Alene mining shares, and Alberta oil stocks, and two other financial institutions, the Bank of Vancouver and the Dominion Trust Company, promised that they, unlike 'eastern' bankers, would support local business by investing British Columbians' deposits at home. Although both the bank and the trust company failed following the collapse of the pre-war real estate boom, the Stock Exchange, with its reputation for dealing in spec-

ulative ventures, survived until the 1990s.[8]

Meanwhile, the CPR was rapidly becoming a vertically integrated conglomerate. In 1905 it bought the West Kootenay Power and Light Company, which produced hydroelectricity. It also amalgamated several smaller Kootenay mining and processing operations, which culminated in the formation of the Consolidated Mining and Smelting Company, a CPR subsidiary, in 1906. The new company renovated the Trail smelter and acquired the Sullivan Mine in 1909.[9] The CPR had already moved into the region, constructing the Crow's Nest Pass line from Lethbridge to Kootenay Landing, near Nelson, in 1898 and acquiring interests in portage lines and steamships that connected the new branch to the main line at Revelstoke. The discovery of rich coal fields in the Crow's Nest Pass led to the establishment of new cities such as Fernie, which became the service centre for nearby smaller mining communities including Coal Creek, Michel, Natal, Morrissey, Hosmer, and Corbin.

Some West Kootenay mining camps such as Nelson and Rossland also became cities, and some smaller towns, such as Kaslo and New Denver, survived as minor service centres. Others, though, remained purely mining towns. Among the latter was Sandon, located high in a mountain valley between Kaslo and New Denver. In its heyday in the late 1890s Sandon had virtually all the modern conveniences: electric lights, 17 hotels, 50 stores, two newspapers, a brewery, entertainment facilities including brothels, bars, and theatres, and a miners' hospital. The town catered to the needs of 4,000 people, mostly men who worked and lived at the silver mines in the mountains above it. In the summer of 1899, like many other Slocan miners, they struck to protest a reduction in their daily

500 FT LEVEL OF THE LEROI MINE
PHOTO BY CARPENTER & MILLAR
ROSSLAND · B.C

'The 500 ft level of the LeRoi Mine', Rossland, c. 1897–9, photo by Carpenter and Millar. Mining, like the other resource industries, experienced a technological revolution at the end of the nineteenth century. Developments in explosives, power hoists, and pumps made it possible to work much deeper underground. But new technologies and tools like the drill in this picture, powered by compressed air, required large capital investments. No doubt these miners were highly skilled, but they would have had no illusions that they could make a living working independently. The image itself is remarkable. Not many photographers ventured 150 metres beneath the surface, as Carpenter or Millar did to make this photo; most pictures of miners show them grouped around the top of the shaft. NAC, PA-51326.

wage when provincial legislation reduced their workday from ten to eight hours. A mob greeted a crew of strikebreakers with 'epithets too profane and obscene to be repeated', but a federal royal commissioner found no evidence of the violence that the mine managers feared; most of the miners, along with their union leaders, wanted 'to settle matters amicably'. After eight months a compromise was reached, but by then many miners had already left. When fire destroyed Sandon a few months later, its economic fate was sealed. It gradually became one of BC's many ghost towns.

In 1901 the largest city in the Kootenay was Rossland, with a population of 6,159. Initially spared the strike over the eight-hour day, Rossland's mines closed for 'repairs' early in 1900. The mine managers then announced that henceforth they would not pay a daily wage; rather, miners would be paid on a piecework basis. The American-based Western Federation of Miners (WFM) reluctantly agreed. Yet according to the historian Jeremy Mouat, mine operators—facing financial problems because of excessive capitalization and declining ore values—'began a determined drive' against the union that culminated in a strike in July 1901. After a four-month standoff, the federal government sent its new deputy minister of labour, William Lyon Mackenzie King, to investigate. King failed to settle the dispute and blamed the union for it. When the international executive of the WFM, concerned about the expense of the strike, seemed likely to withdraw its support, the local union gave in. Legal costs further depleted its resources, and the local went into receivership. Although labour relations seemed to improve, many miners sought more militant and radical ways of redressing their grievances.

Meanwhile, Nelson on Kootenay Lake, which had had rail and water connections to Revelstoke and Spokane since the early 1890s was emerging as the commercial and administrative centre for the West Kootenay. In 1901 Nelson was the first town in the interior to get a high school. By 1911 it was the fifth largest city in the province, with a population of 4,476, a new courthouse designed by Francis Rattenbury, and an electric street railway.[10]

To the west of the Kootenays, in the Boundary district, American prospectors found significant deposits of minerals, especially copper. Grand Forks, Greenwood, and Phoenix sprang up around the mines and smelters, but the branch lines of the Great Northern Railway made the area tributary to the United States. Provincial politicians vied with one another to offer the most attractive loans and subsidies for a railway through the Boundary district that would link the Kootenay to the coast. A score of firms, many of which existed only on paper, responded, but the chief contenders were the Kettle Valley Railway Company (a CPR ally), and the Vancouver, Victoria and Eastern (a subsidiary of the American railroad, the Great Northern). Some British Columbians opposed any extension to the CPR monopoly; others feared further American inroads. On their own, both companies built bits and pieces of line as they fought (in the words of railway historian John Eagle) 'vigorously and unceasingly' to control transportation in southern British Columbia. Occasionally their crews almost came to blows, as at Grand Forks in 1902 when the Kettle Valley Railway parked a locomotive on a diamond crossing that the VV&E had laid across the KVR tracks in order to prevent the VV&E from crossing them.[11] Not until 1916, after the CPR and Great Northern arranged to collaborate on the final link through the difficult Coquihalla Pass in the Hope Mountains, was the line completed. By then the mining boom was over.

Prospectors and investors briefly shifted their attention away from the southern mines after gold was discovered in the Klondike region of the Northwest Territories in 1897. From American ports, Vancouver, and to a lesser extent, Victoria, thousands of prospectors raced north to make their fortunes. Some staked claims in the neigh-

'Attending funeral service of Queen Victoria, Greenwood BC', 1901. Greenwood, a mining and smelting centre in the Boundary District with a population of perhaps 1,200, marked Queen Victoria's death with a day of 'public mourning' during which citizens were asked to 'abstain from their occupations and employments . . . as a slight token of respect and expression of sorrow for our national loss'. City Council arranged a procession from the City Hall to the Auditorium where a thousand people, including visitors from nearby mining camps and the communities of Midway and Phoenix, gathered. The order of the procession, reported in the *Greenwood Weekly Times*, 31 Jan. and 7 Feb. 1901, followed a certain protocol: the local band, the police and fire departments, the mayor and council, former councillors, clergy, Board of Trade, Masons, International Order of Odd Fellows, Knights of Pythias, Foresters, Trades and Labour Council, Western Federation of Miners, trade unions, 'other organizations', American citizens, and—finally—the town's Chinese residents. Every marcher visible in this photo is a man; women and girls watch from the balconies on both sides of the street. NAC, PA-51380.

bouring vicinity of Atlin Lake—a district so remote that at first no one knew whether it was in the NWT or British Columbia. This was a matter of concern to miners because the NWT allowed larger claims than did BC. The surveyors' finding that Atlin was in BC was a boon to lawyers—

'Girl wanted, Atlin, BC', n.d., C.R. Bourne photo. The imbalance in BC's gender ratio was 179 males per 100 females in 1901, after three decades in which development of the province's resource industries had attracted predominantly male migrants. The fact that photographer Bourne, who sold this photo as a postcard, thought that a man doing 'woman's work' made a humorous subject suggests the tenacity of notions about what constituted 'men's' and 'women's' work. NAC, PA-32425.

including a future premier, Richard McBride—who tried to sort out conflicting claims. In 1899 more than 5,000 would-be placer miners rushed to Atlin. Although they found some mammoth nuggets, mining in economic quantities required expensive hydraulic technology. Henceforth, gold would be largely the preserve of corporations rather than individual miners.[12]

The northern gold rushes and the share of the trade that Vancouver merchants got of it encouraged Vancouver entrepreneurs in their efforts to eclipse Victoria and make their city the unchallenged commercial centre of twentieth-century British Columbia. The history of the salmon canning industry provides an early illustration of this trend. From the time it began in the late 1860s until the early 1890s, Victoria commission merchants, with credit links to Britain and San Francisco, dominated the industry. Victoria had the head offices of most canning companies and was the outfitting and hiring centre for the canneries that were scattered along the coast as far north as the Skeena and Nass rivers. The canneries required extensive operating capital to cover the long lag between the purchase of supplies (although the salmon was local, the tin for canning came all the way from England) and the eventual sale in Britain of the brightly labelled product, which became a popular source of protein for working-class families. Large amounts of capital were also needed to finance the installation of labour-saving devices such as conveyor belts. When Canadian chartered banks opened regional offices in British Columbia, they located them in Vancouver. Since the banks were in a better position to provide capital than the commission merchants, the canning companies eventually moved their head offices to Vancouver. Not all the canners depended on Canadian capital, however. A Vancouver-based Scottish immigrant, Henry Bell-Irving, used British capital to begin acquiring canneries in 1890, and two years later his Anglo-British Columbia Packing Company claimed to be the world's largest producer of canned salmon. By 1901 salmon canning was the province's second largest industry and, even with mechanization, employed 15,000 people.[13]

The labour force in the salmon canneries was unusually diverse. Chinese men worked alongside Aboriginal and Japanese women cleaning, cutting, cooking, and packing the fish into cans, although the introduction of butchering machines—most notably the 'Iron Chink', which first appeared in the Fraser River canneries in 1906—reduced the need for Chinese labour, which was then in short supply.[14] Working together did not build class solidarity. In the communities (some permanent, some seasonal) that developed around the canneries, each group had its own little enclave of family cabins and bunkhouses for single men. The fishermen also represented a different ethnic mix: First Nations, Euro-Canadian, and Japanese. In the 1890s so many Japanese immigrants entered the industry that by 1900 they held 45 per cent of the 3,683 gillnet licences issued. The press claimed that 'the little brownies' had driven out Aboriginal fishermen and were threatening to do the same to whites. When the newly consolidated canneries colluded in 1900–1 to cut the prices paid for salmon, all three ethnic groups stopped fishing. But the Japanese, organized in the Japanese Fishermen's Benevolent Society, had fewer employment alternatives than other fishermen did. When, after several weeks, they accepted the canners' offer and resumed fishing, the white Fishermen's Union sent out armed patrol boats to stop them. No one was actually shot, but the threat of violence worked to the advantage of the politically influential canners, who persuaded the provincial government to send the militia, derisively known as 'the Sockeye Fusiliers', to Steveston to protect scabbing fishermen. This demonstration of force persuaded Aboriginal and white fishermen to return to work. Nevertheless, as the historian Paul Phillips points out, the strike was a turning point in BC labour history, marking the start 'of a continuous thread of unionism in the fishing industry'. It also showed the willingness of the provincial government to intervene on the side of capital. Under the leadership of Henry Doyle, a Vancouver-based American immigrant, and using money provided by central Canadian banks, many Fraser River canners formed the BC Packers Association to further reduce competition for fish and labour. BC Packers immediately closed 17 of its 29 canneries on the Fraser River, but still increased its share of the 1903 pack.[15]

'Interior, salmon cannery, Skeena River', c. 1890, by Robert Reford. First Nations women made up a substantial proportion of the workforce in salmon canneries, especially along the north coast. The four women in this photo are doing butchering work that farther south would probably have been done by Chinese men, at least until a mechanical salmon-butchering machine called the 'Iron Chink' began taking over that job in 1906. Reford made this photo with his Kodak rollfilm camera. Unlike his professional contemporary E.S. Curtis, he was not obsessed with recording 'traditional' Native life. NAC, PA-118162.

Salmon canning was no more restricted to the Canadian side of the border than mining and forestry were. Although the Fraser River catch in 1901 was huge, a decline in Oregon's salmon runs served as a warning to Canadian canners. The fisheries of BC, Oregon, Washington, and Alaska all faced supply problems. Inevitably, conservation efforts were complicated by the fact that fish do not respect international boundaries. A salmon hatched in a tributary of the Fraser River makes its way down the river to the North Pacific and spends anywhere from one to seven years (depending on the species) travelling the ocean before returning to its original spawning ground

'Indians bound for cannery work boarding SS Princess Maquinna', 1910s, photographer unknown. Native families migrated with the seasons up and down the coast in search of cannery work. Some were signed up in their villages by labour recruiters working for the canneries; others returned to the same canneries year after year. See Rolf Knight, *Indians at Work: An Informal History of Native Labour in British Columbia, 1848–1930* (Vancouver: New Star Books, 1996), 179–206. BCA, D-06893.

to breed and die. On the homeward journey many salmon pass through US waters and into the nets of American fishermen. As a move towards conservation, the provincial government in 1901 hired John Pease Babcock, an American fisheries biologist, to oversee the fisheries. Babcock spent the next three decades trying to increase the numbers of salmon by promoting the development of hatcheries and temporary closures of varying durations, to allow enough fish to reach the spawning grounds to ensure another generation. Yet even today, not much has changed. The success of the hatcheries project remains open to debate, while closed seasons still cause disputes among different groups of fishermen as well as

between Canada and the United States. Fisheries biologists still do not always agree on the primary cause of the declines in salmon runs that have occurred since early in the last century: degradation of rivers by industrial activities such as the construction of dams, the continuing repercussions of a massive landslide at Hell's Gate in 1913 (caused by blasting during the construction of the Canadian Northern Pacific Railway), urban development, climate, or overfishing.[16]

Before the early twentieth century, the primary conservation concern of many provincial politicians might well have been their own brief careers. The best word to describe provincial politics from 1871 to 1903 is 'confusion'. From 1871

'Fishing fleet at the mouth of the Fraser River', 1895–1900, photographer unknown. Similar fleets worked the mouths of salmon rivers as far north as the Skeena River and into Alaska. Some of the boats in this photo would have belonged to independent Euro-Canadian or Japanese fishers. The canneries owned other boats and would contract fishers, often Native men, to operate them. This photograph appeared in an album illustrating Canada's industries published by the Geological Survey. NAC, PA-51351.

to mid-1903, the province had 15 different governments, of which the longest-lived—headed by William Smithe—lasted only a little over four years (1883–7). In the five years between 1898 and 1903, six different men sat in the premier's chair. The briefest term of all belonged to Joseph Martin, who had moved to British Columbia after a stormy career as Manitoba's attorney-general. Martin was so unpopular that when he accepted Lieutenant-Governor T.R. McInnes's offer of the premiership in 1900, the legislators almost unanimously voted non-confidence. In the subsequent election only Martin and five of his followers were re-elected to the 38-seat legislature. The federal Liberal government of Sir Wilfrid Laurier dismissed McInnes for his unwise choice of Martin and replaced him with Henri Joly de Lotbinière, an experienced Quebec politician.

For its first three decades British Columbia had had no provincial party system. Instead, members of the government and the opposition, whose limited loyalties were attached to individual leaders rather than to parties, competed to attract votes by offering subsidies for railways and by building public works. Largely as a result of this costly practice, by 1903 the province was on the verge of bankruptcy. Then, when Premier E.G. Prior, a hardware merchant, told the lieutenant-governor that he had seen nothing wrong in his firm getting the contract to supply wire rope required to build a bridge after he examined the other bids before submitting his own, Sir Henri asked him to resign. To replace Prior and form a new government, Sir Henri called on Richard McBride, a 32-year-old native of New Westminster and member of the Legislature since 1898, to form a government and introduce party lines. McBride, who had run unsuccessfully as a Conservative in the 1896 federal election, agreed and formed a cabinet that included only known Conservatives. With the guidance of his parsimonious Finance Minister, Robert Tatlow, he reduced government spending, refused further aid to railways, and raised taxes on railways and mining companies. To secure the support of the two Socialist MLAs, J.H. Hawthornthwaite and Parker Williams—who boasted of 'holding the balance of power between "the two great wings of capitalism, the Conservative and Liberal parties"'—McBride introduced legislation to improve mine safety and establish an eight-hour day for coal miners.[17]

McBride also continued his predecessors' fight for 'Better Terms' from Ottawa. At the Dominion–provincial conference of 1906, he convinced Prime Minister Laurier and the other premiers that British Columbia deserved special financial treatment because of its high administrative costs 'owing to the physical character of the country', its distance from eastern Canada, its large contributions to the federal treasury through customs duties, and its disadvantages 'in relation to the markets for its special products'— probably a reference to the fact that most of British Columbia's exports were natural products rather than manufactured goods. When the other premiers agreed that BC had special needs and should get a grant of $100,000 annually, but only for the next ten years, McBride pointed out that the mountains would not disappear in a decade and thereupon stormed out of the conference. Soon after his triumphant return to the province, he called a general election to exploit what the *Canadian Annual Review* called 'that invaluable aid in Provincial contests—a reasonably good grievance against the Federal authorities'.[18] His Conservative party won almost half the popular vote and 26 of the 42 seats.

McBride was exceptionally fortunate to be premier at a time when the province was entering an era of what appeared to be unlimited prosperity. Land sales, timber licences, and mineral taxes all contributed to growing government revenues, and borrowing money in London was easy. British Columbians clamoured for additional railways. As the federally assisted Grand Trunk Pacific Railway 'blunder[ed]' through north central British Columbia, new townsites sprang up along the way. Settlers moved in, and many earned a living cutting railway ties from the trees they felled in the process of clearing their farms. By 1911 the GTP's terminus, Prince Rupert, was 'a town in the process of being born', with some streets made of 'planks on top of muskeg' and others 'blasted out of solid rock'. Eva MacLean, the Ontario-born wife of a Presbyterian clergy-

THE CINDERELLA OF THE FAMILY.

MAMMA CANADA:—What do you want now? you're *always* grumbling!"
Miss BRITISH COLUMBIA:—Please MAMMA I work *hardest* and pay *most*, and my sisters get all the benefits; see how *fat* and fine they are—and then *look at me!"*    H C

Cartoon by Emily Carr from *The Week* (Victoria), April 1905. Before she became British Columbia's most celebrated artist, Carr (1871–1945) reversed the 'spoilt child of Confederation' taunt often directed at BC. Instead,
she depicts the other provinces with full purses, thanks to the generosity of 'Mamma Canada' (Prime Minister
Wilfrid Laurier); even the babies, Alberta and Saskatchewan, are fat and happy. 'What do you want now?' asks
Mamma sternly; 'you're always grumbling!' The emaciated 'Miss British Columbia' replies: 'I work hardest and
pay most, and my sisters get all the benefits; see how fat and fine they are—and then look at me!'

man, recalled that 'small shacks' sat 'side by side
with large new houses, tents, and modest business blocks'. The GTP had an elaborate plan that
included curved streets and generous park
reserves, along with a grand hotel, railway, and
steamship terminal complex designed by Francis
Rattenbury.[19] Economic depression and GTP mis-

management meant that none of these grand
plans came to pass in the end. Nevertheless, the
line was completed in 1914, and even though
the GTP was a federal project, Premier McBride
still contrived to get some political advantages
out of it. Because the province controlled the
land needed for the terminus, he was able to

'Presenting addresses to Sir Wilfred [sic] Laurier at Prince Rupert, August 20, 1910.' Laurier toured the province in the summer of 1910, hoping to soothe regional angst. He failed. In the general election of 1911, BC voters responded to the Conservative party's charges that Laurier was disloyal to the Empire because he did not believe that Canada should contribute to the Imperial Navy. Moreover, BC fruit growers benefited from tariff protection and so opposed the reciprocity agreement that was the centrepiece of the Liberal campaign. Under the leadership of Conservative Premier Richard McBride, a staunch imperialist, British Columbians gave the Conservatives 59 per cent of their votes—the highest percentage of any province—and all seven parliamentary seats. The NAC identifies the photographer as 'I.D. Allen', but this is undoubtedly James Dennis Allen (c. 1880–1966), a commercial photographer active in Prince Rupert 1909–14, who made the photo for sale as a souvenir. NAC, PA-123758.

wrest concessions from the GTP, including a promise not to employ Asian labour and an agreement to build simultaneously from west to east as well as from east to west, since that would allow BC to share in the trade generated by the line's construction.

Throughout British Columbia, people wanted new railways to open up new country, and there was no shortage of promoters willing to build them, if only the province would provide financial aid. Finally, in 1909 the premier yielded to the supplications of the Toronto-based railway magnates William Mackenzie and Donald Mann, whose Canadian Northern Railway had a network of lines on the prairies. Although Finance Minister Tatlow resigned in protest,

McBride agreed to have the province guarantee the bonds that Mackenzie and Mann would issue to finance the construction of the Canadian Northern Pacific (CNPR)—the name they gave their line in BC—and to link it with their lines east of the Rockies. In return, Mackenzie and Mann also agreed to let the BC government regulate CNPR freight rates and promised to lay a line on Vancouver Island from Victoria to Barkley Sound. The CNPR deal and a promise of aid to the Kettle Valley Railway, to serve the southern interior, were the centrepieces of McBride's platform in the 1909 election, in which his Conservatives won all but four seats.[20]

Vancouver's business community, however, wanted access to the Grand Trunk Pacific and the northern interior, fearing that without it the region would fall into Edmonton's economic orbit. To that end, Foley, Welch and Stewart, the Vancouver-based contractors for GTP construction in BC, offered to build a line from Vancouver to Prince George (to be called the Pacific Great Eastern), and McBride also offered a provincial guarantee of bonds for it. He rounded out his railway program with promises of government aid to several shorter lines in southern British Columbia, and went to the electorate in 1912. Voters heartily approved; this time they gave the Conservatives all but two seats.

The 1912 election was the high point of McBride's political career. By then the visions of social reform circulating throughout North America had made their way to British Columbia. In 1909 McBride had responded to demands for prohibition by inviting voters to express their opinions in a plebiscite on a law that would allow municipalities or districts to ban 'the licensed liquor traffic'. A majority favoured such prohibition by 'local option', but

the government made only a few minor changes to the provincial liquor laws. McBride had no more sympathy for the reformers—many of them the same people who advocated prohibition—who demanded the vote for women. 'We have in British Columbia,' he declared paternalistically, 'the right kind of suffragettes, suffragettes who with that peculiar sweet and beautiful charm, which is all their own, say to their men, vote and vote right.' Even if women had acquired the vote under McBride, they could not have exerted much influence on political life, for despite immigration and natural increase, the gender ratio was still unusually skewed. In 1881, 75 per cent of the non-Aboriginal adult population had been male, and even in 1911 the figure was still 70.0 per cent.[21]

Yet the province did have many children, and providing schools and teachers was a challenge, particularly beyond the elementary level. Before the establishment of Provincial Normal Schools in Vancouver (1901) and Victoria (1915), elementary teachers prepared for certification examinations in one of the province's four high schools at Victoria, New Westminster, Nanaimo, and Vancouver. Those schools in 1901 had a total enrolment of 584. With population growth the number of high schools increased rapidly. By 1916, there were 40 of them—though some had only one room—and 4,770 students.[22] High-school teachers usually required a university degree, so most of them came either from elsewhere in Canada or from the United Kingdom. Although the Methodist Columbian College, founded in New Westminster in 1892 and affiliated with the University of Toronto, offered some university-level studies, public university education in British Columbia began when Montreal's McGill University formed affiliations with the high schools in Vancouver (1899) and Victoria (1903). By 1915 McGill University College offered three years of arts and two years of applied science in Vancouver and two years of arts in Victoria. Growing demand for higher education led the McBride government to promise a provincial university. Almost every city claimed to be the best possible site. Acutely conscious of regional rivalries, the premier wisely created a University Sites Commission of outside experts to make an impartial evaluation. The Commission recommended Point Grey, a Vancouver suburb where the government happened to own extensive acreage.[23] Financial exigencies dictated that when the University of British Columbia officially opened in 1915 it was located on the old McGill University College campus in some buildings no longer required by the Vancouver General Hospital.

The creation of institutions of higher education, even on a small scale, reflected the population growth made possible by the transcontinental railways, which had facilitated migration to British Columbia from Europe as well as from elsewhere in Canada. According to the 1901 census, 27 per cent of the non-Aboriginal population had been born elsewhere in Canada. The total population rose from 98,173 in 1891 to 392,480 in 1911 and was still growing rapidly. Perhaps the British Columbians who most felt the impact of this dramatic growth were the First Nations. Although their numbers remained stable at about 25,000, their portion of the total had changed dramatically: whereas in 1891 they had accounted for 27.8 per cent of the total population, by 1911 that figure had dropped to just 5.1. Newcomers moved into areas that Native people had always regarded as their own. The consequences of displacement were most severe along the route of the Grand Trunk Pacific, which offered minimal compensation for its right of way through reserve lands even when ancestors' graves had to be moved. A serious disturbance occurred near Hazelton in November 1909, when local Gitxsan seized the outfits of a road-building crew. Several white families prepared to flee, and wire services circulated sensational reports accusing the Gitxsan of ambushes and murder; the local Omineca *Herald*, however, dismissed the incident as 'a tempest in a teapot', observing that 'the last west . . . wouldn't be really the west without Indian troubles.' When local officials asked for assistance, the provincial government sent in 20 armed provincial police officers and 'specials' from Prince Rupert. In the end, six Gitxsan were found guilty of theft and intimidation: three were sentenced to five months in jail and three were fined. Over the next few years the southern press occasionally carried stories of Native people in the Nass River Valley attempting to halt prospective settlers and of trouble brewing north of Hazelton. In March 1911 a Roman Catholic missionary was reported to have warned that 'There will be blood spilt' in the Skeena and Babine districts: 'Our northern Indians are being starved to death. They will rise against the hand that oppresses them.' Premier McBride was sufficiently alarmed to ask Prime Minister Laurier for a federal investigation, but then the missionary denied the initial report, maintaining that all he had said was that the people in question had refused to work for surveyors except at exorbitant rates. Nevertheless, the federal Indian agent at Metlakatla, a First Nations village near Prince Rupert, saw cause for concern. Noting that McBride had recently told 96 chiefs that 'the title to Indian lands is not vested in the Indians of British Columbia', he reported that they feared 'having their present reserves cut down, should the populations decrease' and warned that they must be 'taken seriously in this matter': 'the sooner some definite steps are taken by the government concerned the better, as delay is predictive of an Indian revolt.' In 1913 the *Omineca Herald* expected bloodshed at Kispiox if negotiations were mishandled, as the local First Nations had quietly acquired arms and ammunition. But white fears proved to be baseless: Aboriginal groups consistently used constitutional means, such as appeals to senior governments, to try to resolve their grievances over the land. Indeed, relations between First Nations and white settlers in British Columbia were remarkably peaceful, especially given the provocations that the former endured. In settlements from Nanaimo to Hazelton, white housewives traded with Aboriginal people who went door-to-door peddling fish or handicrafts such as baskets or blankets in exchange for other food or used clothing.[24] First Nations peoples also competed in local sports events and agricultural exhibitions, although often in separate categories.

The overriding problem for the First Nations was land. Because Victoria insisted that any unused reserve land belonged to the province, which owned all other public lands, the federal government could not allocate more reserves or sell unused reserve land, and the Native people themselves had limited use of the timber, minerals, and water on their reserves. To resolve the impasse, in September 1912 the federal government sent J.A.J. McKenna, an official in the Department of Indian Affairs, to British Columbia. He persuaded McBride to have a joint Dominion–provincial commission examine the reserves in the province and decide whether adjustments in their size would be appropriate.

Any excess or 'cut off' reserve lands would be sold and the proceeds shared by the province and the Dominion, which would hold its share in trust for the Native people. The commissioners, who did not issue their report until 1916, increased the number of reserves and added 87,286 acres (34,920 ha) to them, but also cut off 47,085 acres (18,835 ha).[25] Perhaps not surprisingly, much of the land removed from the reserves was in areas desired by white settlers, and the new land added to some reserves was often of poorer quality than the land 'cut off' from others.

Immigrants also faced discrimination, particularly those who were not white. British Columbians had grudgingly accepted the presence of Chinese workers as long as they were needed to build the CPR, but a new wave of anti-Chinese agitation rose as the railway neared completion. The provincial government passed legislation designed to prevent new Chinese immigration and to regulate the Chinese people already in BC: by introducing an annual ten-dollar tax, forbidding the exhumation of Chinese bodies (by custom, the Chinese returned the bones of the deceased to China), banning the use of opium, and specifying minimum space and ventilation requirements for rooms occupied by Chinese workers. Ottawa disallowed the immigration law and referred the other measures to the courts, which found that the province did not have the power to impose them. Nevertheless, to appease white British Columbians, Prime Minister Macdonald appointed a Royal Commission on Chinese Immigration. Major employers such as colliers and fish canners told the commission that Chinese workers were indispensable to the development of the province, but other white British Columbians complained

'Indian Affairs Commission meeting at Sooke, June 11 1913', photographer unknown. The McKenna–McBride Commissioners had photographs made of every meeting that they conducted with Native people. This pose— the commissioners seated at a table in the centre with their documents in front of them, the Native men standing behind them, and the women and children kneeling in the foreground—captures the power disparity. Still, such images helped to legitimate the expropriation of Native lands by depicting it as the result of a quasi-judicial process. BCA, H-07257.

that the Chinese were 'cheap labour' whose low living standards undercut the ability of white workers to earn a living and whose crowded and unsanitary Chinatowns endangered public health. In addition, Sinophobes protested that by gambling and using opium, the Chinese threatened public morality. The Commission recom-

mended restricting Chinese immigration. Thus on 1 January 1886, just six weeks after the railway was completed, Canada imposed a $50 head tax on all Chinese immigrants.

The head tax merely slowed the pace of Chinese immigration—even after it was raised to $100 in 1902 and to $500 in 1904—but it dramatically skewed the composition of the Chinese community, since only well-to-do migrants, mainly merchants, could afford to bring their wives and families to Canada. In Victoria the School Board tried on several occasions to segregate Chinese children, but was forbidden to do so by the Public Schools Act.[26] Whatever their social position, most Chinese in BC—as in every part of the Chinese diaspora—lived in their own largely self-contained communities. The changing populations of the various Chinatowns reflected the economic fortunes of the cities that surrounded them. Vancouver's Chinatown did not exist in 1884, and by 1911 it had passed Victoria's to become the largest in the province, with 3,559 residents. In the same year Barkerville's Chinatown, home to an estimated 5,000 residents in the 1860s, had all but disappeared.[27]

Yet many white British Columbians believed that the 1886 head tax was not a sufficient deterrent. In response to their complaints, in the early years of the century, BC legislators tried again to ban immigration from Asia, but these efforts too failed: some laws they passed were 'reserved' when the lieutenant-governor refused to sign them, and others were disallowed by the federal government on the grounds that they were contrary to national or imperial interests. The provincial government did, however, have the power to impose some discriminatory legislation on Asians already in BC. It had denied Chinese the provincial franchise as early as 1872. Beginning in 1890, the legislature began amending the Coal Mines Regulation Act in an effort to ban the employment of Chinese underground, but it could not devise a completely enforceable law. Some colliers yielded to pressure from their white miners and did not hire Chinese to work underground; the Dunsmuirs, however, employed both Chinese and Japanese at their Union Mine in Cumberland. Occasionally whites resorted to physical violence and intimidation: in 1887 a Vancouver mob drove a Chinese land-clearing crew out of town; in 1898 and 1901, at Sandon and Phoenix respectively, miners intimidated Chinese cooks and domestic servants into leaving; and in September 1907 a riotous mob attacked Vancouver's Chinatown and the nearby 'Little Tokyo'.

Japanese immigrants, who began arriving in numbers in the mid-1890s, were subject to the same discrimination as the Chinese and for many of the same reasons, including the threat they allegedly posed as 'cheap labour' and the fear that 'hordes' of Asians could overwhelm a white British Columbia. In 1895 the Legislature added Japanese to the clause that denied the provincial vote (and hence the federal vote as well, since Ottawa used the provincial voters list) to Chinese and Aboriginal men living on reserves. After a hiatus in immigration during the Russo-Japanese War, the number of Japanese migrants increased dramatically in the spring and early summer of 1907, when over 5,000 arrived and more were expected. The Vancouver Trades and Labour Council took the lead in forming a Vancouver branch of the US-originated Asiatic Exclusion League, and found ready support from local politicians of all parties. To draw attention to itself, the League organized a parade and rally at City Hall on Saturday, 7 September 1907. One feature of the demonstration was the burning in effigy of the coal baron James Dunsmuir, the largest single employer of Asians in the province, who, as lieutenant-governor, had recently withheld assent from a provincial law designed to halt Asian immigration. The rally attracted so many people that the speakers—local politicians and

'Tomekichi Mayegawa, 264 Powell Street, Vancouver', September 1907. Photographs like this one of a fish market with its windows smashed (case #33130) were used to substantiate owners' claims for damages in the aftermath of the 'anti-Asiatic' riots. Japanese men easily repelled what the *Vancouver News-Advertiser* called 'a gang of hoodlums' when they attacked 'little Tokyo', and these men appear ready to resist any further incursions. See Patricia E. Roy, *A White Man's Province: British Columbia Politicians and Chinese and Japanese Immigration, 1858–1914* (Vancouver: UBCP, 1989), 192–4. NAC, PA-67273.

before considerable property damage had been done. Fortunately no one was seriously injured.

The Laurier government was nonetheless alarmed, fearing the riot would damage Canada's international reputation. It sent the deputy Minister of Labour, William Lyon Mackenzie King, to Vancouver to assess the damage claims; he was shocked to find among the claimants some Chinese proprietors of opium factories, whose business was then perfectly legal. More significantly, Laurier also sent his Minister of Labour, Rodolphe Lemieux, to Japan to negotiate the 'Gentlemen's Agreement' (the Lemieux–Hayashi Agreement, signed late in 1907) under which Japan agreed to limit the number of passports it would issue to emigrants destined for Canada. Most of the details were kept secret, but it was understood that in one category at least—agricultural labourers and domestic servants—Japan would issue no more than 400 passports a year. The number of Japanese immigrants fell to well under a thousand per year, and their composition changed significantly. Whereas most early immigrants were men, now the majority were women, notably 'picture' or mail-order brides who soon began raising families. The presence of women and children saved the Japanese community from complaints about cleanliness and morality, but not from objections based on competition in the work place, supposed inability to assimilate, or the fear that Asians, by the sheer weight of numbers in their homelands, could overwhelm British Columbia.

White British Columbians also objected to immigrants from India, even though they were relatively few and were willing to take on undesirable jobs such as clearing land or stacking lumber. In 1910 Ottawa amended the Immigration Act to require migrants to travel from

clergymen, along with visitors from New Zealand and Seattle—had to repeat their speeches outside the hall to satisfy the overflow crowd. Exactly what happened next is unclear, but a leaderless mob swept towards the nearby Chinatown throwing bricks and stones. By the time it got to 'Little Tokyo' the Japanese had organized to repel the mob with stones, clubs, and knives, but not their homelands by a 'continuous voyage'. The main purpose of the amendment was to prevent Japanese immigrants from circumventing the Gentlemen's Agreement by migrating via Hawaii, but it also effectively checked immigration from India, since no steamship company sold 'through' tickets from India to Canada. In 1914, however, Gurdit Singh, a Sikh entrepreneur, chartered a ship called the *Komagata Maru* to take Indians already in Hong Kong to Vancouver. The plan was clearly intended to test Canadian immigration law, and news of it travelled fast. As the *Komagata Maru* steamed across the Pacific, officials and politicians in Vancouver, Ottawa, and London exchanged telegrams and cables debating what to do when its 376 passengers reached Vancouver. The situation was complicated by the fact that the Indians, like Canadians, were British subjects. When the ship arrived on 23 May, Canadian immigration officials permitted only the 22 passengers who had previously resided in Canada to land. The rest were forced to stay on the ship, which lay at anchor in Vancouver harbour for two months. Finally, on 23 July, the cruiser HMCS *Rainbow*—one half of the Canadian navy's fleet—escorted the *Komagata Maru* and its passengers out of the harbour en route to India.[28]

Asians were the least popular of immigrants, but other non-British immigrants were also unwelcome. Few English-speaking British Columbians had much sympathy for the Eastern and Southern European migrants derisively known as 'Sifton's Pets' (after Minister of the Interior Clifford Sifton, whose immigration policy centred on recruiting experienced farmers to settle on the prairies). Complaints about Italians living on the 'Dago plan' echoed objections to the Chinese, focusing on their willingness to accept

'Hindu in lumberyard, Vancouver'. This 'Hindu', of course, is a Sikh. Although the NAC dates the photo 'ca. 1890–1910', it was probably taken after 1904, when the first Sikh migrants arrived. Distinct ethnic divisions characterized the BC labour market; many Sikhs worked in the lumber industry. NAC, PA-122652.

wages and working conditions that others would reject and their supposed intention to 'sojourn' in Canada only long enough to make their fortune and then to return home. A Dutch-born witness told the provincial Royal Commission on Labour in 1914, 'Italians live on macaroni. . . . That is impossible for us.' Appealing to the stereotypical association between cleanliness and godliness among the Anglo-Canadian middle class, the Kelowna *Courier* spoke of 'our natural repugnance to the great unwashed poured into our land by Europe, such as the Galicians and Doukhobors and certain other people whose love of soap and water is not intense'. A frequent complaint was that the Eastern Europeans lacked respect for the law and degraded the few women in their communities. When a Slav miner at Fernie justified a brutal attack on a Slav woman at a dance on the grounds that 'in their native country a man had a right to beat any woman who refused to dance with him', the Cranbrook *Herald* seized the opportunity to pose a rhetorical question: 'Is this the kind of people that will make the backbone of British Columbia?'[29]

One ethno-religious group, however, caused more consternation than all the others combined. The Doukhobors, or 'spirit wrestlers', were Christian pacifists who, because they resisted compulsory military service and looked to God as their only authority, had been persecuted in their native Russia. Pressed by British patrons of the sect, Sifton arranged to settle 7,300 of them as homesteaders in the late 1890s, mostly in what is now Saskatchewan. In British Columbia, Liberal newspapers welcomed these 'industrious and frugal' people, but the Conservative press criticized Sifton's 'crazy-quilt' communities (a reference to the bloc settlements that European immigrants established on the prairies), and the Vancouver Trades and Labour Council predicted that the new arrivals would be yet another reservoir of cheap labour.[30]

As long as the Doukhobors remained on the prairies, the debate in British Columbia was moot, but trouble was brewing east of the Rockies. Only about 1,000 Doukhobors gained title to their prairie homesteads. The others refused to conform to the homestead law that required them to swear allegiance to the Crown, and insisted on holding land communally. To circumvent the homestead law and isolate his people from secular society, in 1908 the Doukhobors' leader, Peter Verigin, began buying the first of what by 1912 were 14,403 acres (5,828 ha) in southeastern British Columbia around Grand Forks and Castlegar, and in the Slocan Valley. By 1912 Verigin had led approximately 5,000 Doukhobors into this 'promised land'. The Nelson *Daily News* was impressed by the progress they made as farmers, orchardists, sawmill operators, and jam producers, but other newspapers drew attention to the Doukhobors' reluctance to conform to the civil law.[31] In 1912 provincial authorities jailed four men for three months for failing to register a death. The Doukhobor community, which had only recently agreed to send its children to public school, withdrew them and refused to register any births, deaths, or marriages because it regarded the collection of vital statistics as an intrusion on their communal life.

In response to complaints about 'civil disobedience', the McBride government appointed William Blakemore, a Victoria newspaper editor, as a one-man Royal Commission to investigate. Blakemore found the greatest hostility among residents of Grand Forks, who complained that the Doukhobors bought from wholesalers rather than local merchants, sold their vegetables for lower prices than other local producers, and did not conform to provincial laws or standards concerning marriage. Many feared that the Doukhobors' large land-holdings would 'swamp the community' and discourage 'desirable' settlers. Blakemore had little sympathy for such complaints. On the contrary, he found the Doukhobors to be honest

'Doukhobor women haying on community land, Grand Forks, 192?'. By the 1920s, most other BC farmers had abandoned the sort of hand tools used by these women to cut and gather hay. We do not know who made this image or why, but the overexposure suggests an amateur photographer. Koozma J. Tarasoff reproduced the image in his *Pictorial History of the Doukhobors* (Saskatoon: Western Producer, 1969) 124, and deposited it in the BCA. In his Royal Commission Report, William Blakemore noted that Canadian women in British Columbia were 'most sympathetic towards their Doukhobor sisters' and 'spoke in the highest terms of their motherliness and affection, of their domestic virtues, and their devotion to religion'. *Report of the Royal Commission on Matters Relating to the Sect of Doukhobors* (Victoria: British Columbia Legislative Assembly, 1912), T19 and T29. BCA, C-01721.

people and good credit risks. Impressed by the 'majestic and all-powerful' leadership of Verigin, 'a father to his people', he advised the government to be patient and work with him to secure compliance with the law. Nevertheless, Blakemore made one grave error: he recommended cancelling the exemption from military service granted to the Doukhobors as part of the arrangement by which they came to Canada.[32]

That gratuitous recommendation undid any goodwill that Blakemore's report might have gained among the Doukhobors. Moreover, when they responded to Grand Forks residents' continuing complaints with threats to mount mass nude demonstrations or to emigrate (a move that would have been popular locally), the government passed a Community Regulation Act that reiterated laws regarding vital statistics and school attendance, prescribed fines for violations, and empowered the government to seize community 'chattels' to cover any fines. Finally, in 1915 Attorney-General William Bowser negotiated a compromise: the government would not impose religious or military exercises on

Doukhobor children if their families would send them to school.[33]

The largest group of immigrants in the decade before the First World War came from Britain, and most of them blended easily into a province that was, after all, *British* Columbia. British ethnicity was a mark of 'respectability' that transcended class lines. Yet some newcomers did their best to maintain class distinctions by replicating English institutions such as private schools. They were not alone in trying to establish a class structure in the province. Eva MacLean described the aspiring upper-class residents of Prince Rupert in 1911 as 'a miscellaneous group, businessmen and their families, real estate dealers, land developers, construction men, and workers of all kinds—each hoping to make a fortune somehow in this new country.' Some American women, married to railway or construction company officials or prosperous businessmen, tried 'to found a caste of society to offset the more democratic ways of their menfolk', but failed because no one could tell 'who came from which side of the tracks'; as MacLean pointed out, 'the tracks were all but obliterated in the new town.'[34]

Some British immigrants prospered—particularly those who went to the Okanagan Valley and settled on land suited to fruit growing—but others with Arcadian dreams fell victim to dishonest promoters who promised ready-made orchard communities where purchasers would enjoy the fruits of their labours with little physical effort. One such victim was Jack Phillips, a middle-class English army officer who resigned his commission and in 1912 took his new bride, Daisy, to the Windermere Valley in the East Kootenay. For 'about £1000' he purchased land in what Robert Randolph Bruce, the promoter of

the Columbia Valley Irrigated Fruit Lands Ltd, promised would be lush orchards amidst beautiful surroundings with good hunting, sailing, and sports such as ice-skating all nearby. Jack had little knowledge of farming and Daisy had minimal housekeeping skills. No one told them that that they would be unable to find farm labourers or domestic servants to hire even if they could have afforded the high wages that such help commanded. They cheerfully learned to do the work themselves, but no amount of effort could overcome Windermere's altitude, which made the growing season too short to produce a reliable crop. In their case the outbreak of the First World War made this problem moot: before their trees even had a chance to mature, Jack was called back to serve in his regiment and Daisy returned to England.[35]

In another case an entire community was doomed when the climate proved unsuitable for the purpose advertised by promoters. The Walhachin settlement, west of Kamloops in the Thompson River Valley, received its first settlers in 1910 after a London-based firm bought more than 2,000 hectares, subdivided it into 150 town lots, installed an inefficient irrigation system, and began building houses and other facilities, including a luxury hotel for newcomers. The firm's promotional literature, designed to appeal to English gentlemen, was illustrated with photographs of successful orchards elsewhere and quotations from the Governor General, Lord Grey, in praise of fruit farming: 'a beautiful art as well as a most profitable industry'. By the summer of 1910, 56 settlers had arrived and more would follow, but there were probably no more than twenty women at any one time. The majority were bachelor sons of the aristocracy, men with few practical skills and little desire to learn them. Within weeks of the outbreak of the war, all but one of the single men of military age had enlisted. Those who returned in 1919 discovered that their settlement and its irrigation system had deteriorated and the company in charge (which had taken over when the original promoters went broke in 1912) was in severe financial difficulties. By 1922 all the original settlers had gone. Although a provincial historical plaque blames the war for the failure of the Walhachin settlement, a government study in the 1950s showed that extremes of temperature in the deep valley where it was located made it unsuitable for tree fruit in any case.[36]

English settlers were not alone in seeing their dreams disappointed. Some Danes found excellent agricultural land at Cape Scott, at the northern end of Vancouver Island in the late 1890s, but within a decade most had abandoned the dairy farms they established because they had no way to ship their cream to market. A community of Norwegians from Minnesota and North Dakota, who tried to establish a cooperative utopia at Quatsino in 1894, also failed because of isolation, although another Norwegian group from Minnesota, who settled at Bella Coola in the same year, did build a successful cooperative, perhaps because they had better leadership and easier access to coastal shipping routes.[37]

Disappointment contributed to working-class militancy and helped to make socialism unusually popular in British Columbia. Statistics compiled by the Dominion Department of Labour consistently showed BC to be the most strike-prone province in the country, and the Socialist Party of Canada was largely the Socialist Party of BC. R.P. Pettipiece, a socialist and working-class activist from Ontario, offered a simple explanation: 'the province is full of discontented

people who, like myself, came here to get away from existing circumstances'; but, he continued, 'it is of no use.' Historians once maintained that socialism arrived in the cultural baggage of British immigrants. However, more recent research suggests that circumstances in British Columbia itself also created many socialists. E.E. (Ernie) Winch, an English-born bricklayer, and his family arrived to Vancouver in 1910 with 'orthodox views on politics, hoping to better themselves in a land of the future'. Instead, Ernie and his son Harold found 'a more vicious kind of competition and exploitation than they had seen at home'. In 1911 Winch discovered 'a fresh economic gospel' and joined the Social-Democratic Party, an offshoot of the Socialist Party of Canada. In the 1930s the Winches would be among the founders of the Co-operative Commonwealth Federation (CCF), and Harold eventually became its provincial leader.[38]

Socialist influences and union militancy also made their way north from the United States in the form of visiting activists such as Eugene Debs, as well as various American socialist publications, leading some capitalists to blame Americans for exporting socialism to BC. In 1903, when CPR workers belonging to the US-based United Brotherhood of Railway Employees struck in Vancouver to protest the company's refusal to recognize their union and its dismissal of union members, railway workers as far east as Winnipeg joined them in what became a four month-long strike. In Vancouver, strikers alleged that CPR police shot Frank Rogers, a UBRE organizer who immediately became a labour martyr. Coal miners in the Crow's Nest Pass were already on strike for higher wages, shorter hours, and recognition of the Western Federation of Miners, another US-based organization. Two weeks later, coal miners working in the Dunsmuirs' Wellington mine on Vancouver Island also walked off the job. The Laurier government responded with a Royal Commission on Industrial Disputes in British Columbia. The Commission's final report, written largely by its secretary, Mackenzie King, and released in July 1903, showed sympathy with workers' complaints about low pay and long hours, advised employers against behaving in 'tyrannical' or 'arbitrary' ways, encouraged them to accept collective bargaining, and proposed conciliation and arbitration to settle disputes before strikes began. But these sensible recommendations were overshadowed by the report's claim that the coal strike had been instigated by a 'conspiracy' of 'foreign socialistic agitators' in order to deprive the CPR of its essential coal supply and force it to negotiate with the UBRE. Thus the Commission also recommended banning 'radical socialistic' unions like the UBRE and WFM, as well as sympathy strikes and union intimidation of the 'scabs' who replaced union workers during strikes (the report said nothing about the employers' use of intimidation against union organizers and workers who signed union cards).[39]

The Royal Commissioners were not the only ones to identify 'socialist' influences. Keir Hardie, a visiting militant Scottish miner and socialist, noted little interest in socialism among trade unionists in Eastern Canada, whereas in the West, 'beyond Winnipeg, only Socialists need apply.' Of course this was an overstatement.[40] On the other hand, BC's economy—like most of its western counterparts—did differ significantly from those in 'the East' both in the importance of resource-extractive industries and in its increasing domination by large national corporations, notably the CPR and its subsidiaries including the Consolidated Mining and Smelting Company. In addition, Canadian

Northern Railway magnates William Mackenzie and Donald Mann were investing in a variety of provincial enterprises ranging from sawmills and coal mines to fishing companies, and the Granby Company was operating mines. These corporations often offered a fertile recruiting ground for industrial unions such as the United Brotherhood of Railway Employees, the Western Federation of Miners, and the United Mine Workers of America, which endeavoured to organize all the workers in a given industry, both skilled and unskilled, into single unions. It was not unusual for industrial unionists to see their organizations not only as catalysts for improvements in their own wages and working conditions but also as international instruments for broader social change. The most ambitious of these unions was the Industrial Workers of the World (IWW), founded in 1905 at a 'Continental Congress of the Working Class' in Chicago. The 'Wobblies', as they came to be known, sought to build 'an industrial democracy, wherein there shall be no wage slavery, but where the workers will own the tools which they operate, and the product of which they alone will enjoy'. Internationalism was another central principle, and the US–Canada boundary did not exist for the 'boxcar bards' and 'red card men' who carried the Wobblies' message. IWW organizers arrived in British Columbia in 1906 and within a few years had locals in the Kootenay and Boundary mining towns, where they competed with established miners' unions, as well as in Vancouver. Their interests were broad—in Victoria they joined trade unions affiliated with the American Federation of Labour to protest the Empress Hotel's replacement of unionized musicians with non-union members—but their greatest successes came in organizing unskilled workers on the waterfront, in road building, and especially in

'Car of anthracite coal at pit mouth on property of the British Pacific Coal Co. Ltd., Graham Island, c. 1912', photographer unknown. Graham Island is the northernmost of the Queen Charlotte Islands. The well-dressed men standing in the foreground have just inspected the property. This photo was probably created for an investment prospectus issued by Fidelity Securities. NAC, PA-29926.

railway construction. In March 1912, more than four thousand men working on the Canadian Northern Pacific line struck for better wages and living conditions in their overcrowded, foul-smelling camps. The provincial government, in the words of the *Canadian Annual Review*, treated the matter 'with a firm hand'. Following some local violence and the arrival of special police, nearly three hundred men were jailed for crimes ranging from vagrancy to inciting murder. Construction resumed during the summer as the CNPR strike petered out. In the meantime, workers on the GTP struck on 20 July 1912. The GTP workers got some concessions, but the CNPR strike, which was never officially called off, left as

its only real legacy a song by the legendary organizer Joe Hill:

> *Where the Fraser River flows, each fellow worker knows*
> *They have bullied and oppressed us, but still our union grows;*
> *And we're going to find a way, boys, for shorter hours and better pay, boys,*
> *We're going to win the day, boys, where the Fraser River flows![41]*

The railway construction workers' walk-outs were soon overshadowed by a massive and lengthy strike among coal miners on Vancouver

Island. In 1910 James Dunsmuir sold his collieries to a company controlled by Mackenzie and Mann. Miners found it no easier to work for a national corporation, Canadian Collieries (Dunsmuir) Ltd., than for Dunsmuir himself. Unrest began at Cumberland in September 1912, when miners declared a one-day 'holiday' to protest the firing of their colleague Oscar Mottishaw, probably for attempting to organize the United Mine Workers of America on Vancouver Island. In response, Canadian Collieries locked out all its workers and replaced them with strikebreakers, many of them Chinese and Japanese. Although other Island miners joined the protest over the months that followed, production continued, and the highly mechanized Cumberland mine actually increased its output.[42]

As the historian John Hinde explains, the violence that marked the strike's first anniversary at South Wellington, Ladysmith, and, in particular, Extension was a direct result of the fact that the strikers 'had no power'. Rioters—including women—did not spare imported strikebreakers (some from as far away as England) or Chinese from intimidation, physical violence, and property damage, but focused their vengeance on local strikebreakers, management, and supervisory personnel, whose families fled into the bush and whose houses were looted and burned. Astonishingly, the only serious injury occurred when a stick of dynamite that a strikebreaker tried to toss back at the strikers hit a window frame; it exploded and he lost his hand. When the acting premier, Attorney-General William J. Bowser, on 14 August 1913, dispatched militia units—including Vancouver's 72nd regiment, the Seaforth Highlanders—to the Island, the headline in the Victoria *Colonist* proclaimed that the militia would bring 'Order Out of Anarchy' at the

mines, but made no mention of the relative restraint shown by the strikers and their families. After the riot, a total of 213 strikers and sympathizers were arrested, of whom 50 (all of them men) were sent to jail.[43] Nevertheless, the action continued until the summer of 1914, when the United Mine Workers of America announced it could no longer afford to support the strikers by providing them with strike pay.

Strikes like these gave British Columbia a reputation for hostile labour relations and created the false impression that most unionists wanted revolutionary change. But in fact most labour actions were motivated by bread-and-butter issues such as wages, working conditions, and union recognition. Unionized street railway workers in Vancouver and Victoria accepted a profit-sharing plan in lieu of pay raises. The craft unionists who led the Vancouver Trades and Labour Council were labourists, intent not on revolution but on working within the existing political system to introduce progressive reforms such as workmen's compensation, minimum wage laws, and factory inspections. Still, they were not averse to taking direct action against employers: in the spring of 1911 unionized carpenters and some of their allies in the building trades in Vancouver struck, to demand a 'closed shop' in which every worker would be required to be a union member. Although they hoped their action would spark a general strike, not all workers in the industry were prepared to stay on the picket lines for any length of time—if they agreed to strike at all.[44] Only about 10 per cent of the non-agricultural labour force was organized in 1914; in times of prosperity and rapid growth, many workers had seen little need for unions. Despite rapid population growth, mainly through immigration, jobs had been plentiful as

'Maxim Gun crew on flatcar during the miners' strike', Nanaimo, 1913, photo by Frederick Victor Longstaff (1879–1961). BC governments used force to break strikes not simply in order to protect the investments of company owners but to demonstrate to investors that their capital would be safe there. The flatcar on which the heavy machine-gun was mounted illustrates the relationship between the state and capital: it belonged to the Esquimalt & Nanaimo Railway, which the Dunsmuir family had sold to the CPR in 1905. BCA, A-03159.

the province exploited its natural resources and expanded its infrastructure. By 1914, however, a worldwide economic depression that had been developing since 1912 had brought serious unemployment to British Columbia. London money markets dried up, the boom collapsed, and the railways stopped laying track. On the eve of war in Europe, many British Columbians could well describe the province as a land of promises unfulfilled.

# CHAPTER FOUR

## The Limits of Promise: 1914–1941

*I*n early July 1914, most British Columbians were probably not even aware of the crisis developing in Europe. Less than a month later they were at war. Once war was imminent they demonstrated a keen British patriotism, but they were aware of their own vulnerability. The Royal Navy had withdrawn from Esquimalt in 1906, and because of political controversy over Canada's naval policy, the only ship the infant Royal Canadian Navy had on the west coast was HMCS *Rainbow*, an old Royal Navy light cruiser that it had purchased to use as a training vessel. The Anglo-Japanese Alliance of 1902 put the naval defence of Canada's west coast largely in the hands of the Imperial Japanese Navy. Sharing the apprehension of the coastal cities, on 3 August Premier McBride initiated negotiations with a Seattle shipyard to buy two submarines that Chile had ordered but, because of a dispute over specifications, had not fully paid for. As soon as the transaction was completed, the subs headed for Canadian waters, lest the US government cancel the deal in order to preserve American neutrality. McBride might have been hailed as a hero; instead he faced allegations from political opponents in Ottawa that the sub-

marines were unsuitable and that improper commissions had been paid to acquire them before they were sold to the federal government. (He was eventually exonerated by a federal Royal Commission, but by then he had retired from politics.)[1]

In the early days of the war British Columbians enthusiastically contributed to charities such as the Canadian Patriotic Fund. Not all philanthropic gestures were entirely altruistic. When, in September 1914, the province donated 25,827 cases of canned pink salmon to relieve distress in Britain's industrial areas, it took advantage of the opportunity to advertise the qualities of pink salmon, which (unlike the favoured sockeye) was in plentiful supply. The 'free samples' so impressed the British War Office that it ordered large quantities of pink salmon for its troops.[2]

The dark side of patriotism was the xenophobia directed against Germans and their allies. Even Alvo von Alvensleben, once a wealthy promoter of German investment in the province and 'a good citizen', became *persona non grata*. As an enemy alien, he was denied entry to Canada when he attempted to return from a visit to

'Submarine and crew in Victoria Harbour, February 1915', photographer unknown. At 12 noon on 5 August 1914, the Victoria *Daily Colonist* published a one-page special edition devoted exclusively to the following announcement: 'On behalf of the Dominion Government and with their concurrence, Sir Richard McBride, representing the Province of British Columbia, some days ago completed the purchase of two submarines, which are now lying at anchor in British waters ready for action, under the command of Lieut. Jones, R.N., submarine expert. Lieut. Jones is a recognized submarine expert; in fact his knowledge of submarine warfare is not excelled in the Empire. Every preparation necessary for naval warfare is complete. The submarines are newly built and said to be of the most destructive class. Ottawa has been fully advised of the action of the Local Government and the vessels now form part of the national forces.' BCA, A-00267.

Germany shortly after the war had begun; his investments, which ranged from a Vancouver Island coal mine to a holiday resort, were liquidated. A dramatic manifestation of xenophobia occurred after the sinking of the British passenger ship *Lusitania* by a German submarine off the coast of Ireland in 1915. When a rumour circulated in the bar of Victoria's Blanshard Hotel (formerly the Kaiserhof) that local Germans had celebrated the sinking, a mob moved through the downtown streets smashing windows and looting businesses allegedly owned by Germans. Many Germans and Austro-Hungarians lost their jobs, in some cases at the demand of their fellow workers.[3] Enemy aliens had to report to the authorities and some were interned in a camp at

'Demonstrators attacking the Kaiserhof Hotel (Victoria) after sinking of S.S. *Lusitania*, 8 May 1915'. The German U-boat that torpedoed the passenger liner handed the Allies a propaganda coup, touching off waves of outrage throughout both the British Empire and the United States. (The *Lusitania's* secret cargo of munitions remained a secret for a half-century.) Among the 1,201 civilians who perished was the son of James Dunsmuir, the former coal magnate, premier, and lieutenant-governor. To judge by their clothing, the demonstrators who gathered outside the hotel included both working- and middle-class Victorians; five well-dressed women are visible. An hour later, the crowd became a mob. They smashed windows, looted the bar, and tore apart the public areas of the hotel before moving on to attack the local German Club and the German Consulate. The Victoria *Times* (10 May 1915) referred to the hotel as the Blanshard, suggesting that it had already been renamed to deflect anti-German sentiment. The fact that none of the participants seems at all perturbed about being photographed indicates how respectable anti-German sentiment was considered to be in wartime British Columbia. BCA, A-02709.

Vernon or set to work on projects such as road-building through the Monashee Mountains (east of Vernon). Towards the end of the war, however, when labour shortages developed in the min-

ing industry, many internees with the appropriate skills were released to go back to work.

British Columbia had one of Canada's highest rates of voluntary enlistment: 9.5 per cent of its

'Completing the Grand Trunk Pacific Railway near Fort George (now Prince George) B.C., April 7, 1914', photographer unknown. Like the CPR, the GTPR was constructed simultaneously from east and west. The crews met near Fort Fraser, about 80 km west of Prince George. Like mining, logging, and salmon-canning, railway construction had become increasingly mechanized; in 1914 a track-laying machine lowered the rails into position for the track gang. By the time the last spike was driven, the company was almost bankrupt. Glenbow, NA-3658-100.

population. That was not surprising, since many recent British immigrants were men of suitable age with previous military experience. Moreover, the war exacerbated the unemployment that followed the economic downturn of 1912–13. Two local financial institutions, the Bank of Vancouver and the Dominion Trust Company, closed their doors, and many small investors lost their savings. The new railways, then entering the most expensive stages of their construction, were also hard hit. Although the federally sponsored Grand Trunk Pacific managed to drive its last spike at Nechako Crossing in April 1914, it remained the 'Grand Trafficker of Promises' (the name suggest-

ed by the editor of the Prince Rupert *Empire*), as traffic was too light to cover operating costs, let alone interest payments.[4]

The Canadian Northern Railway was even worse off. By the spring of 1914, the province was responsible for more than $47 million of CNR debt, and required federal aid as well as more loans from the Canadian Bank of Commerce to complete the line. William Mackenzie drove the last spike at Basque, just south of Ashcroft, in January 1915. In planning for the formal opening ceremony, to be held in the Fraser Canyon at a later date, Premier McBride suggested that, because of the war, it should not be 'too elaborate'. He got his wish: when the time came, a tunnel cave-in separated the CNR officials from the provincial politicians waiting to give speeches. Fortunately for the province, when the financial disasters of the Grand Trunk and Canadian Northern threatened to undermine Canada's credit, the federal government took over both railways and their debts and formed the Canadian National Railways.[5]

Meanwhile, the Pacific Great Eastern built from Squamish to Clinton but exhausted its funds and became mired in scandals concerning its financing and its relationship with the provincial government. Premier McBride, in failing health, resigned in December 1915 to take up the plum post of British Columbia's Agent-General in London. He left an unhappy legacy to his successor, William J. Bowser, his Dalhousie Law School classmate and long-time attorney general. Dogged by allegations of mismanagement of natural resources and controversy over prohibition, the governing Conservatives lost by-elections in Vancouver and Victoria by large margins, and in the general election of September 1916 the Liberals under Harlan Carey Brewster, a salmon canner, won 36 of the 47 seats in the Legislature and 50 per cent of the popular vote. During the winter of 1918 Brewster went to Ottawa on government business, caught pneumonia, and died. To succeed him, the Liberals chose John Oliver, a Delta farmer.

In a referendum accompanying the 1916 BC election, male voters endorsed the principle of female suffrage by a margin of more than two to one, and in 1917 British Columbia became the last of the four western provinces to grant women the vote.

The suffrage campaign cut across class lines; Evelyn Farris, the wife of a prominent lawyer and Liberal politician, worked alongside the trade unionist Helena Gutteridge. Even with women voting, however, electoral politics remained a largely male preserve. The first woman in the provincial legislature, the Liberal Mary Ellen Smith, was elected in a 1918 Vancouver by-election after the death of her MLA husband, Ralph Smith. Not until 1933 did a second woman enter the legislature, and by 1940 only two other women had won election. Recognizing the importance of women's votes, however, the Oliver government enacted a female minimum wage law (1918) and mothers' pensions (1920). In 1931, in the Sex Disqualification Removal Act, a Conservative government retroactively gave women full civil equality with men.

A second referendum held with the 1916 election gave male British Columbians the chance to express their views on prohibition. Whereas civilian voters tended to favour prohibition, soldiers did not, and the total vote went narrowly against the proposed measure, making BC the only English-Canadian province with a 'wet' majority. Because of irregularities overseas, however, most of the soldiers' ballots were rejected, and on 1 October 1917 British Columbia adopted prohibition after all—the last province apart from Quebec to do so. Based on the Manitoba law, the British Columbia Prohibition Act made it illegal to buy or sell liquor except for medicinal and a few other specified purposes.

The difficulty of enforcing the law became clear almost immediately, with the arrival of the Spanish influenza epidemic, in which almost a third of the province's population fell ill and roughly 1 per cent died. Believing that alcohol could prevent or cure the flu, many British Columbians besieged their doctors for prescriptions. Between March and December 1919, doctors wrote 188,120 prescriptions for liquor in a province with a total population of perhaps 500,000. In a 1920 plebiscite, British Columbia became the first English-Canadian province to put an end to prohibition: 92,095 voters favoured letting the government sell spirituous and malt beverages in sealed packages, and only 55,448 favoured retaining the prohibition law. The government opened the first in what was to become a very profitable chain of liquor stores in June 1921. Among the products it sold was a loganberry wine produced by Growers' Wine Company, a berry-growers' cooperative on Vancouver Island. Although the province's own Board of Health touted it as a 'healthful tonic', one reason for its popularity may have been the price—half that of imported wine.[6] In any event, sales of loganberry wine fell off in the 1930s, when Growers' Wine and the new Calona Wine Company of Kelowna began producing wine from grapes grown in the Okanagan Valley.[7]

The end of the war also brought economic distress. Indeed, BC's wartime experience offers a capsule illustration of the 'boom and bust' cycles characteristic of economies based largely on natural resources. When the war began in August 1914, the metal market went 'to pieces'. The BC Copper Company closed its smelter at Greenwood and the Granby Company closed its copper mines at Phoenix, greatly reducing the demand for coal. Then in the spring of 1915 the demand for artillery in Europe caused

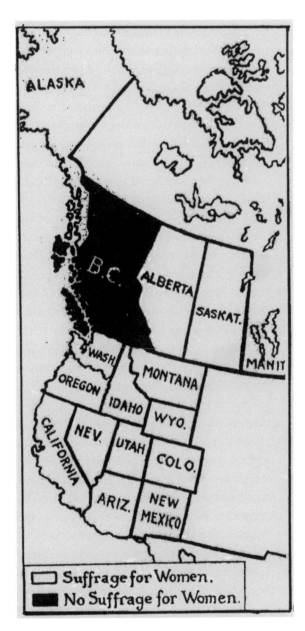

□ Suffrage for Women.
■ No Suffrage for Women.

'British Columbia is One Remaining "Black" Spot', *Vancouver Daily Province*, 12 Sept. 1916. This map accompanied a newspaper article in support of women's suffrage by Mrs. J.A. Clark, 'Chairman Central Suffrage Committee'. In her article, Clark argued that women were entitled to the vote not only as a reward for their contribution to the war effort but also as a consequence of their natural right to equality with men. The map illustrates a striking and largely unexplained fact of North American history. In both Canada and the US, almost all the western provinces and states enfranchised women before their national governments and eastern counterparts did. (This map is not entirely accurate, however; women in New Mexico did not vote until 1920.)

the prices for 'war minerals'—copper, lead, and zinc—to soar. Mines and smelters reopened and in 1916 set production records. As production increased, so did the demand for coal to power the trains used to transport the metals to market, and the Crowsnest Pass region enjoyed full employment and high wages, while on Vancouver Island the mine owners were so short of labour that they rehired men they had blacklisted for their roles in the great strike of 1912–14.[8]

With the end of the war, though, the market for war minerals virtually disappeared. Only a few residents remained in Greenwood after its smelter shut down in November 1918, and Phoenix became a ghost town when the Granby Company closed its last mine there in June 1919; the final act of the local government was to build a war memorial. The Granby Company turned its attention to its more profitable properties around Anyox, a copper mining and smelting town north of Prince Rupert at the head of Observatory Inlet. The total dollar value of BC's mineral production dropped from almost $18 million in 1916 to just under $8 million in 1919 and continued to fall until the mid-1920s, when it began to pick up again; in the last half of the decade it was setting new production records.[9]

The Consolidated Mining and Smelting Company, with its broadly based resources (including its mines, smelter, and a subsidiary, the West Kootenay Power and Light Company) used wartime profits to put itself on a firm footing. Its metallurgists adapted an Australian flotation process that made it economic to extract zinc from the relatively low-grade ore of the Sullivan mine at Kimberley. That contributed handsomely to the company's profits for many years and led to British Columbia's producing

nearly 10 per cent of the world's lead in the late 1920s. (By the time the Sullivan Mine closed in 2001, it had produced 149 million tons of ore.)[10] But coal mining, once central to the BC economy, resumed its decline as railways and consumers increasingly switched to oil for fuel.

Lumbering also experienced severe fluctuations. The end of the long prairie boom, six months before the war began, taught the industry the importance of securing reliable markets. Although the war offered excellent opportunities in Britain, it created a shortage of the necessary shipping capacity. Thus early in 1916 the provincial government responded to requests from the BC Manufacturers' Association and Boards of Trade with a plan to subsidize ships built in provincial yards. The federal and provincial governments also cooperated to send H.R. MacMillan, BC's chief forester, on an international marketing mission. Although he managed to sell 10 million board feet (24,000 cubic metres) of lumber to the British Admiralty, he was less successful in France, South Africa, India, and Australia. MacMillan concluded that major sales required some sort of cooperative trading organization to handle orders more efficiently. Shortly after the war, he formed such an organization himself. It gradually evolved into MacMillan Bloedel and by the 1950s was 'the largest integrated forest company in Canada' with interests in lumber, and in pulp and paper.[11] MacMillan's Export Company and the Associated Timber Exporters of British Columbia, a consortium of mills, helped maintain good sales levels during the 1920s. Taking advantage of the Panama Canal, BC mills sold their products on the east coast of the US, as well as in Europe and Asia.

During the war, the BC forest product of most interest to Britain was Sitka spruce, a

'Anyox smelter and part of the townsite, Anyox, BC, June 1928', by A. Buisson. Anyox was one of the many company towns that grew up around mines, mills, and canneries. They were usually isolated, sometimes accessible only by water or (later) air, and many were ethnically segregated. Japanese, Chinese, and South Asian workers lived in separate bunkhouses in the pulp and paper town of Ocean Falls in a section of the community called Japtown. Similarly, at Youbou on Lake Cowichan the Empire Lumber Co. provided houses for skilled workers and office staff and separate bunkhouses, each with its own cook, for each main group: East Indians, Chinese, and single white men. In many cases the company ran the only store in the area. At Anyox, however, 'Frank-the-Chinaman' had a shop just outside the town limits, and residents could also order groceries by mail from Woodward's, a Vancouver department store. In 1935, faced with a world copper glut, Granby Consolidated shut down its operations; within five years Anyox became a ghost town. See Bruce Ramsey, *Rain People: The Story of Ocean Falls* (Vancouver: Ocean Falls Centennial '71 Committee, 1971), 104; Lynne Bowen, *Those Lake People: Stories of Cowichan Lake* (Vancouver: D&M, 1995), 48, 51; and Pete Loudon, *The Town that Got Lost* (Sidney, BC: Gray, 1973), 56. NAC, PA-14159.

strong, lightweight wood used for airplanes. The Imperial Munitions Board (IMB)—the British agency responsible for procuring munitions in Canada—undertook its own logging operations on the Queen Charlotte Islands. Meanwhile, the provincial government commandeered all spruce for the war effort. A number of First Nations men turned from fishing to logging for the IMB on reserve lands, only to lose their fishing licences the next year because they had not used them.[12]

Like the Sitka spruce enterprise, much of BC's wartime industrial expansion was short-lived. Distance meant that the munitions industry did not move west until it had done all the business it possibly could in eastern Canada. British Columbians manufactured products ranging from wooden ammunition boxes to ships, both wooden and steel. To run the shipbuilding operation the IMB chose R.P. Butchart, a Vancouver Island cement manufacturer best known today for the gardens that his wife Jennie created out of his abandoned quarry. Between 1917 and 1919 Butchart oversaw the production of 27 steel ships and most of their components, including boilers and engines. He had little sympathy for workers who sought higher wages, whether by striking or by heading south to Puget Sound; he suggested that men who refused to work should be conscripted for military service.[13]

Workers' fortunes varied with the booms and busts of the economy. Periods of economic expansion, like the later war years, brought full employment and put workers in a good position to demand the higher wages they needed to keep pace with a cost of living that was rising sharply. The year 1917 was marked by strikes throughout Western Canada, even among groups that had never struck before, such as Vancouver's street railway workers. Union membership grew rapidly, particularly in the more radical and militant industrial unions that were active in mining and shipbuilding.[14] The socialists who had long been active in the labour movement came to the fore in the BC Federation of Labour in the last years of the war, vigorously opposing the Borden government's introduction of conscription for military service in the summer of 1917. In the federal election of December 1917 the Labour party ran anti-conscription candidates in seven BC constituencies. Still, for working-class voters British-Canadian patriotism trumped class solidarity, and no Labour candidate came close to winning a seat.

Tensions between capital and labour increased following the armistice of November 1918. The cost of living continued to rise, but now employment was falling as the munitions industries laid off workers and soldiers returned home. The 1917 Russian Revolution had encouraged radical socialists—their critics called them 'impossibilists'—who believed that only revolution could achieve the social transformation they sought. At a convention in March 1919 the BC Federation of Labour, its membership at a peak of perhaps 15 per cent of the provincial labour force, proposed the formation of a large industrial organization to be called the One Big Union (OBU), and the use of a general strike to secure changes in labour law including a six-hour day. Before the OBU was formally organized, however, workers in Winnipeg launched a general strike on 15 May. Within weeks, many workers in Vancouver, Victoria, and Prince Rupert, as well as interior lumber camps, had struck in sympathy. In the Crowsnest Pass the OBU 'gained a following second only to that of Winnipeg' and a major strike of miners lasted for eight months.[15]

Governments and members of the business community feared that these sympathy strikes were part of a Bolshevik uprising. The Commissioner of the NWMP thought it might 'be necessary to reconquer' British Columbia, especially if railway and telegraph lines were destroyed, cutting it off from the rest of Canada. The army arranged to send an armoured car and to organize machine-gun units in Vancouver. G.G. McGeer, a Vancouver Liberal MLA, believed that some labour activists were 'decidedly inclined to Bolsheviki tendencies' and 'under certain circumstances' would be 'sufficiently powerful to do a great deal of harm.'[16] In both Vancouver and Victoria, businessmen formed Citizens' Committees to maintain essential services that might be interrupted by a strike. Yet in the end the sympathy strikes merely caused inconvenience; they never closed all businesses, and—unlike the Winnipeg strike—they did not involve any violence on the part of either strikers or police. The Victoria strike was over by late June and the Vancouver strike ended early in July.

After 1920, the labour movement in British Columbia, as in the rest of North America, was weakened by conflicts between radical industrial unionists and more conservative trade unionists, post-war unemployment, and a successful counter-attack by employers. Most unions spent the 1920s on the defensive. A 1924 wage strike by Crowsnest Pass coal miners was a dismal failure, as declining demand for coal reduced their bargaining power. Vancouver Island coal miners, badly beaten in the Great Strike of 1912–14, lay low, seeing little to hope for in the remnant of the OBU, and the once-vibrant United Mine Workers locals had disappeared. In the 1920s, most union activity was confined to greater Vancouver.[17] In the province that in the past had seen more dra-

matic working-class militancy than any other, the absence of industrial conflict was remarkable.

Meanwhile, war veterans, many of them

WHO WOULD THE KAISER VOTE FOR?

'Who Would the Kaiser Vote For?' *BC Federationist*, 7 Dec. 1917. This cartoon from the newspaper of the BC Federation of Labour depicts Canada's Unionist Prime Minister Robert Borden as the German Kaiser Wilhelm, and predicts that an electoral alliance of French Canadians, soldiers, and workers will chop down the 'Unionist Tree' in the coming federal election. But on 17 December anti-conscription labour candidates won only 6.1 per cent of the popular votes cast in BC and no seats. The most dramatic protest against conscription occurred outside the electoral arena on 2 August 1918, when thousands of workers struck for a day to protest the death of Albert 'Ginger' Goodwin. A Yorkshireman blacklisted for his role in the Vancouver Island coal strike, Goodwin moved to Trail, where in November 1917 he led a 36-day strike of the Mine, Mill and Smelter Workers. Thereafter, even though he had been ruled unfit for military service because of poor health, he was reassigned to Class A. Rather than report for duty, Goodwin fled to the woods around Cumberland, and on 27 July 1918 he was shot dead by a Dominion Police special constable who was hunting for draft evaders. The precise circumstances of his death will never be known, but overnight he became a labour martyr. In Vancouver on the day of his funeral an estimated 5,600 union workers answered the Trades and Labour Council's call for a one-day general strike (about 10,000 did not). Both the *Vancouver Sun* and the *Daily Province* condemned the strikers as 'pro-German', and a mob of returned soldiers invaded the Vancouver Labour Temple, forcing trade unionists there to kiss the Union Jack. See Roger Stonebanks, *Fighting for Dignity: The Ginger Goodwin Story* (St John's: Canadian Committee on Labour History, 2004).

'News of the armistice, Government and Fort Streets (Victoria), 7 November 1918.' Some Victorians celebrated the Armistice prematurely, but that did not dampen their enthusiasm when the official news arrived four days later. Similar photographs in the BCA collection are the work of John Howard Arthur Chapman (1862–1942); this one is likely Chapman's work as well. BCA F-05321.

wounded either physically or emotionally (by 'shell shock'), were attempting to resume their interrupted lives. The challenges of finding employment for handicapped veterans were especially great in BC because many members of the Canadian Expeditionary Force took their discharges in the benign climate of the coast. Even before the war had ended, veterans' organiza- tions had persuaded the province to establish a Land Settlement Board that made land and development loans available for veterans who wished to establish farms, and the government made a special effort to build access roads. Much of the land provided, however, was of inferior quality. For example, the land set aside at Merville, just north of Courtenay on Vancouver

Island (later immortalized by the novelist Jack Hodgins) was already logged-over and not well suited to agriculture. Some soldier settlers still managed to produce dairy and poultry products for sale to nearby logging and mining camps—until a forest fire in 1922 destroyed not only homes and outbuildings but, most critically, the thin layer of humus required to grow crops. Many of the approximately 400 veteran settlers had to sell out what little remained or find other jobs. Near Creston, the province made land deemed suitable for orchards available to veterans. Unfortunately, provincial officials were not necessarily good judges of land, and drought reduced production to the point that settlers were unable to keep up their payments. By the time the government installed irrigation facilities in 1929, only 21 of the original 70 soldier settlers remained. And although a reclamation project at Sumas, in the eastern Fraser Valley, was very successful, the cost of diking and draining the 134 square kilometres of rich alluvial soil was so great that when the land became available in 1924, few veterans could afford it. Other new settlers continued to arrive through the 1920s, though many of those who moved into the Bulkley and Nechako valleys had to subsidize their 'stump farms' by cutting railway ties. The one advantage of their subsistence lifestyle was that by the time the Depression came, they were well prepared to survive it.[18]

Unlike these newer areas, the Okanagan Valley had by now become an established agricultural region. But its farmers had trouble marketing their produce when many of the early orchards matured at the same time (around 1912), and the difficulties continued. Throughout the 1920s and the 1930s Okanagan farmers tried a variety of cooperative schemes, all of which failed because too many 'fruit-leggers' insisted on selling their fruit outside the cooperatives. The situation was exacerbated by confusion over which level of government should be responsible for marketing legislation. When the Depression destroyed prairie markets for BC fruit, prices fell so dramatically that many orchardists threatened not to harvest their crops at all unless they got at least a penny a pound—their slogan was 'A Cent a Pound or on the Ground'—because lower returns did not cover their costs. By contrast, milk producers in the Fraser Valley had established a very successful cooperative as early as 1917 to buy their milk and market it, along with related products such as butter and cheese.[19] Although they faced competition from New Zealand butter, they could readily ship the more profitable fluid milk to Vancouver via the BC Electric Railway's interurban line.

As an extension of the prairie, the Peace River district in the northeast had the potential to be one of the richest farming areas in the province. Yet the dream of a railway linking it with the rest of British Columbia remained unfulfilled. When the Pacific Great Eastern Railway (PGE) was created in 1912, its boosters expected that one day it would go beyond Prince George to the Peace River. In 1918, however, the province had reluctantly assumed responsibility for the PGE—Premier Oliver called it an 'unwelcome foundling'[20]—and for the next few decades premiers regularly sought in vain for Ottawa, or the Canadian Pacific, or the Canadian National Railways, to take over what cartoonists frequently portrayed as the province's 'white elephant'. Certainly there were no funds to extend it to Prince George, let alone the Peace country. The Provincial Party—an unholy alliance between the tiny United Farmers of British Columbia and

'Okanagan—apple pickers', c. 1930. As with many archival photographs, we know nothing about this photo but what we can see in it. We do not know who the photographer was, and the date and location are merely informed guesses by the BCA archivist who catalogued it. As for the relationships among the people in the photo, the smiles on two of the women suggest that they were more likely family members than hired help, but the frozen expressions on the other six faces are not easy to read. Perhaps the only other thing we can tell from this photo is that tasks here were assigned according to gender: the men load and drive, while the women climb and pick. BCA, B-06875.

major businessmen, led by the dissident Conservative General A.D. MacRae—attacked the government for its handling of the PGE, claiming that Oliver had mismanaged the railway and been involved in corrupt dealings in letting construction contracts, and that both Oliver and Conservative leader W.J. Bowser had received campaign funds from the PGE in 1916. In the 1924 election the Provincial Party won 24 per cent of the popular vote but only three seats. The Liberal government first elected in 1916 won a plurality large enough to stay in office with a minority, and the Provincial Party soon disappeared.

Without any links to external markets, the few farmers in the Peace River country were forced to rely on activities like trapping for their livelihoods. To stimulate economic development, beginning in 1919 the provincial government sponsored a 'reconnaissance' of possible petroleum resources, since oil had been found in adjacent parts of northern Alberta. Geologists determined that oil or gas might be present, though

'Climbers at station awaiting train. Possibly Alta Lake, Pacific Great Eastern Railway, 1922–1926', photographer unknown. These climbers were not the only British Columbians in the 1920s who waited for the Pacific
Great Eastern, the provincially owned 'white elephant' that was supposed to have reached Prince George but
in the 1920s went only as far north as Quesnel. BCA, I-61688.

without extensive and expensive drilling they could not be sure it existed in commercial quantities.[21] Late in the 1930s, Liberal Premier Duff Pattullo, who shared McBride's northern vision, would sponsor test drilling. Meanwhile, the population of the Peace district grew as refugees from the drought-stricken southern prairie took advantage of the completion of the Northern Alberta Railway to Dawson Creek in 1931 to move to an area where the climate might still allow them to grow grain.

While Oliver did not solve the problems of the PGE, his campaign for lower freight rates on the transcontinental railways did succeed. According to the Crows' Nest Pass Agreement of 1897, under which the CPR built a line into the West Kootenay from Lethbridge, eastbound grain shipments enjoyed special freight rates. Alberta grain farmers had begun asking for lower rates on westbound shipments as well even before the Great War, once they realized that the Panama Canal (opened in 1914) would make it practical to ship their produce to Europe by sea. During the war, problems in operating the Canal, shipping shortages, and the temporary lifting of the Crow rates had made the issue academic; however, when the Crow rates were restored in 1922, groups such as the Vancouver Board of Trade joined Alberta farmers in demanding reductions for westbound grain. Recognizing a political issue that would let him 'fight Ottawa' without directly attacking the Liberal government there, while promising economic benefits for the province, Premier Oliver took up the challenge. As the Board of Railway Commissioners reduced rates, the volume of grain shipped through Vancouver rose from just over a million bushels in 1921 to more than 97 million bushels by 1929. 'Stevens's Folly'—a Vancouver grain elevator built by the federal government in 1914 in response to agitation by local Conservative MP H.H. Stevens—ceased to be a 'folly' and became a busy place. (Still, the elevator at Prince Rupert, built by the federal government in 1920, served little purpose apart from long-term storage, and the same was true of the elevator in Victoria.)[22]

Although railways continued to handle most of the transport within the province, trucks and automobiles came into widespread use in the 1920s. In 1916, 9,457 automobiles were registered in BC; by 1921, there were 32,000, and by 1925, 56,000. The Department of Public Works began paving provincial highways in 1917, but four years later only 69 kilometres, mostly near Vancouver and Victoria, had been completed. Federal funds provided under the Canada Highways Act, 1919, were used to pave some highways on southern Vancouver Island and in the lower Fraser Valley and to grade and gravel others, including the north–south Cariboo road.[23] In the same period the federal government opened national parks in the Rocky Mountains to cars entering from Alberta.

Cars also brought American tourists attracted by BC's fishing waters and perhaps by certain other liquids that prohibition made illegal in the United States. It was the presence of those tourists that motivated BC to give up one of the last vestiges of its colonial past: left-hand drive. The legislature agreed to the move in 1919 and the changeover was accomplished the following year in the interior; it took a little longer on the Lower Mainland and Vancouver Island because the BC Electric Railway wanted compensation and time to change switches, signals, and the doors on its streetcars. Despite a history of confusion at the border as Americans switched from right- to left-hand drive, not a single accident was reported at Hope during the months when coastal and interior drivers followed different rules. The reason was simple: the road through the Fraser Canyon—the only road link between the coast and the interior—was closed until the summer of 1927, when the Department of Public Works finished rebuilding parts of the dirt road that had been destroyed during the construction of the CPR. The Fraser Canyon toll road was less than six metres wide and full of twists and turns; the approach to one bridge required three 180-degree switchbacks.[24] Although the road was open only from May to mid-November, in 1929 almost 15,000 cars passed through the toll gate, of which more than 3,000 were from outside the province (mainly the American west coast).

Another landmark in the province's development came in 1925, when the University of British Columbia finally opened the doors at its own campus in the Vancouver suburb of Point Grey. By 1922 students were complaining of rats running through the classrooms at the old McGill University College campus and the risk of fire in the tents that housed chemistry labs. That sum-

'Great Trek at the Science Building'. In 1922, UBC students organized a province-wide campaign to persuade the provincial government to provide the funds to open the Point Grey campus. One of the final publicity measures, a parade on 28 October through downtown Vancouver, culminated in the Great Trek to the skeleton of the Science Building, where construction had been halted early in 1915 because of severe financial stringency. Although most of the banners visible here earnestly emphasize the value to the province of engineers, nurses, and science and agriculture graduates from the province's own university, one wag interpreted 'UBC' as standing for 'United But Crowded'. UBC Special Collections and Archives, 1.1/1315.

mer they collected 56,000 signatures on a petition calling for completion of the new campus, and in the fall they set out on a 'Great Trek' to Point Grey. They made their point. The job was finished within three years.

A new university campus was only appropriate for Canada's fastest-growing province. The 1931 census revealed a total population of almost 694,000, as compared to 525,000 a decade earlier—an increase of more than 30 per cent over a period when the national increase was only 18 per cent. During the 1920s there was some new immigration from Britain and Europe as well as from other parts of Canada, but the impact was much less obvious than that of the immigration in the decade before the war. Although the census categories for ethnicity were imprecise, they suggest that the composition of the population shifted only slightly in the 1920s as the proportion of residents claiming 'British' origin declined from 75 to 70 per cent. Indeed, the provincial government was no longer courting British immigrants, and when British promoters sought to encourage emigration to the province in the 1930s, the

'Entrance gateway to Kootenay National Park, Kootenay National Park, BC, October 1929', by W.J. Oliver. This image is probably a still from a series of tourist promotion movies that Oliver—a Calgary photographer turned film-maker—made for the Dominion government to encourage tourism in national parks. NAC, PA-58657.

provincial government gave them little more than polite attention. The same census recorded a tiny increase in the numbers of 'Native Indians', to 24,599; yet in relative terms Native people continued to decrease, making up only 3.5 per cent of the population. People of 'Continental European' origin—the census category that grew most rapidly—numbered 127,000 in 1931, rising from 14 per cent of the total in 1921 to 18 per cent ten years later.[25]

Despite a modest increase in absolute numbers, 'Asians' declined slightly as a percentage of the population in the 1920s (from 7.5 to 7.3 per cent). There was some sympathy for the approximately 700 Sikhs in the province in 1918, and for the decision of the federal cabinet in 1919 to let them bring in their wives and children under 18. Such a journey was costly and many Sikhs were sojourners; during the 1920s, only 488 South Asians, mainly Sikh women and children, immigrated to Canada.[26]

Other Asian immigrants, however, faced renewed hostility from many white British Columbians. Adding fuel to the old anti-Asian arguments was the fact that during the war both Chinese and Japanese had begun opening small grocery stores and fruit and vegetable shops in white neighbourhoods, especially in Victoria and Vancouver, while Japanese farmers had taken advantage of a wartime real estate slump to buy land in the Fraser Valley, where they were now raising poultry and growing berries. During the war many Chinese who had gone back to China to visit family or escape unemployment had been unable to return to Canada because of wartime reductions in shipping. As a result, the numbers who arrived back in 1919 seemed to represent a large influx. By the time of the 1921 federal election, anti-Asian sentiment was widespread and politicians took advantage of it, Liberals and Conservatives alike claiming that they would do the most effective job of keeping British Columbia white. Meanwhile, on the national level, the Retail Merchants Association of Canada, fearing that Asian retailers might move east of the Rockies, lobbied members of Parliament to put an end to Asian immigration. Together the Merchants lobby and the British Columbia MPs who set aside their party differ-

'Sutekichi Miyagawa and his four children Kaloko, Mitsuko, Michio and Yoshiko, in front of his grocery store, the Davie Confectionery, Vancouver, B.C., March 1933', photographer unknown. The regulations imposed by the Gentlemen's Agreement meant that most of the Japanese immigrants to Canada after 1907 were women of childbearing age, many of them 'picture brides'. As a result, the number of Canadian-born Japanese increased dramatically. By the late 1930s anti-Japanese agitators in Vancouver, including Alderman Halford D. Wilson, were complaining about the 'fecundity of the Japanese race' and especially the competition of Japanese merchants in many parts of the city who operated small businesses such as confectioneries, which sold some groceries in addition to sweets. NAC, PA-103544.

ences to support it saw their efforts rewarded with the passage of the Chinese Immigration Act of 1923—in effect, a Chinese exclusion act.

Canada had no compunctions about insulting China, which was a weak and divided country. It was not so ready to alienate Japan. Nevertheless, during the 1920s it renegotiated the Gentlemen's Agreement to reduce the number of Japanese immigrants to a total of 150 per year, of whom no more than half were to be female. The latter clause was a response to the 'picture brides' whose arrival had produced a

large natural increase in the Japanese population. Whereas only 1,422 Japanese children had been enrolled in provincial schools in 1923, by 1930 there were 4,014. The federal government also responded to complaints about increasing Japanese participation in the fisheries; in 1919 Japanese fishers held nearly half the fishing licences issued in BC. Since the Royal Commission appointed to investigate this situation included several BC MPs who had been among the most vocal critics of Japanese competition, its recommendation for a gradual decrease in the number of licences issued to Japanese was not surprising. Ottawa implemented the recommendation, and although the courts ruled in 1929 that the federal government did not have the authority to discriminate in issuing licences, by that time many Japanese fishers had switched to farming or lumbering. The Male Minimum Wage Act, 1926, which forbade the lumber industry to pay lower wages to Asian workers, accomplished its goal of encouraging sawmills to replace Asian workers with white men.[27]

Nevertheless, the people hit hardest by interwar xenophobia were the Doukhobors. During the Great War they had exercised their legal right not to perform military service (although some did contribute to the Red Cross and various patriotic funds), and with full employment and good markets they had enjoyed relative prosperity. As a consequence, their non-Doukhobor neighbours were increasingly resentful. In 1919, for example, the Trail Reconstruction Board reminded BC's attorney-general that 'these people came to this country to farm and clear land—not to enter the labor market in competition with those who are endeavouring to live as honest "WHITE" men, in decency and respectability.' Local merchants continued to complain that Doukhobors would not trade with them, and returned soldiers around Nelson and Grand Forks suggested that Doukhobors should be deported and their land given to veterans. In response, a group of radicals who called themselves the Sons of Freedom decided to prove their willingness to suffer for their faith by mounting protests in the form of nude parades. Then, when the government began enforcing school attendance laws, demanding the payment of school taxes and fining parents who did not send their children to school, the Sons of

Freedom set fire to some schools. Naturally, that upset the government. Premier Oliver recognized that the Doukhobors were industrious and successful farmers but warned that they must obey the law 'or drastic action will be taken to make them do so.'[28]

The situation became more complicated. Post-war unemployment and poor crops had created serious financial problems for the Christian Community of Universal Brotherhood, the corporation formed by the Doukhobors to hold their land communally. Then in 1924 their leader, Peter 'The Lordly' Verigin was killed in a mysterious explosion on a CPR train. The same explosion killed the MLA for Grand Forks-Greenwood, and during the by-election that followed, the provincial government seized Doukhobor property, including provisions and even kitchen utensils, in lieu of payment for truancy fines. As the Doukhobors of Nelson put it in a letter to Prime Minister Mackenzie King in April 1925, these were 'very cruel measures to compel our children to attend schools'.[29]

Verigin was succeeded by his son, 'Peter the Purger'. The new leader temporarily quieted the Sons of Freedom and tried to restore the community's finances. But he had a fondness for drinking and brawling, and many Doukhobors rejected his leadership. When the radicals resumed their protest activities, the government responded to public demands for punishment by jailing 104 men and women for public nudity and disfranchising everyone who had claimed exemption from military service. Perhaps not surprisingly, increasing numbers of Doukhobors began to see themselves as martyrs and joined the Sons of Freedom, while others, who disapproved of the radicals' illegal activities, broke away from the community and became Inde-

Many salmon labels featured either First Nations stereotypes or images suggesting imperial solidarity between producers in British Columbia and consumers in Britain. 'Indian Brand', BCA, I-51544; 'Flagship Brand', BCA, I-51973; 'Capital Brand', BCA, I-51969.

CANADIAN APPLES
FOR THE
UNITED
KINGDOM

Empire Marketing Board posters advertising BC apples in the United Kingdom: left, by Charles Pears (1873–1958); below, by George Sheringham (1884–1937). The purpose of the Board (1926–33) was to increase trade by encouraging consumers in Britain, the dominions, and the colonies to 'Follow the Flag in all your purchases.' NAC, C-126224, NAC, C-109410.

МИРНАЯ ЖИЗНЬ
ГОСПОДНИЙ

AND PEACEFUL LIFE
P. LORDLY VERIGIN

'In Memorium'
Peter Lordly (Virigin)
Brilliant, BC, Nov. 2nd 1924

Hughes Bros
Trail BC
(copyright applied for)

The funeral of Peter Verigin, Brilliant, BC, 2 Nov. 1924. An estimated 7,000 mourners, many of them from Doukhobor communities in Saskatchewan, attended the funeral of 'Peter the Lordly'. This photo is number 8 in a series documenting the event, made by Lelsoe or Robert Hughes, two brothers who were partners in a Trail studio. They made the photos to sell as souvenirs. An unnamed federal employee purchased this copy, which wound up incongruously in the records of the Department of Mines and Natural Resources and went from there to the National Archives. NAC, PA-17425.

pendents. Internal turmoil led to more nude parades and arson. Finally in 1932 the federal government rounded up some 600 Sons of Freedom, both men and women, and tried them again for public nudity—a formerly minor charge that had now been raised to a criminal offence. Accordingly, those found guilty were sentenced to three years in a special penitentiary on Piers Island near Victoria. The province put some of their children in non-Doukhobor foster homes or provincial industrial schools, although—to save money—eventually most were placed with Doukhobor foster parents.[30]

Since August 1928 the provincial govern-

'Doukhobors on railway tracks, location unknown, 193?' During May 1932, almost 600 Sons of Freedom were arrested in the course of five nude demonstrations. Four of the five actions were mounted on provincial highways. According to newspaper accounts, it was the third of the five actions, on 12 May, that blocked the CPR line between Castlegar and Nelson. On that occasion BC provincial police arrested 48 women and 39 men and placed them under guard in the curling rink at Grand Forks because the jail at Nelson was already overflowing. The first protest, on 1 May, had resulted in a violent confrontation, with police using 'itching powder and short lengths of rubber hose' to subdue the protestors, but this photo suggests that by mid-month the two sides had established a routine: the Doukhobors stand patiently as the police calmly take their names. They carry their clothing not out of modesty, but so that they will have something to wear once they are in police custody: the 118 men and women arrested in the first demonstration spent three days in jail naked (Toronto *Globe* and *Winnipeg Free Press*, 1–30 May 1932, quotation from the latter, 2 May 1932, 1). VPL, 1719.

ment had been in the hands of the Conservatives under the unfortunate Dr Simon Fraser Tolmie. A native of Victoria, a veterinarian, and a one-time federal Minister of Agriculture, Tolmie had been in office little more than a year when the Great Depression struck, and he was not well-equipped to meet the challenge. How bad were the 'dirty Thirties'? Booms and busts had marked the BC economy since the 1860s, and at first the crash of 1929 seemed to herald just another of the economic downturns that had become familiar across western North America. But the decline of the 1930s—actually two massive 'recessions', one lasting 43 months (August 1929 through March 1933), and one 13 months (May 1937 through June 1938)—turned out to be unprecedented.

'Distribution of food to unemployed, September 1931.' Members of the Revd Andrew Roddan's congregation at the First United Church in Vancouver distribute food to unemployed men living in a 'hobo jungle' at the city dump. This image is one of several made by a professional photographer, W.J. Moore, who was commissioned to document Roddan's efforts to help the homeless unemployed and to reassure Vancouverites that the 'relief problem' was under control. VPL, 12748.

Although the repercussions were felt around the world, they hit hardest in the US and Canada (its principal trading partner). Within Canada the western provinces suffered proportionately more than the rest. Between 1929 and 1933, the value of minerals produced in BC declined by more than half, and the value of forest, farm, and fishery production by more than two-thirds.[31]

As mines, mills, and logging camps closed or cut back on production, provincial revenues from taxes and royalties dropped from $26 million in 1929–30 to $20 million in 1932–3. British Columbians were not even drowning their sorrows in liquor; provincial liquor store profits in 1932–3 were less than half what they had been in 1929–30. As unemployment mounted, the numbers of British Columbians on relief rose. The government introduced some public works

'Clearing deadfall in No. 2 landing field area, Salmo, BC, 25 May 1933', photographer unknown. These carefully posed workers on DND Relief camp project #RP-24-14 were building an airstrip in the Kootenays. Not all the tasks assigned to relief campers were as worthwhile as this government-commissioned photo suggests. NAC, PA-35072.

schemes and set up work camps for single unemployed men, but found it increasingly difficult to cope as industries continued to lay off workers and unemployed workers from other provinces continued to arrive in BC. Though no part of the province was immune to unemployment, the problem was worst in Vancouver, where single male transients established four 'hobo jungles' under city bridges and along the waterfront. At first, authorities tolerated the 'jungles' and even provided their inhabitants with modest aid. Then four Communist-led demonstrations in Vancouver in the summer of 1931 changed their minds. That fall, police destroyed the 'jungles' and forced most of the men into work camps.[32]

The federal Conservative government of R.B. Bennett took over the work camps in November 1932. Nevertheless, the strain on provincial finances was severe and many municipalities were in even worse shape. In the Canadian federation of the 1930s, the municipalities had the primary responsibility for unemployment relief, even though they had much smaller tax bases than the provincial and federal governments. Towns and cities were caught in a vicious cycle: those with the largest numbers of unemployed also had the largest number of residents unable to pay their property taxes. The Vancouver suburbs of Burnaby and North Vancouver both plunged into receivership.[33]

'J. Minal leaning against stoop at relief camp,' date, location, and photographer unknown. Given that Canada had some 200 such camps by 1935, there are remarkably few photographs of life inside them. This scene suggests the boredom that made their residents easy targets for the organizing efforts of the Relief Camp Workers' Union. As one wrote to the Vancouver *Sun* in May 1935, 'we have no laughter in our hours, no hope in our young lives' (quoted in Michiel Horn, *The Dirty Thirties*, 339–40). VPL, 8834.

Tolmie's slashing of government expenditures did not satisfy an influential group of Conservative businessmen headed by George Kidd, the recently retired president of the BC Electric Railway Company—the provider of electricity, gas, and public transportation throughout the Lower Mainland and greater Victoria. The businessmen persuaded Tolmie to let them investigate the province's finances and recommend further reductions. Among the proposals they put forward were to shut down the PGE; cut the size of the civil service, the legislature, and cabinet; reduce the number of years of free public schooling; and eliminate the provincial grant to the university.[34]

Having lost control of the financial situation, Tolmie also lost control of his fractious party. In the provincial election of November 1933, not one candidate represented the Conservative Party. Tolmie himself ran for the Unionist Party of British Columbia; other Tories ran as Independents, Independent Conservatives, or Non-Partisans. (The latter gathered around W.J. Bowser, who complicated matters by running in both Vancouver Centre and Victoria, and then dying suddenly shortly before election day; the elections in both constituencies were postponed for four days so that new candidates could be nominated.)

The 1933 election was the first in BC history to be depicted as a clear conflict between socialism and capitalism. A new political party, the Co-operative Commonwealth Federation (CCF), formed in Regina that summer, gave new life to the BC left, which had won only 5 per cent of the vote and a single seat in the provincial election of 1928. Representing a broad range of socialist and labour traditions, the activists who formed the BC branch of the CCF did not always see eye to eye. Yet from the veteran Ernest Winch of the radical Marxist Socialist Party to Lyle Telford—an energetic medical doctor who, as leader of the more moderate Reconstruction Party, criss-crossed the province signing up members in 'CCF clubs'—they managed to work together. The party fielded candidates in 46 of the province's 47 constituencies, and eight 'irreconcilable socialists' ran as Independent CCFers.[35]

The Liberal leader was T. Dufferin Pattullo, a native of Woodstock, Ontario, who had worked as a civil servant and then a real-estate dealer in Yukon before moving to Prince Rupert in 1909. There he bought land from the government with the intention of re-selling it at a profit, but when sales proved disappointing he decided to make a new career in politics. Service on city council as an alderman (1910–11) and as mayor (1913) whetted his political appetite. In 1916 he was elected as the Liberal MLA for Prince Rupert and immediately became Minister of Lands. He survived the Conservative victory of 1928, secured the Liberal leadership, and assiduously rebuilt the party. Pattullo's career had imbued him with a healthy respect for the power of the state. Pattullo offered voters what he called 'socialized capitalism'—a middle road between Tolmie's business-based conservatism and the socialism of the CCF. To describe his objective he drew on the idiom of the poker table: 'not so much to change

the game as to redistribute the chips.' Campaigning with the slogan 'Work and Wages', and inspired by the progressive program of US President Franklin D. Roosevelt, Pattullo promised voters a 'New Deal' that included massive public works, better schools and hospitals, reduced freight rates, and a solution to PGE problem (through a takeover by the CNR). Other Liberals, however, took a more negative approach, turning the CCF into a socialist bogeyman in hopes of frightening voters away. Gerry McGeer, for example, warned that a CCF government would force British Columbia's sons to attend 'a school that propagates Socialism and Atheism', and force its daughters into 'the heinous system of companionate marriage.' Warnings against socialist ideas became a staple of BC politics.[36] The Liberals won a comfortable 42 per cent of the popular vote, which translated into 34 of the 47 seats in the Legislature. The CCF, on the other hand, with 31.5 per cent of the popular vote, won only seven seats, although it also gained the status of Official Opposition.

Pattullo's 'New Deal' proved more difficult to implement than his campaign speeches had suggested it would be. His proposals depended on the cooperation of the federal government, whether in the form of direct financial assistance or of indirect aid through reallocation of income taxes to the province, and the Conservative government of R.B. Bennett (not surprisingly) refused to play along. Instead Pattullo and his colleagues across the country saw their federal support cut by 20 per cent in 1934.

The unemployment problem refused to go away. To the alarm of authorities, the Communist Party of Canada moved to the forefront of popular protests. In Vancouver the May Day labour parade to Stanley Park became an annual rite of

'Gerry and Tom leading the Mothers' Council Section of the May Day Parade, Vancouver', c. 1933, photographer unknown. Numerous photos in the NAC and the VPL depict Vancouver May Day parades organized by the Communist Party of Canada and its affiliates between 1931 and 1935. 'Gerry and Tom'—costumed as a liquor-swilling capitalist and the capitalists' ally, a professor—demonstrate the CPC's skill at political street theatre. The parades (and the images) stopped in 1936, when party strategy shifted from directly confronting capitalism to forming a 'popular front' with other progressive groups. NAC, PA-125042.

spring. In British Columbia, as elsewhere, men in the federal government relief camps protested the strict discipline imposed on them and the insulting 20 cents a day they were paid. The Communist-led Relief Camp Workers' Union organized them. When the Bennett government ignored their complaints, in April 1935 the RCWU led about 3,000 of the 7,000 men in the BC camps in a mass exodus. Some 1,800 of them headed to Vancouver, where they rattled empty tin cans on street corners for donations to support themselves and snake-danced through the Hudson's Bay Company's department store before gathering at Victory Square. Claiming that

Vancouver was 'up against a Communist revolution', Mayor Gerry McGeer read the Riot Act—although in fact no riot took place at any time in the two months that Relief Camp strikers stayed in the city. Finally, on 3 and 4 June a cheering crowd waved goodbye as some 1,200 strikers boarded freight trains and set out for Ottawa. At the time, no one could have known that the 'On to Ottawa Trek' would be stopped short in Saskatchewan on Dominion Day by a bloody confrontation that came to be known as the Regina Riot.[37]

In October 1935 voters from Alberta east emphatically rejected Prime Minister R.B. Bennett

May Day Parade in Michel, BC, 1934(?). A number of photos in the Glenbow portray much grimmer May Days in the coal-mining towns of the Crowsnest Pass. This parade, bringing together workers from both the BC and Alberta sides of the pass, was photographed by Thomas Gushul, a commercial photographer who had studios in Coleman, AB, and later in Blairmore, AB. Gushul came to Canada from Ukraine in 1906 and worked as a labourer until he started his business in 1917. He earned his living from portraits, weddings, and funerals, but throughout his 45–year career he also recorded 'the lives and work of the immigrant miners'; Brock V. Silversides, *Waiting for the Light: Early Mountain Photography in British Columbia and Alberta, 1865–1939* (Saskatoon: Fifth House, 1995), 3–4. It is difficult to imagine a market for this photo and the many others like it. Glenbow, NC-54-2011.

and his Conservative government. British Columbians, however, gave their support to three different parties. Although Mackenzie King's Liberals won a massive national victory, they took only six of the 16 seats in BC. The Conservatives, crushed in every other province except Ontario, won five BC seats, and the maverick Tory H.H. Stevens, running as the leader of the Reconstruction Party, won a sixth. CCF candidates collected a third of the popular vote—more than either of the traditional parties—but won only three seats.

The King government was no better equipped than its predecessor to solve the economic crisis. Yet recovery gradually came on its own. Despite the setback of a sharp recession in 1937, and even though there were still not many new jobs, the Liberals shut down the relief camps in the spring of 1938 and offered to send 1,600 unemployed men who had come from the prairies to do winter work in provincial forestry camps back to their homes. The men protested and, with other relief camp workers, resorted to staging sit-down strikes in Vancouver's Art Gallery and main Post Office and 'tin-canning' on city streets. After a month, on 'Bloody Sunday', 19 June 1938, city police in cooperation with the RCMP evicted the sit-downers. Because the Pattullo government still refused them relief, approximately 700 men marched on the Parliament Buildings in Victoria. The capital had been spared major demonstrations because it was easier to keep stowaways off boats than off railway freight cars, but they could not stop marchers who paid the fare. Although Pattullo refused to meet with the men, his government advanced each of them $6.40—the equivalent of two days' pay, enough to sustain them for ten days—on the condition that they look for work.[38]

Pattullo's initial promises of reform had been more than just rhetoric. He set up a 'brains trust' of experts (modelled on Roosevelt's) to provide information and advice about economic policy. He also took steps—spurred on by the reformist provincial secretary, George M. Weir, who had been the professor of education at UBC—to pursue the recommendations of two earlier Royal Commission studies (1921 and 1932) that had reported favourably on the idea of health insurance. But the plan devised by Harry M. Cassidy, an expert in social welfare, had many problems, and not all cabinet members supported it. Many medical doctors disliked both of the compensation systems proposed for them (one was based on a salary, the other on per capita payment), while employers and employees alike objected to the payroll tax that would be required to help pay for the plan. In a referendum at the time of the 1937 provincial election, 56 per cent of the voters indicated that they favoured the idea of health insurance, but the margin was too small and the opposition too sustained for the re-elect-

'Strikers from Unemployment Relief Camps en route to Eastern Canada during "March on Ottawa", Kamloops, BC, June 1935', photographer unidentified. The history of this much-reproduced image shows how easily the cropping of a photo can lead to misinterpretation; at the same time it underlines Roland Barthes's argument that 'it is not the image which comes to elucidate or "realize" the text, but the latter that comes to sublime or rationalize the image' (quoted in Williams, *Framing the West*, 27). The NAC caption merely identifies these men as being 'en route' to Eastern Canada'. Yet when George Woodcock used the photo in *British Columbia: A History of the Province* (Vancouver/Toronto, 1990), his caption stated that they were boarding a train. Such is the power of text that since then several reproductions of this image have made the same claim. In fact, a glance at the complete image, including the parts outside the white lines along which it has been cropped, shows that the Trekkers are not boarding but getting off the train. The men on top of the boxcar have gathered their gear and are awaiting their turn to descend. The man on the ladder in the foreground looks down to place his foot on the next rung, taking care not to tumble; if he were climbing to the roof of the car, he would look up, and one of his comrades would offer him a hand. But the most obvious visual evidence comes from the dozen men already on the ground: they are walking away from the boxcar, not towards it. NAC, C-029399.

'Man evicted from Post Office, Vancouver, BC, 1937 [actually 1938]', photographer unknown. A tear-gassed and bloodied post office sit-downer surrenders. The police, following specific instructions from Prime Minister Mackenzie King, stormed the building early on a Sunday morning in hopes of limiting the numbers of on-lookers. NAC, C-79026.

ed government to pursue it any further. Pattullo had better success with several more modest projects. In 1935, for example, with federal financial help, his government established programs to train unemployed men aged 18 to 25 in placer mining or forestry. In addition, the province itself sponsored 'Pro-Rec', a province-wide Provincial Recreation program that offered young men, especially those who were unemployed, and later women, an opportunity to engage in healthful physical exercises and team sports.[39]

Pattullo alienated some voters, however, with the Special Powers Act, 1934 (which gave the cabinet the powers of the legislature when that body was not sitting). Many voters also objected to the expense of Pattullo's projects: his grandiose plans to annex the Yukon Territory and build a highway through BC to Alaska, and

'Queen Elizabeth with Premier Pattullo at foot of steps of Parliament Buildings, 30 May 1939', photographer unknown. King George VI descends the steps and Prime Minister William Lyon Mackenzie King brings up the rear as the royal tour visits Victoria. BCA, G-03703.

his decision to build a much-needed bridge across the Fraser River at New Westminster at an estimated cost of $4,000,000—roughly three times the entire annual budget for roads, bridges, and wharves. People in the interior and on Vancouver Island thought roads in their regions were more important, and Lower Mainland residents objected to paying to cross what they called the 'Pay-Toll-a' Bridge.

Pattullo had hoped to get more help from Ottawa after William Lyon Mackenzie King—an old family friend—became prime minister again in 1935. But King was so shocked by the size of the federal deficit that he was not prepared to offer any province much more money. Instead,

he created a Royal Commission to investigate Dominion–Provincial Relations (often referred to as the Rowell–Sirois Commission). Pattullo had his 'brains trust' prepare a 354-page submission entitled *British Columbia in the Canadian Confederation*. This 'economic anatomy' of the province traced its claims for 'Better Terms' since Confederation and documented with voluminous statistics the inadequacies of its tax revenues in the face of the increasing cost of social services and the difficulties that federal trade, tariff, and transportation policies posed for British Columbia. But Pattullo had misread public opinion. In the past, 'fighting Ottawa' had been a useful strategy for provincial politicians; now, after almost a decade of economic depression, regionalism had lost much of its appeal. As Commissioner Newton Rowell observed, the private groups who made submissions at the Commission's hearings in Victoria in March 1938 were 'ahead of the government in national sentiment'.[40] By the time the Commission's report was published, a new world war had made British Columbians nationally rather than provincially minded. They were not amused when Pattullo and the premiers of the other 'have' provinces, William Aberhart of Alberta and Mitchell Hepburn of Ontario, walked out of the January 1941 conference to discuss the Commission's proposal that they help the 'have not' provinces establish minimum standards of social services.

In the October 1941 provincial election Pattullo's Liberals won only 21 of 48 seats. The Liberal convention in December 1941 decided that a coalition with the Conservatives was the only way to carry on and ensure that the CCF, which won 14 seats and a marginally higher percentage of the popular vote, would not form a government. Predicting that the Liberals would rue the day they entered a coalition, Pattullo resigned as party leader and premier, leaving John Hart, his long-time Finance Minister, to form a coalition administration. Ironically, the outbreak of the Pacific War a few days later meant that one of Pattullo's dreams—the Alaska Highway—was realized after all.

By then Canada had been at war for over two years. In 1914 British Columbians had greeted the Great War with an outburst of patriotic enthusiasm. But when 'Hitler's War' began in September 1939, their zeal was restrained by memories of the last conflict's horrors. By increasing spending on coastal defences in the late 1930s, Ottawa had temporarily allayed fears of spies and illegal immigrants arriving from across the Pacific. Moreover, in contrast to the situation in 1914, the province's economy was improving in 1939. In the course of its preparations for war, Britain had increased its purchases of BC lumber, and shortly after the war began, it announced it would purchase all the lead and zinc that the province could produce. The primary industries on which the economy depended were once again offering full employment. The tragedy was that war was necessary to restore prosperity.

# CHAPTER FIVE

# The Two Sides of Prosperity: 1941–1972

When the Second World War began, British Columbia was still very much part of the British Empire, both in its ethnic composition—70 per cent of the population was of British origin, according to the 1941 census—and in its sentimental attachments. As in the First World War, the province had the highest rate of enlistment in Canada: 90,976 women and men—one British Columbian in seven—joined one of the armed services. War against Hitler's Germany had almost universal support, and regionalism temporarily vanished from provincial politicians' rhetoric. Even Premier Pattullo, noted for his fights with Ottawa, assured Prime Minister King that the provincial government would 'co-operate with you to the fullest extent in the war which is being thrust upon us.'[1]

For British Columbians, however, war started in earnest with Japan's surprise attack on the US fleet at Pearl Harbor on 7 December 1941. Residents of coastal British Columbia, where more than 95 per cent of the 23,149 Canadians of Japanese ancestry lived began to panic.[2] It did not matter that 13,309 of them were Canadian-born and another 3,223 had been naturalized, so that almost three-quarters were Canadian citi-

zens.[3] Within hours of the Japanese attack, the Royal Canadian Navy began impounding 1,200 fishing boats owned by Japanese-Canadians, lest they be used to assist in a Japanese invasion. The federal government now made the registration of all Japanese over the age of 16, which had begun earlier in 1941, compulsory. False rumours of a Japanese fifth column operating in Hawaii inspired public hysteria, as did Japan's rapid conquest of Hong Kong. Following advice from the British Columbians (mostly municipal or provincial politicians) it had appointed to a Standing Committee on Orientals, the federal government announced in mid-January that male Japanese nationals of military age would be required to leave the coast by 1 April. As Japan's forces marched toward Singapore, which fell on 15 February, public pressure mounted for the removal of all Japanese from the coast. Finally, fearing that planned public rallies might lead to a repetition of the anti-Japanese riot of 1907, on 24 February the cabinet used the War Measures Act to issue an order-in-council commanding that all Japanese move at least 100 miles (160 km) away from the coast. A few days later, it created the British Columbia Security Commission, which began moving Japanese-Canadians and taking them to an assembly centre in the livestock buildings of the Pacific National Exhibition in Vancouver. From there, the Security Commission gradually moved able-bodied men to road-building and railway maintenance camps in the interior. Women, children, and elderly men were moved to old mining towns like New Denver, Kaslo, Sandon, and Greenwood, and when the housing available in those places proved insufficient the Commission built some shacks along Slocan Lake and at Tashme, a settlement on a ranch just 22 kilometres east of Hope—barely outside the protected zone. Almost 2,000 other Japanese-Canadians moved to sugar beet farms in Alberta and Manitoba, and a few hundred, most of them well-to-do, established 'self-supporting settlements', mainly around Lillooet.

In the early phase of its dispersal program the federal government tried to encourage young Japanese-Canadian adults to move east by offering them free transportation and jobs, but only a few took advantage of the offer. Ian Mackenzie, the province's representative in the federal cabinet, had repeatedly promised white British Columbians that after the war there would be no Japanese left between the mountains and the sea. To fulfill this promise, in 1944 the government announced that any Japanese who did not agree to move east of the Rockies would have to accept 'voluntary repatriation' to Japan after the war.

'"Wait for me, Daddy": Private Jack Bernard, BC Regiment (Duke of Connaught's Own Rifles) saying goodbye to his five-year-old son Warren, New Westminster, 1 Oct. 1940', by Claude Dettloff. This is surely the most widely reproduced photograph ever taken in BC. Dettloff (1899–1978) of the *Vancouver Daily Province* captured 'Whitey' Bernard running after his soldier father as the regiment marched down Eighth Street to board a troopship. The *Encyclopedia Britannica Year Book* used it to illustrate Canada's war effort, it was extensively reprinted in Britain, and in 1946 the mass circulation US magazine *Life* named it one of the finest news photos of the previous decade. Unlike several celebrated 'candid' photos made famous by *Life*, Dettloff's image was not staged. Yet text-oriented historians do not always treat even iconic images with the care they deserve. A recent monograph that included this one got most of the details right but credited an Ottawa newspaper on 2 September 1939! The photograph made 'Whitey' Bernard a poster boy for Victory Bonds. He later recalled how 'they'd put me up front in my short pants and blue blazer and tell them I hadn't seen my Dad for a long time and would they please buy bonds to help get him home soon' (*Province*, 20 July 1978). Returning home as a sergeant in 1946, Jack Bernard worked as a log grader and died in 1981 at the age of 74. NAC, C-038723.

J.E. Roy (right) and another army reservist from New Westminster in military camp at Nanaimo, Fall 1940, photographer unknown. When George Woodcock used the photo of Warren and Jack Bernard in his *Picture History of British Columbia* (Edmonton: Hurtig, 1980), he reported that the men of the British Columbia Regiment were embarking 'for Europe and war'. In fact, the troopship that Jack Bernard boarded sailed to Nanaimo, where these two citizen-soldiers from New Westminster also trained in the autumn of 1940. Private collection.

'Naval rating prepares to hoist the Union Jack on a Japanese-Canadian fishing boat, New Westminster, BC, 29 Dec 1941', photographer unknown. The Department of National Defence may have commissioned this photo to reassure Euro-Canadians who feared that Japanese-Canadian fishermen and their boats might assist a Japanese invasion force. The shadow across the stern of *Kuroshima No 2* is that of a second seaman, on guard with a rifle and a fixed bayonet. NAC, PA-170513.

Many who wished to stay in British Columbia—especially in several interior towns where they were now accepted as members of the community—signed on for 'repatriation', expecting that they could change their minds after the war. But the government meant what it said, and the courts backed it up. After the war, public protests, especially from Ontario and Manitoba, against sending Canadian citizens to a foreign country convinced the government to cancel the 'repatriation' plan in 1947. Not until 1 April 1949, however, did it allow Japanese to return to the coast without police permission.[4]

No part of the province was more dramati-

'Large sleeping accommodations prevent crowding in the homes built by the B.C. Security Commission in Japanese camps, c. 1943', by Jack Long (NFB). Despite the comforting caption, possibly intended to prevent any complaints from Japan about ill treatment of its nationals, the accommodations were small and cramped. The standard hut, intended to accommodate two families, measured 14 by 28 feet (just over 4 by 8 metres) and consisted of three rooms: a room like this one for each family and a small shared kitchen/sitting room. NAC, C-44943.

cally affected by the war than the north. The American army, in cooperation with Canada, took on the biggest project, the construction of the Alaska Highway from Dawson Creek to the Yukon border and beyond. Prince Rupert, a staging point to Alaska, became a largely American community. To protect the Prince Rupert–Terrace corridor, the Canadian army ran an armoured train with a small mobile strike force that could assist the infantry in case of an enemy landing.

Meanwhile, Canadian and American troops built a road between the two centres, although it did not become fully accessible to the public until 1950, when the province arranged to use part of the Canadian National Railway's right of way for the highway.[5] The military strengthened its bases at points such as Ucluelet on Barkley Sound and Alliford Bay, southeast of Skidegate on the Queen Charlotte Islands.

For British Columbians not in military ser-

'Group of Japanese who had been interned during WW II, waiting for train which is to take them to ships waiting to take them to Japan, Slocan City, B.C., 1946'. During 1946, 3,964 persons of Japanese ancestry were 'repatriated' to Japan. Tak Toyota, who learned photography as a teenager in the camp at New Denver even though cameras were officially proscribed, took this photo. After the war he stayed in the Kootenays and became a successful businessman in Creston. NAC, C-47398.

vice the war brought steady jobs at good pay. European demand for BC resources had surged with war preparations, and by 1940 the resource industries had regained the production levels of 1928–9. With European supplies of forest products cut off, Britain turned to BC. But most of the freighters that in the past had carried goods from Pacific ports to Europe through the Panama Canal were now working exclusively on the Atlantic, and shipping overland by rail was prohibitively expensive. Although a special reduc-

tion in rates for BC lumber was eventually negotiated, by the time the backlog was cleared some mills had been forced to close temporarily when they ran out of storage space. Professional foresters were proud of the province's contribution to the war effort, but warned that high production was reducing the number of virgin timber stands and recommended establishing new stands on logged-over lands. Wartime demand also stimulated manufacturing. Having learned its lesson during the First World War, when it

'Air Raid Protection Officers Jones and Denten calling on Mrs Pratt in their sector. Purpose: to acquaint occupants with blackout regulations and see if they have articles such as hoses or step ladders useable in a fire caused by bombs, Vancouver, B.C., January 1943', photographer unknown. Air-raid warnings and blackouts reflected wartime anxieties on the home front. This image is a still from a NFB documentary promoting civil defence. NAC, PA-133261.

expanded, while the Prince Rupert dry dock got a new yard and West Coast Shipbuilders established itself on Vancouver's False Creek. At the peak of the shipbuilding boom, more than 24,000 men and women were employed in the industry, building corvettes, minesweepers, and especially freighters. With financial help from Ottawa, Vancouver became the site of a large branch of Seattle's Boeing Aircraft Company, which built 362 Catalina Flying Boats for the US Navy, as well as components for other planes.[6]

Shipbuilding, military construction, and war contracts created so many jobs that most of those left on unemployment relief were either aged or infirm. By 1943 BC led the other eight provinces in per capita income. High wages in the munitions industry, however, attracted workers away from the mines—leaving that industry in 'critical condition'—and luring teenagers away from their schools; authorities did not recognize the extent of child labour in the shipyards until a 14-year-old was killed in an accident. In addition, many women entered the labour market, some in occupations closed to them before the war, although they usually earned less than men for similar work, and were the first to be laid off when wartime demand ended. Social workers blamed increased juvenile delinquency on working mothers who left 'many children with the merest shreds of home life', and they warned of problems to come when soldiers returned 'almost as strangers', in some cases to find their wives with children they had not fathered.[7]

High wartime employment stimulated the growth of labour unions. In 1942 only 29 per cent of non-agricultural workers belonged to a union; yet by 1955 union members made up more than half—53.21 per cent—of BC's non-farm workers. British Columbia was Canada's

did not secure significant munitions contracts until relatively late, British Columbia was the first province to appoint an official 'to advance its interests in Ottawa'. The Burrard Dry Dock Company grew from 200 workers in 1939 to more than 10,000 at its North Vancouver and new False Creek yards. In addition the Yarrows and Victoria Machinery Depot in Victoria

'U.S. Army Personnel Working on the Alaska Highway attending dance at Dawson Creek, B.C., 22 April 1942', by Harry Rowed (NFB). This photo is one of more than a hundred made by the National Film Board's Still Photography Division (1941–84) to show Canadians and Americans working happily together as the Alaska Highway pushed northwest from Dawson Creek. According to the CBC Museum, the still division was charged with 'constructing a government-endorsed portrait of nationhood through documentary photographs'. The images were made available to newspapers and circulated across Canada through travelling NFB exhibits. NAC, PA-113197.

most unionized province: nationally, union membership increased only from 21 per cent to 34 per cent over this period. In BC before the war, the International Woodworkers of America (IWA)—an industrial union covering all the workers in an industry, as opposed to a craft union covering only workers with a particular skill—was active in only a few logging camps on Vancouver Island. A failed strike of affiliated quarry and sawmill workers at Blubber Bay in 1938 left the IWA near-

ly bankrupt when the war began. Nonetheless, it vigorously recruited new members, sending organizers in a 'loggers' navy' of small boats to remote logging camps, and sponsoring a radio program, 'Green Gold'. During the war strikes were rare and short. But in 1946 the Canadian Congress of Labour (the national federation of industrial unions affiliated with the American Congress of Industrial Organizations) decided that the invigorated IWA should set a pattern for wages through-

'Woman lumber worker peavying logs, on the BC Coast, 1943'. This photo, by an unidentified NFB still photographer, is one of a series showing women doing non-traditional jobs in response to wartime labour shortages. Although this 'lumberjill' seems to be acquitting herself well, the woman posing stiffly with a peavey on the far left of the photo was more representative. Jeff Keshen concludes that 'By the end of 1942, over 1,000 women had been recruited to work in logging and sawmill operations in British Columbia, although they were usually given comparatively light jobs and were paid about half the amounts men earned.' Ruth Roach Pierson's research has shown that women loggers were largely a propaganda invention. See Pierson, *Canadian Women and the Second World War*, vol. 66 of *Canada's Visual History* (Ottawa: Museum of Civilization, 1984), 15-6, and Keshen, *Saints, Sinners, and Soldiers* (Vancouver: UBCP, 2004), 103. NAC, PA-116932.

out industry, seeking '25–40 Union Security' (a wage increase of 25 cents per hour, a 40-hour week, and union security) along with a 'dues check-off' (payroll deduction of union dues). When employers offered a 12.5-cent raise and refused all other concessions, 37,000 IWA members struck province-wide against 4,167 separate employers. Union solidarity was so firm that in some communities no pickets were needed. When more than a million man-days had been

'March of IWA Strikers Victoria, 1946', by Duncan Macphail. The International Woodworkers of America (international because it had locals in Oregon, Washington, and British Columbia) was organized as an industrial union in 1937. During the war it became the largest such union in the province, covering most workers in every part of the industry, from the forest itself to the retail lumberyards. When its 37,000 members struck in 1946, the federal government appointed Chief Justice Gordon Sloan to arbitrate. According to historian Paul Phillips, the agreement settling the strike was 'a landmark in B.C. industrial relations' because it set a new pattern for bargaining between large industrial unions and large corporations; see *No Power Greater: A Century of Labour in B.C.* (Vancouver: BC Federation of Labour, 1967), 148. BCA, I-01403.

lost to the strike, the federal government began to worry that fruit growers would not have crates to ship their harvest in, and appointed Chief Justice Gordon Sloan to arbitrate. The union got only a 15-cent raise, but it won the 40-hour week, concessions on union security, and an industry-wide contract covering the coast and the interior. It also gained 10,000 members; after the 1946 strike, the IWA covered 'all woodworkers from the stump to the finished product, including logging, saw-milling, plywood plants, shingle mills, sash and door factories and retail lumber yards'.

Despite internal problems that saw the 'white' faction drive out Communist 'reds', the IWA remained a formidable force in the provincial economy. In the summer of 1952 alone 1,035,000 man-days were lost when its coastal members struck for higher wages and benefits, compared to fewer than 50,000 in many other years, when the industry-wide bargaining system worked to prevent conflict.[8]

The IWA was able to press its post-war demands in part because jobs were still plentiful as many industries converted to peacetime production, and a huge pent-up demand for new construction, especially of residential housing at home, and for rebuilding in the United Kingdom created a high demand for lumber. Despite occasional setbacks (because of weather or strikes) and shifts in overseas markets, the value of timber production soared. New mills appeared in the central interior, where the PGE improved access to markets; on the coast new technology such as the self-dumping log barge made the industry more efficient. Before long, however, these developments began to mean trouble for workers and smaller operations. New technology made it possible to produce more lumber with fewer workers, and the high cost of new mills and machinery helped to accelerate a trend in which big, vertically integrated companies supplanted the small, independent loggers and sawmill operators who had once dominated the industry.

That tendency was well exemplified by the 1951 merger of the H.R. MacMillan Export Company with Bloedel, Stewart, and Welch to form the giant MacMillan Bloedel Limited, known popularly as MacBlo. It grew even larger when, in 1960, it acquired the Powell River Company, which had dominated newsprint production in the province but was facing increasing competition both from the US and from newer, more efficient mills such as Mac-Blo's Port Alberni plant.[9] Among the other new mills established in the 1950s were the American Celanese Corporation plants at Prince Rupert and Castlegar, Crown Zellerbach's operation near Campbell River, and BC Forest Products' Crofton Mill on Vancouver Island. Expansion resumed in the late 1960s with new mills at Gold River on Vancouver Island, Kamloops, Prince George, and Skookumchuck near Cranbrook.[10]

Unlike the forest industry, mining in British Columbia had been a corporate domain since the later days of the gold rush. Mineral production increased after the end of the war as more workers became available, and the Korean War caused prices to rise sharply in the early 1950s. Yet mining did not regain the significance it had had in the provincial economy before the First World War.[11] Labour disputes, changes in world demand, and diminished or newly discovered ore bodies caused many local fluctuations. The Sullivan lead and zinc mine at Kimberley remained the most important in the province, but its production began to decline in the early 1960s. And whereas the Britannia Mine, only 50 kilometres north of Vancouver, had led the British Empire in copper production in the 1920s and 1930s, by the 1960s low copper prices meant that its dwindling reserves were no longer worth mining. After 1960, however, Japanese investment led to the opening of several major open-pit copper mines, including Highland Valley south of Kamloops, Craigmont near Merritt, and Brenda near Kelowna. Other mining companies—almost all of them foreign-owned—exploited new minerals such as asbestos at Cassiar and molybdenum at Endako. The last commercial coal mine at Nanaimo

'Accidental', cartoon by Meadows, *Vancouver Sun*, 23 April 1947. The 'Big Operators' who came to dominate the BC forest industry after the war did not do so all by themselves. Forestry legislation intended to support a 'sustained yield' granted large companies larger holdings and longer-term cutting rights. In his 1980 autobiography, timber entrepreneur Gordon Gibson accused the BC Forest Service of handing 'a few companies . . . a heritage that rightfully belongs to everyone'; Gordon Gibson with Carol Renison, *Bull of the Woods* (Vancouver: D&M, 1982 [first published 1980], 213).

closed in 1954, after a steady decline caused by the loss of markets to other fuels, depletion of reserves, and high production costs. New strip mines at Princeton were harbingers of the changes to come in coal extraction.

The salmon industry prospered during the war, when Britain was prepared to buy every salmon that could be caught and canned and every halibut liver that could be processed into vitamin capsules. Production was not greatly

'Strike – Mine Mill. Millmen and Power Plant Workers of the Granby Co. Operations parade to the tune of bagpipes in Princeton', c.1951. 'Mine Mill'—the International Union of Mine, Mill, and Smelter Workers—was among the many industrial unions that expanded during the Second World War. By 1946 it had approximately 8,000 members. Three years later, however, the union became a casualty of the Cold War when it was expelled from the Canadian Congress of Labour, the national federation of industrial unions, because of its Communist party connections. The strikers in this photo are from the Granby Consolidated operation at Copper Mountain near Princeton, opened in 1920 and shut down in 1957. As an example of how the archival record can be skewed by the simple availability of some photographs and the absence of others, the BCA index lists 71 photos of Granby Consolidated copper mines and smelters, but not a single image of this union, even though it was active in the province from 1916 until 1966, when it merged with the United Steel Workers. This photo comes from *The Canadian Tribune,* a newspaper published by the Communist Party of Canada. NAC, PA-93853.

affected by the removal of Japanese Canadian fishers because white and Aboriginal fishermen acquired many of their boats. The Native Brotherhood of British Columbia, formed in 1931, though mainly concerned with Aboriginal rights in hunting, trapping, fishing, and forestry, as well as better schooling, also represented its members in negotiations with the canners. Meanwhile, militant leaders emerged among white fishermen and

formed the United Fishermen and Allied Workers Union (UFAWU) in 1945. In addition to addressing the usual issues such as prices, wages, and working conditions, the UFAWU advocated conservation, particularly of salmon.

British Columbians knew how easy it was to eliminate a fishery. Until the 1930s the pilchard—a small member of the herring family—had been a significant part of the economy on the west coast

'Kimberley Sullivan Mine', 1954, by an unknown BC government photographer. Many photographs were created to celebrate the expensive new machinery introduced into the resource industries after 1950, but few of them are as artistic as this one. Collectively, such images showed pride in the machines. Yet they could also suggest that mechanization would soon supplant troublesome union workers. BCA, I-27683.

of Vancouver Island, but overfishing depleted the stock and by 1948 it had disappeared. Many seiners started casting their nets for herring instead, and by 1967 that fishery in turn was so depleted that it had to be closed. After five years the government decided that the herring population had recovered to the point where the fishery could be reopened—under strict regulations—specifically to supply the lucrative Japanese market for herring roe. Some openings were as short as twelve minutes, but in that time a lucky crew could make

a small fortune in 'silver gold'. According to one sociologist, the cost of administering the fishery was probably close to the total value of the annual catch.[12] As in other resource industries, technological change and corporate reorganization led major fishing companies to consolidate their operations. With the closing of smaller canneries, some of the coastal communities that depended on them, such as Klemtu (on Finlayson Channel, about half-way between Prince Rupert and Port Hardy) virtually disappeared, and even larger

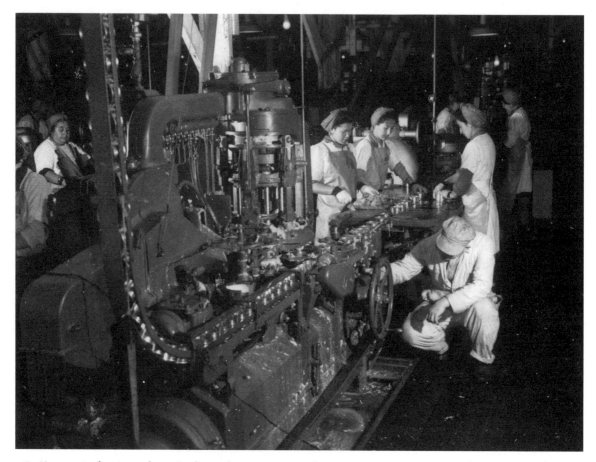

'Automatic cleaning and canning line, salmon processing plant, Namu, B.C., August 1945', by John Mailer. Compare this 1945 NFB photo with the 1890 photo on page 81. The machinery is much more sophisticated, but the workforce remains ethnically diverse and tasks continue to be gendered. The man in coveralls bending to examine the canning line would have earned about twice as much as the 'cannery girls'. NAC, PA-114826.

cities such as Prince Rupert, where halibut was most important, suffered.

Unlike the fisheries, agriculture served mainly local markets. The exceptions were apples, grain, and some meat products. The war was a boon to Peace River farmers who used their grain to produce pork both for export to Britain and to feed construction workers on the Alaska Highway. The completion of the PGE to Dawson

Creek and Fort St John in 1958 gave them easier access to seaports for the export of grain. In the south, the federal government's Veterans' Land Act, 1942, allowed some veterans to acquire reasonably sized holdings in the Okanagan and Creston valleys and to borrow the money to pay for the land and equipment at favourable rates. Others were able to take up berry farms in the Fraser Valley, some of which had been leased by

Mennonites from the prairies during the war, after the Japanese-Canadian farmers who had established them had been removed.[13] Many of the berry fields in the lower Fraser Valley were soon to vanish, however, under the tidal wave of suburbanization that accompanied Greater Vancouver's post-war boom.

In part, that boom reflected the fact that many mining and forestry companies had their head offices in Vancouver. Symbolic of the new growth was the strikingly modern BC Electric building. When it opened, in 1957, it dominated the West End landscape; but within a decade it was dwarfed by the office and apartment towers of the West End, which by the late 1960s was well on its way to becoming Canada's highest-density urban area. Meanwhile, the removal of tolls on older bridges and the construction of new bridges and highways encouraged developers to subdivide farmlands into town lots in the nearby municipalities of Richmond, Surrey, Delta, and Coquitlam. As new regional shopping centres appeared to serve the new communities, they drew trade away from older shopping districts like Hastings Street in downtown Vancouver and Columbia Street in New Westminster, where increasing numbers of stores stood empty. Yet despite the astonishing growth of Vancouver and the lower mainland, the interior still carried significant political clout. As early as 1942, the Coalition government had sent a committee of MLAs, called the Post-War Rehabilitation Council, on a tour of the province, and the government eventually did implement many of its recommendations: creating the publicly owned BC Power Commission in 1947 to provide rural areas with relatively inexpensive electricity; contracting to build the PGE from Quesnel to Prince George, with a possible extension to the

'Eric H. Brown carrying irrigation sprinkler pipes to be laid in the orchards of his 12-acre farm in the Lakeview Heights V.L.A. project at Westbank, BC, summer 1951', by Gar Lunney (NFB). Irrigation has always been the key to success for Okanagan orchards. New to fruit farming, Brown secured this relatively expensive land through the federal government's Veterans' Lands Act. The dream of building an independent life on a family farm had never completely died, and an NFB photographer was there to capture it on film. NAC, C-49433.

Peace River; and building new provincial roads.

Communication and travel were difficult in a province that was still sparsely settled and partly unmapped. The Department of Social Welfare, for example, used a motor launch to visit clients on parts of the coast; other social workers travelled by railway speeder or on foot. Even where there were roads, the population was often scattered. The social worker at Williams Lake had a district that extended 378 kilometres to the west and more than 300 to the south. In the Peace River, workers had to go 965 kilometres to the northern border; travel on the Alaska Highway was relatively easy but side roads, some up to 120 km long, were 'thick with dust during the summer months, and practically impassable because of thick gumbo during the spring'. Because the only road access was from Alberta, the Public Utilities Commission exempted the Peace River district from the operation of the British Columbia Motor Carriers Act.[14] To improve communications, the Coalition completed the Hope–Princeton Highway (1949), which reduced the distance from Vancouver to Penticton from 590 to 410 kilometres, built the Hart Highway from Prince George to Dawson Creek (1952), and improved other roads. The provincial surveyors who did some of the preliminary work investigating resources and laying out boundary lines were pioneers in aerial surveying but also travelled by foot, pack train, and raft.

In addition to providing the infrastructure for economic development, the Coalition government encouraged the development of new industries. Most important was the Aluminum Company of Canada, which employed more than 5,000 workers to build a hydroelectric plant at Kemano and an aluminum smelter at Kitimat. Together the two projects formed what was then the world's largest construction project. During the construction phase men seemed to outnumber women by at least a hundred to one, and the shortage of women led to some 'spirited fights' at community dances. By the time the smelter began shipping aluminum in 1954, Kitimat was an incorporated city, but its economy remained that of a company town, vulnerable to changes in the world market for aluminum until the Eurocan pulp and paper mill in opened 1969 and provided a second industry. Not until the

1970s did many people worry about flooding behind the Kenney dam, which stored water for the Kemano plant, and its impact on the flow of the Nechako River and the subsequent impact on the Cheslatta people, the fisheries and wild life, and Tweedsmuir Park.[15]

By the early 1950s, it seemed that the promise of the north would be fulfilled. New pulp and plywood operations, as well as new mines, drew people to Prince Rupert, Quesnel, Vanderhoof, Smithers, Terrace, and Burns Lake, but the centre of the boom was Prince George. Not only did it get new industry, but with the PGE and new highways it became a transportation hub and attracted branches of Vancouver wholesalers as well as regional offices of eastern banks. The city laid cement sidewalks and paved most of its downtown streets, while at last people were buying homesites in subdivisions laid out before the First World War. Yet the forest industry was also dependent on weather and international markets, and as a result Prince George suffered serious slowdowns from time to time.[16]

Industrial investment was not confined to the north. Construction of the Trans-Mountain oil pipeline from Edmonton to Vancouver led to the establishment of a new oil refinery at Kamloops and the expansion of existing refineries along Burrard Inlet. In 1951, with the easing of British currency restrictions, British investors bought most of Annacis Island near New Westminster to create a large industrial park.[17]

At the same time, the Coalition government was undertaking social and administrative reforms. It completed the consolidation of over 800 school districts, many of them consisting of a single one-room school, into 74 districts. By 1949 only one in ten of BC's teachers was still working in one-room school—the lowest pro-

'He's Rolling!' *Vancouver Sun*, 15 Feb. 1949. Three months before a provincial election, *Sun* cartoonist Meadows depicted Premier Byron Johnson as the engineer driving the train of BC progress. Although W.A.C. Bennett and his Social Credit government later took credit for much of the expansion of the provincial infrastructure, most of the work had been started by the Coalition, partly on the advice of the Post War Rehabilitation Council. Grateful British Columbians gave the Coalition 61 per cent of the popular vote in 1949.

portion in Canada.[18] School consolidation and a growing population enabled rural districts to build or improve secondary schools and provide transportation facilities or dormitories. The Coalition also replaced the Provincial Police with the federal Royal Canadian Mounted Police, in the hope of providing more economical and efficient police services.

In 1952, however, another social innovation played a major role in the Coalition's defeat. That innovation was hospital insurance. People liked the idea—some had been attracted to British Columbia precisely because of its social benefits—but not the compulsory premiums, the (small) co-insurance charge, or the provincial sales tax that was instituted in part to help pay for it. Some complaints focused on administrative inefficiencies and operating deficits; others, on overcrowded hospitals that could not accommodate all the patients who sought care. Hospital construction had not kept pace with population growth during the Depression and war; many people had put off elective surgery until the insurance scheme went into effect; and some sought admission to hospital for laboratory services that were covered for inpatients but not outpatients. By 1952 the Coalition government had solved most of the administrative problems and the hospital insurance scheme even had a slight surplus, but voters remembered only their aggravation.

Before British Columbians went to the polls in June that year, the Liberal–Conservative Coalition disintegrated. Since 1947 its leader had been Byron Johnson, a Liberal who had succeeded to the premiership on Hart's retirement. The relationship between the Liberals and Conservatives within the Coalition was seldom problem-free, but fear of the CCF had kept them together in a marriage of convenience. Ignoring the fact that most CCFers rejected communism, it took advantage of the North America-wide Red Scares of the late 1940s to accuse the CCF of flirting with the Soviets. During the 1949 provincial election campaign, for example, Coalition supporters reported that the audience at a CCF rally in Vancouver had sung the 'Red Flag'—the Communist anthem.[19] Fearing that the CCF might win if the Coalition collapsed and voters split between Liberal and Conservative candidates, the Coalition introduced a new ballot on which voters, instead of simply marking an 'X' beside the name of their choice, were to rank the candidates in order of preference. If no candidate won an absolute majority of first choices, the last ranking candidate was dropped and the second choices of the voters who had placed that person first were added to the totals of the remaining candidates. If necessary, this process would be repeated until one candidate emerged with 50 per cent of the vote. Since both Liberals and Conservatives opposed socialism, the Coalition

expected that Liberal supporters would favour Conservative candidates as their second choice, and vice versa. What neither of the old parties foresaw was the emergence of a fourth contender: Social Credit.

Some British Columbians had been discussing Social Credit as a monetary reform ever since the idea caught fire in Alberta in the 1930s, but they were very much on the political fringes. By the 1950s Alberta's Social Credit government had shed its radical origins to become a model of orthodox business-like administration, and its approach appealed strongly to W.A.C. Bennett, a discontented Conservative Coalitionist. A Kelowna hardware merchant and MLA for South Okanagan, Bennett broke with the Coalition, joined the Social Credit party late in 1951, and ran under its banner in the 1952 provincial election. The movement in BC had had no organization, but the Alberta movement sent in an organizer (the Revd E.G. Hansell) and the nascent party soon developed a good grass-roots organization, including a very active Women's Auxiliary. By the time the election was called it had yet to select a leader, but was able to nominate candidates in 47 of the 48 constituencies. Denouncing the discredited former Coalition partners as 'two stale eggs' and the CCF as 'a pink copy of what is going on in Russia', the Socreds positioned themselves as the alternative between the Liberal–Conservative right and the CCF left.[20]

Counting the transferable ballots took more than six weeks. The surprising result reflected the fact that the electoral map favoured the interior, where major new developmental projects and forest policies that seemed to favour large corporations were not always appreciated.[21] Only four seats were decided by absolute majorities on election night. The CCF won a plurality of the first choices (just over 34 per cent). The Socreds came next with just over 30 per cent, while the Liberals took 25 per cent, and the Conservatives only 10. When the votes were finally tallied, Social Credit had won 19 seats and the CCF 18, leaving the Liberals and Conservatives with just 10 between them and the Labour party with one (the Fernie seat held since 1920 by Tom Uphill). The lieutenant-governor decided that the premier should be the man the Social Credit caucus had selected as its leader: W.A.C. Bennett.

Bennett had the exceptional good luck to gain power at a time when British Columbia was entering a 20-year period of almost uninterrupted growth. Prosperity translated into Socred majorities in every general election between 1953 and 1969. Even though it never won a majority of the popular vote, the party usually took at least 40 per cent of it. With the sharp decline of the Liberals and Conservatives, Social Credit became the undisputed representative of 'free enterprise', to the frustration of the official opposition, the CCF (renamed the New Democratic Party in 1961), which usually attracted about a third of the popular vote.

Bennett's government initiated a myriad of programs for provincial development. By 1959 the premier, who usually acted as his own finance minister, boasted that British Columbia was debt-free. At Kelowna, on the seventh anniversary of his government, he shot a flaming arrow into a barge anchored in Okanagan Lake and carrying $70 million worth of cancelled bonds. He had not counted as part of the debt the many 'contingent liabilities' acquired by government agencies such as the PGE and the Toll Bridges and Highways Authority.

Regardless of the provincial balance sheet, BC workers enjoyed the highest per capita incomes in Canada, whether their jobs were in the resource industries or in city offices. To attract skilled workers and a stable labour force to out-of-the-way places, companies offered high wages and in many cases built 'instant towns' complete with shopping centres, recreational facilities, and attractive homes. One such community was Mackenzie, officially opened in 1968 as the townsite for workers in two pulp mills, five sawmills, and logging operations in the area 190 kilometres northeast of Prince George. A visiting sociologist remarked that it looked like 'a suburb in search of a town'.[22]

Bennett expanded on many programs inherited from the Coalition, often in a spectacular way. Like such electorally successful predecessors as Richard McBride, Bennett recognized the need to serve the whole province. He first gave responsibility for the provincial Highways Department to P.A. Gagliardi, a flamboyant Pentecostal minister and Social Credit MLA from Kamloops who, in the words of one engineer, blew into the department 'with the force of rare Northwest Pacific Typhoon'. Bennett praised Gagliardi as 'the greatest road builder since the Romans'. Before 'Flying Phil'—a reference to his indifference to speed limits—was forced to leave the cabinet (over his sons' timely purchases of land along proposed highway routes and the use of a government jet to take his daughter-in-law to Texas), he added thousands of kilometres to the provincial highway system. Among the roads the province improved were the southern trans-Provincial Highway through the Kootenay and Boundary districts, the Trans-Canada Highway through the Fraser Canyon, Highway 97 through the Okanagan and Cariboo, and Highway 16, the Northern Transprovincial.

The Bennett government took advantage of whatever federal aid was available, but Bennett

W.A.C. Bennett in the cab of a piece of heavy equipment. This photo is listed as 'Untitled' in the BCA, but Bennett's grin is unmistakable. Terry Reksten, in *The Illustrated History of British Columbia* (Vancouver: D&M, 2001), 244, dates the photo to September 1967 and identifies the location as the Peace River Dam (later renamed the Bennett Dam). BCA, H-01741.

did not always acknowledge it. When the final link in the Trans-Canada Highway, the expensive Rogers Pass section between Revelstoke and Golden, was completed in July 1962, the province had its own ceremony without federal participation; Prime Minister John G. Diefenbaker called it 'one of the most peculiar, self-cen-tred actions' he had ever known.[23] To add further insult, the province erected signs designating the Trans-Canada as 'B.C. No. 1'. A few weeks later the federal government held its own opening ceremony in Glacier Park. Whether federal or provincial, the new highway was an immediate boon to the tourist trade, and prairie vacationers poured over it every summer on their way to the lakes of the Okanagan.

Bennett's government also expanded the Coalition's plans for the PGE. He was at the centre of the ceremonies marking the inaugural run of the PGE to Prince George (a project initiated by the Coalition) on 1 November 1952, and in 1956 he presided over the driving of the last spike for the southern link from Squamish to North Vancouver. By then, natural gas was being produced in commercial quantities around Fort St John and the PGE was building from Prince George to Dawson Creek and Fort St John. When he left office in 1972, the railway, which he had renamed the British Columbia Railway, extended to Fort Nelson and work was underway on a 563-km line toward Dease Lake.

That the PGE was a government agency did not temper Bennett's repeated endorsements of free enterprise. Paradoxically, Bennett did more than any other premier to involve the government in the economy. In 1958, after labour disputes halted ferry service between Vancouver Island and the mainland, Bennett created the BC Ferry Corporation. More spectacular still was his expropriation of the BC Power Corporation, popularly known as the BC Electric, in August 1961—a move that the CCF had advocated for years. Formed in 1897, this company produced and distributed electricity and gas and operated most public transit systems on the Lower Mainland as well as in Greater Victoria. Bennett wanted to develop hydroelectricity on the Peace River, but BC Power, the only likely large customer, had no interest in buying power from the Peace. Bennett had become involved with the plan through Axel Wenner-Gren, a Swedish multimillionaire who, in order to demonstrate a revolutionary type of monorail, proposed that his firm build a pulp mill, along with a hydro plant to power the railway. Shortly before the 1960 provincial election, Bennett officiated at the turning of the first sod for the Pacific Northern Railway, now transformed into a conventional railway. But that first sod proved to be nearly the last. The Wenner-Gren project was no more than what Bennett's biographer called 'the Wizard of Oz approach to economic development'. Wenner-Gren faded from view, but Bennett went ahead with power on the Peace River, even though damming the river would cause massive environmental change. Construction of what became the W.A.C. Bennett Dam near Hudson's Hope began in 1963. By the time the power flowed in 1968, the project had flooded the valleys of the Finlay and Parsnip Rivers and created Williston Lake—the largest man-made lake in Canada.[24]

Bennett also wanted to develop hydroelectricity on the Columbia River, but because it is an international waterway, the federal governments of both Canada and the US were involved, and when they signed a treaty on its development, early in 1961, Bennett refused to ratify it. Ottawa wanted the US to pay for downstream benefits in the form of power; Bennett wanted cash to build dams. Personality conflicts between Bennett and the federal cabinet minister who acted for Ottawa, his fellow British Columbian E. Davie Fulton, added to the problem. The discussions dragged on, but Bennett eventually got his way. On 16 September 1964, in a ceremony at the Peace Arch in Blaine, Washington, President L.B. Johnson proclaimed the treaty in the presence of Prime Minister L.B. Pearson and Bennett. Construction of the necessary dams flooded out several small settlements on the Arrow Lakes but created a short-term employment boom.

The Bennett government inherited one in-

'Now here's the deal, Phil blacktops the road from California to the Aleutians, Mike gives up the Yukon, Lyndon gives me Washington and Oregon . . .', by Len Norris, *Vancouver Sun*, 16 September 1964. President Lyndon Johnson and Prime Minister Lester Pearson listen to Premier W.A.C. Bennett's latest grand scheme and hang on in terror as BC Highways Minister 'Flyin' Phil' Gagliardi, known for his propensity to speed on the highways his department had built, outraces his motorcycle escort. Norris (1913–97) drew cartoons for the *Vancouver Sun* from 1950 until 1988. In an honourable cartooning tradition, Norris swiped his style from the British satirist Giles, but his pithy observations on BC society are entirely original.

tractable problem from its predecessors: the radical Sons of Freedom Doukhobors. The bombings and burnings that had begun in the 1920s had increased in intensity since the end of the war. In 1950 approximately 400 Sons of Freedom were in jail, yet the bombings and burnings—described by the Attorney General as being 'in the nature of an insurrection'—continued, as did the nude parades, and most Sons of Freedom refused to send their children to public school. Social Credit candidates in the 1952 provincial election pledged to solve the 'Doukhobor problem' by force if necessary. In 1953, the provincial government rounded up 104 truant children and turned a former Japanese tuberculosis sanatorium at New Denver into a boarding school for them. Parents required permission to enter the dormitory; instead, most visited with their children through the eight-foot chain-link fence that surrounded the compound. Some children were later released to parents or other relatives, and in time the children remaining in the dormitory were sent to the local public school. The dormitory remained in operation until 1959, when the last parents swore an oath promising to send their children to school.[25]

But the release of the children did not end the problems for the Sons of Freedom. Terrorism peaked in 1962 with 474 separate incidents, of which the most serious was the destruction of a power line serving the Bluebell mine. Some Sons of Freedom, found guilty of conspiring to commit 'depredations', were sent to jail. To draw attention to the prisoners' plight, roughly 1,200 'zealots', mainly women and children, began a march from the Kootenay to the coast. At Hope, where they stopped for the winter, they found considerable hospitality. Although some younger marchers ventured to Vancouver and stayed there, most drifted back to the Kootenay, where some took high-paying jobs in dam construction. Except for a handful of fanatics, the march was the last outburst of the Sons of Freedom. Most Doukhobors had long since assimilated into mainstream society.

Whereas the Sons of Freedom garnered countless headlines, Native people had been largely out of sight and mind of white British Columbians for decades, but as their population grew, many began moving to cities such as Prince Rupert, Port Alberni, and Victoria. Having hovered around 25,000 since the 1880s, the Aboriginal population reached a low point of 22,605 in 1929; the 1941 census showed the beginning of a dramatic increase in absolute terms, although the proportion of the province's total population identified as Native continued to hover around the 2.4 per cent mark. By 1963 the number of registered 'status Indians' in the province had reached 41,000, largely because of improvements in living conditions and health care, and possibly, as anthropologist Wilson Duff speculated, a 'hybrid vigour' resulting from interracial marriages. There

'A service held at the New Denver institution for the "Sons of Freedom" children incarcerated there, 1956', photographer unknown. This photo is one in a series of three held by the BC Archives. The talented photographer who made the images clearly intended them to arouse sympathy for the Freedomites. The most famous (and most maudlin) of the three shows a mother kissing her child through the chain-link fence. Koozma J. Tarasoff reproduced the photo without crediting a photographer in his *Pictorial History of the Doukhobors,* 170, and then deposited it in the archives. BCA, C-01738.

was now some recognition that, as wards of the state, they had not been treated well, receiving inferior schooling and medical care. Yet even sympathetic editorialists generally maintained that the best hope for Native people lay in assimilation to the mainstream. The provincial government agreed. In 1949 it amended the Public Schools Act to allow Native children to attend local public schools; the federal Department of Indian Affairs

'Haida ceremonial costume, Skidegate Mission, 1949.'
This photo is one in a series made by an unidentified BC
government photographer at Skidegate Mission (on
Graham Island in the Queen Charlottes, or Haida Gwaii)
and apparently intended to demonstrate the progress
made by Indian Act towards its goal of leading 'the Indian
people by degrees to mingle with the white race in the
ordinary avocations of life'. To that end, almost all the
children are shown in contemporary Euro-Canadian
dress, looking as 'un-Indian' as possible. This photo is the
only one that suggests any sense of 'tradition'. Yet even
here the 'Haida ceremonial costume' is worn over neatly
creased trousers and penny loafers. BCA, I-28940.

paid tuition fees. In 1955 British Columbia boasted that it had more Native students attending its
schools and universities than any other province,
that they mixed well with other students, and that
they were being prepared to mix with their 'white
neighbours in adult life'.[26]

Native people were not idle bystanders to
Euro-Canadian plans for their future. Early in
1947, the Native Brotherhood of British Columbia staged a mock legislature in which they made
white settlers wards of the state. That impressed
the provincial legislators, and in 1949 they granted Native people the vote without requiring that
they abandon their Indian status. Activists like
Andrew Paull, the Squamish leader of the North
American Indian Brotherhood, objected, fearing
that enfranchisement would lead to assimilation
and the loss of privileges and rights. Others,
however, welcomed the chance to join the mainstream. Among them was Frank Calder, a Nisga'a
who ran successfully for the CCF in Atlin in 1949;
although he later switched to Social Credit, he
remained an MLA for 30 years, until he was finally defeated by a single vote in 1979. Gradually,
First Nations people secured more civil rights.
Shortly after Ottawa amended the Indian Act to
let provinces regulate Native access to drinking
places, BC gave them the right to drink in beer
parlours, the only public places where drinking
was legal in the province. Despite a 'howling dis-
order' in Terrace when a number of local men
took advantage of the new law, the provincial
advisory committee on Indian Affairs reported
that the majority 'used their new freedom from
prohibition with discretion.'[27]

Beginning in the 1930s, British Columbia
surpassed the national average in population
growth, reaching a million in 1951, and two million in 1971. From Canada's sixth largest

province in 1931, BC leapt to fourth in 1941 and third in 1951, where it has remained. The province was a magnet for migrants from other regions, particularly the prairies; over 800,000 new residents arrived between 1941 and 1971. Many wartime workers who had come to BC from other provinces stayed, and soldiers from across the country took their discharges there. Overseas immigrants were a minority among the newcomers in the first three decades after 1945; however, chain migration continued, with Italians, for example, heading to the existing Italian communities such as the 'Little Italy' in Trail. The 'Continental European' group in the population grew to 35 per cent by 1971—reflecting the ethnic roots of many prairie migrants—and gradually the British segment of the population shrank as a proportion of the total. People of Asian ancestry, however, accounted for only 3.5 per cent in 1971—half the level reached 40 years earlier. Even though the restrictions on Chinese immigration were eased slightly in 1947, it is estimated that BC received only 11,624 legal immigrants from China between 1946 and 1965, most of whom were joining family members already living in the province. In 1960, when Nanaimo's Chinatown was destroyed by a fire, it was not rebuilt: instead, two new senior citizens' residences were built to accommodate the ninety or so elderly men who had lived there. Reflecting the change in attitudes, one local businessman at the time remarked that 'There is no color bar in Nanaimo. The modern Chinese live anywhere and everywhere here.' The small Chinatowns that were once a feature of almost every community faded away as their residents died, returned to China, or moved to the larger Chinatowns in Vancouver and Victoria, which survived in part by catering to tourists.[28]

'Mungo Martin and Helen Hunt presenting ceremonial copper crest to Elizabeth, the Queen Mother, London', 1958, Barratt's Photo Press Ltd. In a bizarre convergence of traditions, Kwakwaka'wakw carver and chief Mungo Martin (Nakapemkim) and his adopted granddaughter Helen Hunt present a potlatch copper to Her Majesty Elizabeth the Queen Mother on the centennial of the creation of the colony of British Columbia. 'Coppers'—hammered copper shields, decorated with crests—were highly valued ceremonial gifts. The ban on the potlatch had been lifted in 1951. The presentation took place at the foot of the 'Royal Totem' in London's Windsor Great Park. BCA, I-51777.

Internal migration during and immediately after the war created severe housing problems despite the hundreds of modest but efficient houses constructed by the federal government's Wartime Housing Limited near places like the North Vancouver shipyards, the Boeing Aircraft plant at the Vancouver Airport, and shipyards in Victoria. So desperate was the situation in 1946 that veterans, with the help of the Labour Progressive Party—the name adopted by the Communist Party in 1943—occupied the old Hotel Vancouver, which was slated for demolition, and quickly persuaded federal authorities to turn it into a hostel for veterans and their families. As the economy returned to peacetime conditions and building supplies became more readily available, the federal government, through its Central Mortgage and Housing Corporation, built tracts of rental housing for veterans in Vancouver's Renfrew Heights and Fraserview subdivisions. By the 1960s increasing numbers of urban residents were living in apartments rather than houses, and in Victoria, where the proportion of senior citizens was higher than in most cities, more apartment units were constructed than single-family dwellings.[29]

Traditionally, British Columbia's birth rate had been below the Canadian average (24.1 for BC and 27.2 for Canada as a whole in 1951). As early as 1940, however, the superintendent of Vancouver schools noted an increase in births and warned that it would have implications for the schools in 1946. With the advent of the 'baby boom', natural increase exceeded immigration as a source of population growth as early as 1949. Provincial birth registrations almost doubled in the 1950s, from 161,769 in 1949–50 to 302,204 in 1959–60.

Within a decade or so, immigration was once again the most important source of population increase. Few parts of the province did not experience some growth, but the increases were

greatest on the lower mainland and southern Vancouver Island. By the early 1950s, 68 per cent of British Columbians lived in urban communities. The populations of Vancouver, New Westminster, and Victoria spilled over into suburban municipalities where housing was less expensive. Bus companies began to run 'commuters' specials' from Maple Ridge and White Rock to Vancouver and New Westminster and, through a subsidiary, the BC Electric Railway introduced buses to replace its Fraser Valley interurban line in 1950. As new roads and river crossings in the early 1960s made commuting to Vancouver easier, the agricultural centre of the Valley moved ever farther to the east.[30] In 1960 the Deas Island tunnel under the Fraser River opened to serve a new four-lane highway from Vancouver to the American border, and in 1964 Vancouver gained a new Second Narrows bridge that linked with a four-lane section of the Trans-Canada highway from the eastern Fraser Valley. (Since 1994 it has been known as the Iron Workers' Memorial Bridge, in honour of the 18 men who lost their lives when the partially built span collapsed in 1958.) Despite the new highway and bridge, Vancouver residents vehemently opposed the idea of a freeway within their city, and in 1968 City Council finally shelved its plans to build such a road.

W.A.C. Bennett may be best remembered for highways, railways, and power developments, but he did not ignore education; perhaps he recalled his experience on the Post-War Rehabilitation Council, which in 1943 had called for the establishment of junior colleges.[31] In the early 1960s, when the first of the baby boomers were approaching university age, Bennett charged John B. MacDonald, the new president of the University of British Columbia, to investigate the

'Crest subdivision, showing 4 year old National Housing Act (NHA) housing, Burnaby', n.d. Like other Canadians, British Columbians urbanized and suburbanized in the decades after the Second World War. As sterile as this development seems, many Canadian families in the 1950s dreamed of owning a house in a similar setting, with a massive television antenna to pull in US television signals. The Crown corporation responsible for meeting mortgage needs—Central Mortgage and Housing (CMHC)—commissioned an unidentified photographer to show Canadians what a good job it was doing. NAC, PA-170065.

needs of higher education. On his recommendation, the province decided to build a new university in greater Vancouver, named after Simon Fraser; to turn Victoria College into a degree-granting institution; and to establish 14 regional colleges to provide university transfer programs and technical and vocational studies to comple-ment the work of the new British Columbia Institute of Technology in Burnaby.

Yet growth and prosperity also had negative consequences. They attracted people to British Columbia in search of work, but sometimes the job seekers outnumbered jobs, and often the work that was available required skills that the

'Dancing class, Fort Langley Elementary School, 1960', by an unknown BC government photographer. Children of the 'baby boom' dance beneath the photo of Queen Elizabeth II that presided over every provincial classroom. Several of the girls wear the BC Centennial tartan, introduced in 1958. In 1960 a provincial Royal Commission on Education headed by S.N.F. Chant declared that the main aim of Physical Education should be to provide 'healthful exercise' for all students rather than to develop a high level of skill in competitive games for a few. This photo was one in a series presumably intended to show that the Social Credit government was providing the province's children with a well-rounded education. BCA, I-23701.

new arrivals did not have. In older communities the influx of people caused severe housing shortages, particularly for inexpensive rental units. The Department of Social Welfare, renamed the Department of Rehabilitation and Social Improvement in 1969, did not cope well with such problems. A cynic might suggest that the 'rehabilitation' was that of the department's new minister, Phil Gagliardi, now back from political purgatory. In 1971 Gagliardi's department reported that immigration and nationwide unemployment had contributed to the largest number of

An Anglican priest explains to the touring Archbishop of Canterbury: '. . . our great problem in BC, Your Grace, is the widespread local belief that this *is* Heaven . . .'. Len Norris, *Vancouver Sun*, 28 Sept. 1966.

people on provincial social welfare rolls since 1932. Through its agency, the Provincial Alliance of Businessmen (another Gagliardi creation), the department bluntly told the unemployed to get to work. An even greater challenge were 'incipient drug problems' associated with young people, many of them hippies, who began drifting into BC from across the country in the late 1960s.[32]

Many hippies settled in the Kootenays but they had their highest profile in Vancouver, where the perceived threat to law and order posed by protest groups like the Youth International Party ('yippies') led Mayor Tom Campbell to speculate about resorting to the War Measures Act.

In 1972 W.A.C. Bennett went back to the electors confident of a seventh consecutive major-

'Don't turn "left",' urged this full-page Socred advertisement, which appeared in many provincial newspapers just before the 1972 election. The text below the image warned against splitting 'your free enterprise vote', highlighted major accomplishments of the W.A.C. Bennett government, and concluded by promising 'a broad, straight road ahead . . . to a better life for every person in this province'. Voters, however, decided that it was time for a change. Vancouver *Province*, 30 Aug. 1972.

ity mandate. Part of the Socred campaign was a short film called 'The Good Life'. Broadcast on television stations throughout the province, it drew attention to the roads, railways, and buildings that the government had constructed over the previous twenty years and suggested that if voters wanted continued prosperity, Social Credit was the party to provide it. But British Columbians were tired of Bennett and his government. Labour was particularly incensed by legislation that prevented the use of union dues collected by payroll deductions for political purposes (a blow to the New Democratic Party, which relied on union support) and set limits on picketing and the circulation of 'do not patronize' lists. In the spring and summer of 1972 major strikes hit both the forest and construction industries. Even so, people were surprised on election night when the count revealed that the New Democrats under David Barrett had won 38 seats to just 10 for Bennett and the Socreds. (The Liberals and Conservatives shared the remaining seven seats.) Regardless of Bennett's admonitions about 'socialist hordes', apparently British Columbians were ready to try out a new version of 'the good life'.

# CHAPTER SIX

✍

# A New British Columbia?
# 1972–2004

*L*ike many of his predecessors as premier, Dave Barrett was a flamboyant character. Whereas most of them were businessmen, however, he was a social worker by profession. A member of the legislature since 1960, he presented himself as 'fat little Dave', an ordinary Jewish boy from Vancouver's East side, and showed his populist touch by arriving for his first day on the job in a five-year-old Volvo (W.A.C. Bennett had used a chauffeured Cadillac). Yet the malice directed at him by his opponents created an impression of radicalism that was at odds with his actual objectives. Dave Barrett's NDP had travelled a long way from Ernie Winch's CCF, which Barrett himself dismissed as 'five people in a room with sixteen ideas on how to construct socialism'. The party that succeeded Social Credit in September 1972 was social democratic, not socialist. In addition to the usual lawyers, Barrett's cabinet included teachers, accountants, and a few trade unionists. But anyone who thought this diversity might be a promising sign was soon disappointed, for instead of seeking out talent or practical experience Barrett chose to reward a number of NDP stalwarts who had sat in the legislature before the election. Even sympa-

thetic critics suggested that some of his ministers were weak at best, and his failure to name either Emery Barnes or Rosemary Brown—the first Black British Columbians elected to any public office since Mifflin W. Gibbs served on Victoria City Council in 1866—disappointed the province's small Black community.[1]

One of the lasting reforms made by the Barrett government concerned the operations of the legislature, which for the first time was to have a full Hansard (the daily stenographic report of debates) and an oral question period. The new government also extended the length of legislative sessions from 40 to 50 days per year, and—because members would be spending more time on legislative business—increased their salaries and expanded their staffs. In a reaction against the all-night sessions that had been a hallmark of the Bennett era, Barrett also promised to end daily debate at 11 p.m. One commentator has suggested that these reforms—the product of the NDP's long experience in opposition—were actually were more beneficial to the opposition than to the government itself.[2]

Instead of moving slowly in the hope of broadening their base of support, Barrett and his

'Number one on the hit parade', by Roy Peterson, *Vancouver Sun*, 20 Sept. 1972. 'Fat Little Dave' Barrett and his NDP government enjoyed an initial surge in popularity because of programs like the 'Mincome' plan for senior citizens. Roy Eric Peterson (b. 1936) has drawn for the *Sun* since 1962, and succeeded Len Norris as its principal cartoonist on Norris's retirement in 1988. Not confined to local issues, Peterson's work has won national and international audiences. Simon Fraser University Library, Special Collections, Peterson Collection, MsC 25.PET.2.9

cabinet chose to legislate a social democratic agenda as rapidly as possible. As Barrett explained, 'We knew we would probably not get another shot, so we decided to try to do everything.' His government pressed ahead with promised social legislation including a 'Mincome' plan guaranteeing senior citizens (over 65) a minimum monthly income of $200, and

Pharmacare, to provide them with free prescription medications. A new system of subsidies quadrupled the number of day care centres, from 67 to 280, and education generally benefited from greatly increased budgets. To 'keep capitalism honest', a new Department of Consumer Services enforced Canada's most effective consumer protection legislation, and in 1974 the government froze rents and established the Rentalsman's office to regulate them. A new Human Rights code banned discrimination in housing or employment based on race, religion, sex, ancestry, or place of origin. The NDP government also remembered its political base in the union movement, repealing laws that favoured compulsory arbitration, removing restrictions on secondary picketing during a strike, banning the use of professional strike-breakers, and reducing the percentage of workers in a company that had to sign up in order to qualify for a union certification vote. The government also extended the right of free collective bargaining to provincial civil servants, and for the benefit of hourly workers increased the minimum wage from $2.00 to $2.50 and then, in 1975, $2.75 per hour.[3]

In a province where even conservative governments had been prepared to countenance some public ownership (W.A.C. Bennett himself had nationalized the BC Electric and created the BC Ferry Corporation), the new government faced criticism from commentators on the left for not 'attacking capitalism head on' with a bold program to nationalize private industry. Barrett dismissed his leftist critics as 'leather seat bound university socialists' and followed the examples set by earlier NDP governments in Manitoba and Saskatchewan, which had combined modest ventures in public ownership with provincial regulation of private capital. One such venture, the government's purchase of the financially troubled Ocean Falls pulp and paper mill from Crown Zellerbach, was intended mainly to preserve threatened jobs. More clearly motivated by a public enterprise vision were the provincial purchase of Columbia Cellulose (renamed Canadian Cellulose) and the creation of the BC Petroleum Corporation to market natural gas

exports. Angry mining companies attacked the Mineral Royalty Act of 1974 as 'socialism', though in fact it was part of a business-like effort to increase the province's return from natural resources. A comment that Barrett made shortly after becoming premier summed up his attitude towards corporations that would sooner reduce production than pay royalties to the province: 'Resources won't go rotten if left in the ground.'[4] Other NDP interventions into the economy, however, did challenge private property. Farmers who expected large gains from urban development were outraged when the BC Land Commission froze the sale of agricultural land for non-farm purposes without the approval of the new Environmental and Land Use Committee, created to establish guidelines for land-use planning in various regions of the province. The greatest controversy of all arose when the Barrett government (following Saskatchewan and Manitoba) created the Insurance Corporation of British Columbia (ICBC) and gave it a monopoly on the sale of automobile insurance.

Barrett spurned his predecessor's calculated hostility to Ottawa and indifference to the other Western provinces, refusing to play 'cheap regionalist politics'. An early gesture was to restore the signs identifying the Trans-Canada Highway that Bennett had removed. His goal, he said, was 'to break down the many barriers erected by the former administration to reflect fully that British Columbia is a part of Canada'. Whereas Bennett had refused the Prairie premiers' invitations to join them on the Western Canadian Economic Council, Barrett readily accepted. Unlike Bennett, Barrett never complained about BC's contribution to federal equalization payments. In 1974 he joined the other western premiers in objecting strenuously when

public ownership of natural gas and oil).[5] When, in October 1975, the federal Liberal government of Pierre Elliott Trudeau imposed wage and price controls in an attempt to contain serious inflation, Barrett accepted the controls in principle and imposed a temporary freeze on the prices of food, drugs, and other essential goods and services, including energy. He raised Mincome and the minimum wage while freezing the salaries of MLAs and senior civil servants.

A buoyant economy cushioned the Barrett government during its first two years. Both the BC Petroleum Corporation and Canadian Cellulose reported substantial profits. As Finance Minister, Barrett in February 1974 introduced a 'resource dividend budget' that invited school boards and universities to ask for more money, put funds aside to purchase land to construct family housing, and promised to reduce school taxes and build new ferries. But the good news stopped with an economic downturn later that year. In response to falling profits, BC Hydro raised rates for residential electricity and natural gas. Then in late 1975 ICBC announced that it would have to raise automobile insurance premiums by 19 per cent after a number of its workers won a wage increase of almost 40 per cent the previous summer. Hence the public mood was already souring when the Barrett government proposed a dim-witted plan to adopt Daylight Saving Time in the winter to save energy, and attributed a $100 million overrun in the welfare budget to a 'budgeting error'.[6] The NDP even alienated its union base, first legislating striking firefighters back to work and then calling a special session of the legislature to pass a law (the Collective Bargaining Continuation Act) that forced striking workers in the propane industry, BC Rail, supermarkets, and the pulp industry

'Everybody stay calm', by Roy Peterson, *Vancouver Sun*, 26 February 1973. After six months in office Barrett had become a scarecrow, his Land Commission Act frightening away not only 'developers' and 'promoters' but also farmers. Simon Fraser University Library, Special Collections, Peterson Collection, MsC 25.PET.2.12

Ottawa cut the price for natural gas (although he offered to accept federal jurisdiction over non-renewable resources if Ottawa would agree to back to work for a 90-day 'cooling off' period. Although provincial labour leaders reluctantly agreed to obey the law and the BC Federation of Labour reaffirmed its support for the NDP, the legislation did not endear the NDP to the union rank and file.

Just over three years into his government's term, Barrett surprised the province by calling an election for December 1975. Campaigning under the banner of 'the Barrett Government' rather than the New Democratic Party, the NDP claimed to represent 'the people against the big, vested interests'.[7] Barrett emphasized his government's social and economic programs, warning that Social Credit would repeal them, and promised new ones. For their part, the Socreds stressed their party's program rather than its inexperienced leader: William Richards 'Bill' Bennett, the son of W.A.C. They blamed the NDP for the province's 'economic nose-dive' and promised to 'Get BC Moving Again' through reduced government spending and 'tough but fair taxation', which reduced provincial royalties on minerals. Yet Social Credit also pledged not only to maintain Mincome and Pharmacare but to improve them (when the economy permitted), and to ensure that the jobs of those employed by Crown corporations would not be threatened, even if a Socred government decided to privatize them. The election results were clear enough. Although the New Democrats won virtually the same percentage of the popular vote that they had in 1972, they were rewarded with only 18 seats, and seven cabinet ministers, including Barrett, were defeated. The Progressive Conservative vote collapsed from almost 13 per cent to less than 4, and the Liberal vote from 16 per cent to 7; together they elected only two members, compared to seven in 1972. By contrast, the revived Social Credit Party

under Bill Bennett captured 49.3 per cent of the popular vote—more than his father's party had ever won—along with 35 of the 55 seats in the legislature. Among the 35 Socred members were three incumbents who had been elected as Liberals in 1972 (Patrick McGeer, Garde Gardom, and Allan Williams), one former Conservative (Hugh Curtis), and one disgruntled former New Democrat, Frank Calder.[8]

W.A.C. Bennett had retired in 1973, soon after the defeat of his government, and when his son Bill was chosen to replace him, journalists quickly dubbed the younger man 'Mini-Wac'. With the assistance of Grace McCarthy, who had been a member of his father's cabinet, Bill Bennett appealed to the business community for financial help in rebuilding the party's base. The mining industry was especially generous. The Socreds kept up their campaign rhetoric after the election, and talked about 'Barrett plundering the provincial piggy bank' and a 'foreign socialist' ideology controlling the province. By 1975 the party had 75,000 paid-up members.[9]

The new government made administrative reforms, appointing an auditor-general, an ombudsman, and a legislative committee to oversee Crown corporations. It also attempted to undo some NDP policies. At the swearing-in of the cabinet, Bill Vander Zalm—a former Liberal mayor of Surrey who was now the Minister of Human Resources, responsible for welfare—had made the Socreds' position clear, declaring that 'if anybody is able to work, but refuses to pick up the shovel, we will find ways of dealing with him.' (The shovel became Vander Zalm's trademark, and, as his biographers note, it didn't hurt his family's gardening business.) In his first press conference as premier, Bill Bennett hinted at spending cuts. Yet despite some retrenchment in

1976 and 1977, and transfers of government employees to Crown corporations, the numbers of public servants continued to rise, and government spending increased at a rate beyond that of inflation. In 1977, Social Credit privatized Canadian Cellulose (one of the companies the NDP had nationalized) and some other provincial assets to create the British Columbia Resources Investment Corporation (BCRIC). Shortly before the 1979 election, every British Columbian was issued five BCRIC shares, with the chance to buy more at an issue price of $6. The announcement of the market price of BCRIC shares became a regular feature on the staunchly Socred BCTV (a privately owned television channel) just before the weather report and sports scores. BCRIC soon went on a buying spree, purchasing shares in MacMillan Bloedel and buying more shares in a coal export business, Kaiser Resources. But the high price paid for the Kaiser shares, BCRIC's failure to develop new industries, and allegations of insider trading soon put a halt to the spree. Shares that had sold for $9.25 in 1980 fell to $3 by the autumn of 1981. (Multimillionaire entrepreneur Jimmy Pattison, whose business interests ranged from supermarkets to automobile dealerships to neon signs, purchased what was left of the corporation in 1995.)[10]

Bennett had made BCRIC the centrepiece of his spring 1979 election campaign, asking British Columbians to choose between 'individual ownership' as represented by BCRIC and 'state ownership' as favoured by the NDP. Behind the scenes, however, Social Credit organizers were advising party members to write letters to the newspapers signed with fictitious names, praising the Socreds and criticizing the NDP. Certainly the NDP was not hurt by this amateurish effort: they won 26 seats in the election, while the Socreds took the

other 31, and the popular vote was even closer: 48 per cent for the Socreds and 46 per cent for the NDP. The Liberals and Conservatives had become electorally irrelevant. As political scientist Donald Blake put it, 'a substantial realignment had taken place in the mass electorate.'[11] Before 1970 the BC NDP had been confined to the lower mainland, the Kootenays, and Vancouver Island; now both parties had province-wide electoral bases.

Bennett responded to this intensely competitive environment by hiring professional political organizers. Progressive Conservative apparatchik Patrick Kinsella arrived from Ontario to become his deputy minister, and when he was named principal secretary to the premier, another Ontario Tory, Norman Spector, succeeded him. Bennett ignored the resentment expressed by his party and cabinet that outsiders should be given such influential positions. With the help of Kinsella and Spector, among others, Bennett built 'a high-powered institution with centralized authority over both the Socred party and the provincial government'.[12]

British Columbia's pronounced economic cycles made retaining political power a delicate business. Between 1976 and 1980, increases in the province's exports—lumber, coal, metal concentrates, pulp—almost tripled the government's revenues. By the summer of 1981, however, rampant inflation had reduced housing starts in the US, and hence the demand for BC lumber, while international demand for copper, coal, and natural gas was also falling. By 1982 much of the western world was in recession. The blow to BC was especially harsh, because of its dependence on outside markets. Unemployment soared from 5.8 per cent in July 1981 to peak at 16.1 per cent in January 1983—the highest rate since the

Depression of the 1930s—and the highest in Canada west of the Maritimes. Meanwhile, as the numbers on the welfare rolls increased, the government's revenues continued to fall.[13] In February 1982 Bennett announced that the government would cut spending to match revenue, in part by limiting wage increases in the government sector. Hospitals, school boards, and municipalities, their provincial revenues frozen, began to lay off employees.

In the spring of 1983 Bennett sought a third majority on a program of 'restraint' that echoed Ronald Reagan in the United States and Margaret Thatcher in Britain. Opinion polls told him that people would vote for someone they perceived as a 'tough guy in tough times'. British Columbians still liked big projects, and Bill Bennett took a page from his father's script, pointing to his government's development of BC Place, a domed sports stadium in downtown Vancouver capable of seating 60,000 people; the upcoming Expo '86; Vancouver's 'Skytrain' Light Rapid Transit system; the Coquihalla highway, which cut hours off trips from Vancouver to Kelowna and Kamloops; and the development of northeast coal. Critics charged that the province was diverting federal funds earmarked for health and higher education to fund such 'extravaganzas'. Bennett promised more money and increased attention to education, while Education Minister Bill Vander Zalm—who thought BC students should learn to 'write good' and recommended using the strap for discipline—conveniently decided to take a 'sabbatical' from politics. Nevertheless, the NDP seemed to be winning the campaign until its leader Dave Barrett announced that he would end wage restraint. As the journalist Allen Garr recalled, the Socreds and the media interpreted this to mean the NDP were 'profligates shovelling

'It appears to be another letter of resignation over the Dirty Tricks affair . . . but the signature's been forged', by Roy Peterson, *Vancouver Sun*, 15 November 1979. Socred stalwart Grace McCarthy, then Minister of Human Resources, briefs Premier Bill Bennett on the scandal. Simon Fraser University Library, Special Collections, Peterson Collection, MsC 25.PET.3.17

money out of the back of the government truck, blowing a bundle on their friends in the trade-union movement while everyone else suffered'.[14]

In the May 1983 election, Social Credit took 49.76 per cent of the popular vote and 35 seats, leaving the NDP with the remaining 22 seats and 44.94 per cent of the vote.

With a renewed majority, the Social Credit government radically escalated its program of restraint, introducing 17 bills aimed at shrinking the size and the cost of government. Bill 2, the Public Service Labour Relations Amendment Act, gave the government, as management, the right to eliminate positions and assign duties throughout the civil service. Bill 3, the Public Sector Restraint Act, restricted collective bargaining in the civil service (and in its original version would have given the government the right to terminate any employee without cause). Other bills set maximum wage increases at 5 per cent; eliminated the Rentalsman's office and motor vehicle inspection; removed budgetary authority from local school boards and assigned it to the Minister of Education; gave the Medical Services Commission greater authority over physicians; and restricted doctors' access to billing numbers. Bill 27, the so-called Human Rights Act, repealed the Human Rights Code and abolished the independent Human Rights Commission; in its place, a government-appointed council would enforce much narrower definitions of discrimination. Within hours, the government employees who had administered these programs had been dismissed. The Ministry of Human Resources fired 599 employees, most of them child welfare workers. Given the modest cost of many of the purged programs, and the government's lavish spending on Expo '86, some suspected that financial restraint was not the only item on the agenda. Critics charged that 'restraint' masked a broad ideological assault on the provincial welfare state.[15]

Widespread opposition to the Socred program gathered behind Operation Solidarity, a mass movement that usurped the role of the NDP as the official opposition and further undermined Dave Barrett, who had already announced that he would be resigning as party leader. Although the Solidarity coalition's membership extended well beyond organized labour, Art Kube, president of the 250,000-member BC Federation of Labour, reluctantly took on the role of official leader. A clear sign of the province's ongoing transformation from a resource to a service economy was the fact that white-collar unions in the public sector, such as the BC Government Employees' Union, now had more members than the blue-collar unions in the private sector such as the International Woodworkers of America. Whereas organized labour feared that legislation to circumscribe the BCGEU would be the first step towards major changes that would affect all workers, community groups such as Women Against the Budget were more concerned about measures affecting human rights and social services. For trade unions the era of mass rallies and parades was long past, but Solidarity was able to attract wide popular support. In July 25,000 protestors converged on the legislature's lawn; in August 40,000 gathered at Vancouver's Empire Stadium; and in October some 60,000 marchers bearing banners such as 'General Strike! Stop Bennett's War on the Poor' paraded outside the Hotel Vancouver, where the Socreds were holding their annual convention. Smaller demonstrations took place in Kelowna, Nanaimo, and Prince George.[16]

But the protests seemed to embolden Premier Bennett. To push its program through, his government held marathon sessions—at least one ran through the night to nine o'clock in the morning—and in some cases used closure to end debate and force a vote. Twice, when Dave Barrett objected to arbitrary changes in procedure imposed by the speaker, he was ordered out of the chamber; on the second occasion, at 4 a.m., he was dragged from his seat by the sergeant-at-arms and suspended for the rest of the session. Once all the controversial measures had been passed, Bennett announced in a television address that he was adjourning the legislature indefinitely.[17] While Operation Solidarity publicly pondered a general strike, Bennett tried to mollify unionists with a contract concession that ferry workers could not be fired without cause, and promised to postpone the threatened dismissals of civil servants. At midnight, 1 November 1983, the BCGEU strike went ahead all the same. The next week, 90 per cent of the province's teachers followed suit, defying both court injunctions and threats that they would lose their teaching certificates.

But secret negotiations were already underway between the premier's deputy, Norman Spector, and the president of the IWA, Jack Munro. Munro worried that, 'drunk on their own power', the 'well-meaning' supporters of Operation Solidarity threatened to undermine the trade union movement. The IWA executive made clear that the union was not about to picket for causes like the inclusion of sexual preference in the human rights code. In his memoirs Munro recalls how the discussions he initiated with government officials and labour leaders culminated in 'the Kelowna Accord', announced by Munro and Bennett together from the porch of the premier's Okanagan home.[18] The BCGEU dispute was settled when the government agreed that reductions in the numbers of civil servants would be carried out in a fair and equitable manner. Although

'The people are behind me', by Bob Krieger, *The Province* (Vancouver) and reprinted in Marjorie Nichols & Bob Krieger, *Bill Bennett: The End* (Vancouver: D&M, 1986), 75. Krieger brilliantly captured Premier Bill Bennett's stubbornness in refusing to acknowledge the massive protests mounted by Operation Solidarity. Behind Bennett, the legible signs read, 'Human Rights', 'Democracy', 'Stop the Cuts', and 'Save the Rentalsman'. In his style, Krieger is reminiscent of the Montreal *Gazette*'s Aislin (Terry Mosher).

Bennett refused additional funds for education or any concessions on matters of concern to the community groups, he abandoned the bill that would have undercut the collective agreement of the BCGEU. Government workers and teachers went back to work, and for all practical purposes Operation Solidarity disappeared. The brief

Expo Centre under construction, Vancouver, 1985. The uncredited BC government photographer who made this image probably did not intend the threatening sky in the background to be allegorical. Although Expo '86 at times looked like a disaster in the making, in the end it was generally considered a success. BCA, I-21684.

dawn of a new mass politics had ended with an informal backroom deal brokered between the premier and a union boss.

Bennett's subsequent actions demonstrated that the Kelowna Accord was, as Stan Persky has put it, 'not worth the paper it wasn't written on'.

The government reduced the public service by a quarter, from 46,000 in 1982 to 35,000 in early 1984, cut spending on education, and fired uncooperative school boards. As if to demonstrate its contempt for its opponents, the government slowly began to increase spending on major projects such as the Coquihalla highway, a new bridge across the Fraser River, the Skytrain mass transit system, and construction of the site for Expo '86 under the direction of Jimmy Pattison. Revisions to the Labour Code created a special economic zone for Expo that permitted the employment of both union and non-union crews without the risk of strikes. Further labour code revisions made it more difficult for unions to organize and easier for workers to leave unions, and effectively banned secondary picketing and secondary strikes such as those used by Operation Solidarity.[19] W.A.C. Bennett—who had died in February 1979— would have been proud of his son.

Unlike his father, however, Bill Bennett was willing to take an active part in national affairs. As Kim Campbell, who served briefly as executive director of the premier's office, recalled, he 'never played fast and loose with the country for the sake of political gain'. (When observers outside the province commented approvingly on the younger man, his father's response had been cautious: 'They seem to like you in Ottawa. And in Toronto they're writing glowing editorials about you. But what do they think of you in Spuzzum?') Bill Bennett played a supporting role in the negotiations that led to the 1982 patriation of the Constitution and the passage of a charter of rights, but made it clear that, as chairman of the premiers at the national constitutional debate in Ottawa, he was, in his own words, 'chairman in name only'—the ones who ran the show were Peter Lougheed of Alberta and Bill Davis of Ontario.[20] Still, like most of his predecessors in the premier's office, he did not hesitate to play the regional card if circumstances seemed to require it. When his 1984 budget cut education and most other services, and included measures to discourage welfare recipients from other parts

of Canada from moving to his province, he blamed Ottawa for 'short-changing' BC on transfer payments.

Perhaps the most striking difference between Bill Bennett and most of his predecessors was the fact that he left office voluntarily. In May 1986, after Expo '86 had opened to great acclaim and he had taken the inaugural drive, in his yellow convertible, along phase 1 of the Coquihalla highway, he announced his retirement. Except for John Hart, every other BC premier in the twentieth century had been forced out of office, whether by death, political defeat, or scandal. After he left office, however, Bennett faced a long investigation into the fact that he and his brother sold their shares in Doman Industries hours before bad news concerning the company was released and its stock price fell dramatically.

In the 34 years before 1986, British Columbia had had only three premiers. In the 18 years to follow, it would have seven: two Socreds (Bill Vander Zalm and Rita Johnston); four New Democrats (Mike Harcourt, Glen Clark, Dan Miller, and Ujjal Dosanjh); and one Liberal (Gordon Campbell). Only Johnson and Dosanjh were defeated in general elections; Vander Zalm, Harcourt, and Clark left office under the shadow of scandal (although all were later exonerated); and Miller was never more than a caretaker. Why British Columbia has experienced such instability is a question that has no simple answer. Some observers, like journalist Geoffrey Molyneux, maintain that the more recent leaders lack the vision of giants like McBride and the two Bennetts; a more likely explanation is that political, social, and economic changes have made British Columbia a much more complicated place than it was in the past, and hence a more challenging one to govern.[21]

The competition to succeed Bill Bennett made the Socreds' 1986 leadership race one of the most fiercely contested in Canadian history. Bill Vander Zalm, back from three years on the sidelines, won on the fourth ballot over eleven other candidates, including Kim Campbell, who came last in the race and made a prescient comment: 'charisma without substance is a dangerous thing.' The two-thirds of the grassroots delegates who chose Vander Zalm overwhelmingly supported Bill Bennett's neo-conservative policies, but emphatically rejected the modern party that Bennett and his experts from Ontario had created to implement those policies. Those delegates, half of whom had joined Social Credit before 1975, chose Vander Zalm in hopes of turning back the clock and restoring the comfortable party they had known under W.A.C. Bennett.[22] Even though almost all of the elected Social Credit MLAs opposed him, the party elected Vander Zalm as its leader and hence as premier. Vander Zalm was sworn in on 6 August 1986, and in October won a snap election, with an increased majority, over an unprepared NDP.

In his approach to Canadian federalism Vander Zalm preferred the traditional BC regionalist line to the constructive engagement of Dave Barrett and Bill Bennett. However, the need to incorporate Quebec into Canada's new Constitution increased the stakes at federal–provincial conferences in the late 1980s. At Meech Lake, Vander Zalm did not get the Senate reform he wanted, but—fearing fiscal punishment from Ottawa—reluctantly supported the agreement. He conceded that Quebec was a 'distinct society'—and then proceeded to suggest that each province was also distinct (a variation on an old BC theme). Alarmed by an opinion poll suggesting that 46 per cent of British Columbians

thought he was too cozy with the Mulroney Conservatives in Ottawa, Vander Zalm saw to it that the March 1988 Throne Speech enumerated BC's grievances and gave notice that his government would 'evaluate areas of federal jurisdiction'. He had his bureaucrats prepare a confidential report called *The Economics of Canadian Confederation: A British Columbia Perspective*—an updated version of Duff Pattullo's 1938 brief to the Rowell–Sirois Commission. He also had them draft a Confederation Equity Act and study the possibility of a separate tax system for BC, parallel to Quebec's. At the same time, he mused about creating an advisory council on Confederation, to be charged with ongoing review of 'the situation of the province *within* Canada'. Vander Zalm enthusiastically endorsed free trade—the centrepiece of the 1988 federal election—after the Mulroney government gave the province some modest grants. But the honeymoon was short. On the one hand, Vander Zalm maintained that Canada should be a united country; on the other, as a fan of decentralization, he sympathized with the Quebec government's Allaire Report's plan to reduce federal powers.[23]

Yet Bill Vander Zalm bitterly disappointed those Socreds nostalgic for the political stability of the first Bennett era. In less than five years, he steered the party into oblivion. Vander Zalm governed from the right, privatizing public corporations and provoking confrontation with the trade union movement through changes to the labour code. In June 1987, some 300,000 unionized workers joined a one-day general strike to make their protest known. Vander Zalm's penchant to speak out on moral issues like abortion attracted embarrassing national attention to the province: one of his speeches in the legislature was described in the *Globe and Mail* as 'a gore-dipped

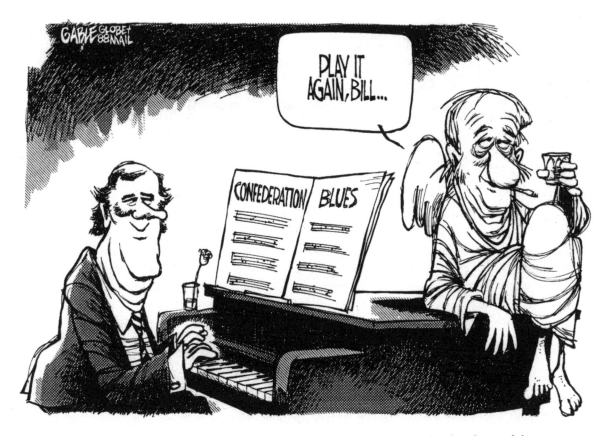

'Play it again, Bill,' by Brian Gable, *The Globe & Mail*, 17 March 1988. Vander Zalm plays the 'Confederation Blues' with encouragement from the ghost of René Lévesque. Born in Saskatchewan in 1949, Brian Gable drew for the Regina *Leader Post* before becoming a regular cartoonist for the *Globe* in 1987. This cartoon is unfair—no BC premier has advocated that the province leave Confederation—but it does suggest how other Canadians perceived British Columbia and its politicians.

attack on abortions, and the women who have them'.[24] Charges of conflict of interest dogged the premier, among them allegations that he tried to steer the sale of the Expo '86 site to a personal friend, multi-millionaire businessman Peter Toigo. It was another such charge that drove him from office. Having been accused of using his position to facilitate the sale of his Christian theme park, Fantasy Gardens, to a Taiwanese investor, Vander Zalm resigned as premier on 2 April 1991.

The fact that his successor, Rita Johnston, was the first woman to govern a province in Canada did not turn the tide. Six months later the voters emphatically dismissed Social Credit, which won only 24 per cent of the popular vote and returned only seven candidates. Even so, the NDP won its large majority (51 of the 75 seats in the expanded legislature) with only 40.7 per cent of the popular vote—less than it had received in the defeats of 1979, 1983, and 1986! Almost all the remaining votes—32 per cent—went to the resurgent BC Liberal party. Liberal leader Gordon Wilson had accomplished the impossible. In 1989, a veteran journalist had quipped that a Liberal revival remained 'on a par with sightings of the mythical Ogopogo monster of Lake Okanagan'.[25] Yet Wilson quietly rebuilt the party, and then attracted wide public attention to it during the televised leaders' debate. As Rita Johnson and NDP leader Mike Harcourt bickered, Wilson suggested to voters that bickering was all they would get if they elected either one of his opponents. Vancouver's CTV outlet, the most widely watched television station in the province, replayed the clip almost incessantly throughout the campaign; and the Liberals came from nowhere to win 17 seats and form the official opposition.

Like Bill Vander Zalm, Mike Harcourt had a short and troubled tenure as premier. One problem was the ongoing constitutional issue that culminated in the national referendum on the Charlottetown Accord. The seemingly endless federal–provincial negotiations that preoccupied politicians irritated the public and intensified debate about BC's place in the Canadian federation. Harcourt wanted to settle the constitutional issue, get on with addressing economic and social problems, and prove to the rest of the country that not all British Columbians were 'flakes'. He plunged into the post-Meech constitutional swamp with a made-in-BC agenda, including a distinct society clause for Quebec, Aboriginal self-government, a social contract, a 'Double-E plus L Senate' (elected and equitable but limited in powers), increased representation for British Columbia in the Commons, and more provincial powers over economic matters. British Columbia did get one concession when the other premiers and the federal government devised a plan to increase its

representation in Parliament. Unfortunately, some journalists misinterpreted the proposal as meaning that British Columbia would lose seats.[26] Despite the government's efforts to explain how parliamentary reform would give the province a stronger voice, many British Columbians were more inclined to believe the popular hot-line host (and former Social Credit cabinet minister) Rafe Mair, who claimed that Harcourt had simply given in to Quebec. Pat Carney, a senior federal cabinet minister from BC at the time of the referendum, agreed that Ottawa's apparent preference for Quebec was an important factor in the province; however, she also blamed hostility to undefined Aboriginal rights for the fact that in the national referendum of October 1992, 68 per cent of British Columbians—the highest proportion in the country—voted against the Charlottetown Accord, 'The Canadian Unity Agreement'. Ottawa took note. A Privy Council Office investigation concluded that although British Columbians did not have a 'collective cultural sense of separateness', they felt distinct because of their growing Asian population and Pacific Rim ties, their frustration at not getting what they considered a fair share of federal expenditures, their geographic isolation, and their growing self-confidence based on the province's economic growth. Despite murmurs of separatism in the province, by 1997 a public opinion poll found that British Columbians were 'firmly Canadian'. So too did studies and public forums organized by the provincially sponsored BC Unity Panel.[27] Nevertheless, in federal elections from 1993 to 2004, many British Columbians, especially those outside Vancouver, appeared to express a certain sense of 'regional alienation' by rejecting national trends and electing a majority of Reform, Alliance, or Conservative candidates.

Reform Party leader Preston Manning shakes hands with a butcher during a campaign visit to Vancouver's Chinatown, 1 May 1997, by Frank Gunn. British Columbia was second only to Manning's home province of Alberta in its support for Reform, giving the party 24 of 32 seats in the 1993 federal election, and 25 of 34 in 1997. In 2000 Manning's otherwise hapless successor Stockwell Day and the re-named 'Canadian Alliance' won 27 seats (including his own in Okanagan–Coquihalla) and a remarkable 49.4 per cent of the popular vote in British Columbia. CP Archives PLS Image 322701.

Even more divisive than constitutional issues was the place of Aboriginal people in British Columbia. The number of people who reported 'Native Indian' origins to the census enumerators increased from 52,430 in 1971 to 73,670 in 1981 and 169,040 in 1991. Instead of disappearing into Euro-Canadian society, as a century of 'Indian policy' had confidently assumed they

would, Native people were taking a new pride in their ancestry—which partly explains the dramatic increases in their population numbers. As Paul Tennant has pointed out, their 'greater familiarity with the larger society [had]. . . resulted not in assimilation, but rather in a redoubling of efforts to revive aboriginal culture and to pursue aboriginal claims.' The immediate stimulus to the political resurgence of Native people in the 1970s was a spectacular miscalculation by the Trudeau government in June 1969. In an infamous 'White Paper'—the actual title was 'A Statement of the Government of Canada on Indian Policy'—Minister of Indian Affairs Jean Chrétien had proposed to abolish the Indian Act, end the distinctive legal status of indigenous peoples, dissolve reserves, and assign reserve lands to individuals as their private property. In British Columbia, the White Paper was the spur that that drove formerly divided Native organizations to join forces as a united front. In November 1969, 140 bands sent representatives to a conference in Kamloops to create the Union of BC Indian Chiefs. Whereas previous umbrella organizations had concentrated their efforts on the federal level, this one targeted the provincial government as well. Its 1970 *Declaration of Indian Rights: The BC Position Paper* was followed in 1971 by the more portentous *Native Title to BC*.[28]

British Columbia had been at the centre of Aboriginal political and legal struggles ever since it joined Confederation. Only a handful of Native people around Victoria and in the northeast had ever surrendered their lands to Europeans by treaty. As it had since 1871, the provincial government insisted that Native bands without treaties—all but a handful of the First Nations in BC—had no legal claim to compensation for their land. The landmark legal decision that triggered a flood of land claims litigation came in 1973, when the Canadian Supreme Court, in a case brought by Nisga'a plaintiff Frank Calder (the former CCF-NDP and Social Credit MLA), ruled that Aboriginal people did hold title to their lands, because 'when the settlers came, the Indians were there, organized in societies and occupying the land as their forefathers had done

for centuries'. The next year the federal government agreed to negotiate with the Nisga'a, and in 1976 the BC government joined the negotiations, while insisting that it did not acknowledge the existence of Aboriginal title.[29]

British Columbia's Social Credit governments stood almost alone among provincial governments in their truculence on Aboriginal issues. The ministers who spoke for the Socred governments during the 1980s—in turn Allan Williams, Brian Smith, and Garde Gardom—argued sometimes that they had no legal obligation to negotiate, and sometimes that they could not negotiate because of the excessive financial demands made by the Native peoples. The province found itself a pariah in national discussions. In March 1987, at a first ministers' conference devoted to defining Aboriginal rights, Premier Bill Vander Zalm tried to justify his opposition to constitutional entrenchment of Aboriginal rights on the grounds that with 197 bands and 1,628 reserves, BC had one-third of all the bands in Canada and 72 per cent of the reserves: hence satisfying Native claims would place an unfair economic burden on the province. He did not mention that those statistics might have supported a different conclusion: that the reason BC had so many reserves was that, instead of negotiating comprehensive settlements by treaty, as had been done elsewhere in Canada, its governments had insisted on piecemeal arrangements with individual bands. Two months later, in May 1987, the case of Delgamuuk'w vs. British Columbia went to court in Smithers before BC Supreme Court Justice Allen McEachern. The plaintiff Delgamuuk'w, also known as Earl Muldoe, had initiated the case on behalf of the Gitxsan and Wet'suwet'en (formerly known as Carrier), whose 7,000 people claimed 57,000 square kilometres in the watersheds of the Bulkley and Skeena Rivers. The political theatre

George Manuel, president of the National Indian Brotherhood, shakes hands with Pierre Elliott Trudeau, Ottawa, 6 July 1972, by Peter Bregg. In the background are members of the Union of BC Indian Chiefs, who had just presented the prime minister with a claim for the loss of their territory to 'the White Man'. BC Native people found it much easier to get the ear of politicians in Ottawa than of their counterparts in Victoria. CP Archives PLS Image ID 1756661.

involved in the trial, which lasted for four years, brought the land claims issue to public attention as never before. The Crown sought to prove that the Gitxsan and Wet'suwet'en were no longer 'authentic Indians' because they worked for wages, drove cars, and ate 'white' food; Crown lawyers repeatedly questioned Native witnesses about how many times they had eaten pizza, Kentucky Fried Chicken, or Big Macs. These arguments were enough to persuade McEachern, who in March 1991 declared that Native peoples had had no political organization before Europeans arrived, ruling that 'aboriginal rights exist only at the pleasure of the Crown, and . . . may be extinguished

And on Thurs. Evening Oct. 10 Did you or did you not order a pizza in SMITHERS Mr. Alfred? Proving that you have abandoned your birthright!

'Pizza test', by Don Monet from Monet and Skanu'u, *Colonialism on Trial: Indigenous Land Rights and the Gitksan-Wet'suwet'en Sovereignty Case* (Philadelphia: New Society Publishers, 1992), 66. Geoff Plant, the Crown counsel satirized here, became Attorney General and Minister Responsible for Treaty Negotiations in the Liberal government of Gordon Campbell. Cartoonist D.H. Monet lived and worked in Hazelton, BC, for 13 years and now teaches at the University of Ottawa.

whenever the intention of the Crown to do so is plain and clear.' McEachern's misreading of history immediately drew the wrath not only of Native people themselves but of many anthropologists and historians.[30]

The NDP government of Mike Harcourt took an unprecedented step towards provincial action on land claims when it created the BC Treaty Commission in 1992, with two commissioners selected by the BC First Nations Summit, one by

each level of government, and a chief commissioner selected by all three parties. But even with a more sympathetic provincial government in office, movement towards resolution of Aboriginal land claims in BC continued to be painfully slow. Thus it is surprising to note how rarely these issues have given rise to violence. When the *Globe and Mail* drew up a list 'major confrontations' in 1990, only one of ten had taken place in BC (a 1985 road blockade in Haida Gwaii protesting forestry practices). A second 'major confrontation' took place west of 100 Mile House in the summer of 1995, when Secwepemc traditionalists at Gustafsen Lake occupied a ranch on land sacred to their people; after exchanging automatic weapons fire with RCMP they were disarmed without casualties. Thirteen of the protestors received prison terms ranging from six months to more than four years.[31]

Three events over the next years suggested progress in the glacial land claims process. Early in 1997, after five years of hearings, the federal Royal Commission on Aboriginal Peoples delivered its report, which recommended 'nation-to-nation' discussions with more than 50 Aboriginal 'First Nations' to negotiate forms of self-government. In December of the same year the Supreme Court of Canada overturned BC Chief Justice Allan McEachern's decision in the Delgamuuk'w case, affirming both Aboriginal title and the validity of the oral evidence used by the Aboriginal plaintiffs to prove it. 'BC Indian Chiefs Lay Claim to Entire Province, Resources,' claimed the headline in the *Vancouver Sun*, despite reassurances from First Nations that their only intention was 'to assume our rightful place and to fully participate in the economy and future of this province'. Finally, in 1999—three years after an agreement in principle had been reached—the NDP govern-

Lucille Martin, a member of the Neskonlith band, speaks to skier Ken Balter during a protest at Sun Peaks in Kamloops, 28 Dec. 2000, by Brendan Halper. With surprisingly few exceptions, Native protests in British Columbia have been non-violent. Note the text on the second sign: 'Environment not development.' CP Archives PLS Image 2064241.

ment approved the first modern-day treaty in BC, despite loud protests from the Liberal opposition and angry editorials in most of the province's newspapers. The Nisga'a Treaty provided the Nisga'a with some 2,000 square kilometres of land in northwestern BC and a limited form of self-government, as well as a cash settlement of almost a half-billion dollars.[32]

In the last three decades of the twentieth century BC's population growth outpaced Canada's by far: from barely two million in 1971 to more than four million in 2001 despite some out-migration, particularly to Alberta, between 1997 and 2002. More significant than total growth was the demographic transformation within that four million. Those of 'British' origin, who had made up the majority of the provincial population until the 1970s, accounted for barely a quarter by the late 1990s. No doubt part of the reason for the decline was the inclusion, after 1996, of 'Canadian' as an acceptable 'ethnic origin' in the census questionnaire in 1986. But the change could be perceived everywhere in the province. 'Suddenly—and I like this—the Brits are just another ethnic group,' wrote journalist Ian Haysom in 2003, three decades after his arrival from Britain. Even if Victoria was still 'hanging on for dear life to a kind of desperate colonial kitsch', he added, 'this too will pass.'[33] In 1981, for the first time in its history, British Columbia ceased to be a 'masculine' province, at least in terms of demographics: in that year, the number of males per 100 females, which had peaked at 179 in 1901 and remained at 105 in 1951, reached momentary balance. Since then the ratio has steadily favoured women. It was 98.3:100 in 2002, and by 2031 is expected to reach 94.9:100, (assuming that female 'Baby Boomers' will outlive their male counterparts).[34]

British Columbia has been an 'old' province since the 1940s, in the sense that the percentage of residents over age 65 has been higher than the national average. While it is true that seniors migrate to BC in disproportionate numbers, so do younger Canadians, moving the province closer to national averages. The gap between BC and the national average actually declined, after reaching a peak the 1960s, so that by the mid-1990s BC's 13 seniors per 100 residents barely exceeded the national average of 12. In some parts of the province, however—the Okanagan and parts of Vancouver Island—the concentration of seniors is closer to one in five. In the twenty-first century this pattern may become more typical of the province as a whole. The ratio of those under 18 and over 65 to those 18–64— the 'dependency ratio', in demographer's jar-

gon—has grown from .162 in 1971 to .204 in 2002.[35]

Nor is British Columbia any longer a 'White Man's Province'. The absolute numbers of Native people have increased rapidly from 74,000 in 1981 to almost 200,000 in 2001. More than 35 per cent are under 15 years of age, as compared to 19 per cent of the total provincial population. Between 1931 and 1951, the number of Asians counted in British Columbia by the census declined by almost half, from 50,954 to 25,644, as a result of the exclusion of Chinese immigrants during many of those years and the dispersal of the Japanese during and immediately after the war. The absolute numbers grew over the next two decades, to 76,695 in 1971, but Asians remained a small percentage of the total BC population, just 3.5 per cent in 1971—less than half the level (7.3 per cent of the total population) in 1931. In the next two decades, largely because of immigration, the province's Asian population grew rapidly, to 204,856 in 1981 and 370,835 in 1991. In the 1991 census, BC's 181,185 ethnic Chinese became the second-largest ethnic group in the province, at 5.6 per cent of the total, and they retained that position by a greater margin in 2001. These growing minorities are concentrated; more than nine in ten of the ethnic Chinese in British Columbia live in metropolitan Vancouver. In a series of articles in 2003 on 'Our Changing Face', the *Vancouver Sun* observed that the city had been 'completely transformed by the rise of visible minorities' and quoted a 36-year-old woman, born in India of Chinese ancestry, who migrated to Canada as a teenager: 'People from all these different cultures, they are becoming one. They're not saying, I'm this or that. They say, "I'm Canadian."'[36]

It is much easier to depict the dimensions of

this demographic transformation than to comprehend its broader implications. The notion that diverse groups that originated in Asia can be collectively described as 'Asians' is itself a North American construction. The young woman quoted above is only of many 'Chinese' who have come from neither China nor Hong Kong. Indeed, many Canadian-born 'Asians' speak English as their mother tongue. Of the 141,000 immigrants who arrived between 1991 and 1996, 21 per cent came from Hong Kong, 13 per cent from the People's Republic of China, 11 per cent from Taiwan, 10 per cent from India, 7 per cent from the Philippines, and 3 per cent from South Korea. Nevertheless, the 342,665 individuals of Chinese background living in the Lower Mainland in 2001 account for more than half of the visible minority population in the region. Their visibility is enhanced by the presence of Asian shopping malls in the suburbs, three Chinese-language daily newspapers, and Chinese-language radio and television. The durable stereotype of the Chinese community as cut off from the mainstream, isolated by white prejudice, has no validity in post-1970 Vancouver. In contrast to their pre-war counterparts, who were overwhelmingly male and limited to low-paying jobs, many of the high-profile Chinese immigrants of the 1980s and 1990s were wealthy investors from Hong Kong. More numerous, however, have been middle-class professionals with backgrounds in engineering, technology, and financial services.[37]

These changes in occupational patterns reflect broader structural changes in the provincial economy. Eighty per cent of BC workers—almost two million—now produce services, and only 399,000 produce goods. Workers who actually extract natural resources are a minority within this second group: only 26,000 in forestry, and

Sylvie Durand, a striking member of the Public Service Alliance of Canada, rollerblading in front of federal offices in Kelowna, 15 Aug. 2001, by Gary Nylander. The image of the typical trade unionist had changed significantly by the turn of the twenty-first century. CP Archives PLS Image 2597339.

10,000 in mining.[38] For the 30,000 who work in agriculture the focus has shifted over the past three decades. While dairy and cattle raising remain important, especially in the Fraser Valley and the Cariboo–Chilcotin region respectively, specialty crops such as greenhouse tomatoes and cucumbers, mushrooms, and ginseng now account for the largest portion of legal agricultural income (unofficially, 'BC bud'—marijuana—may have a larger dollar value). And while fruit growing remains important in the Okanagan, new vineyards have replaced many older orchards, producing wines that are now winning international awards. Though always subject to the hazards of weather and disease, agriculture seems more stable than the resource-extracting industries, which are vulnerable to changes in external markets. As a result of the continuing US tariff on Canadian softwood lumber, for example, BC counted 11,000 fewer forestry workers in 2002 than in 2000.

British Columbia's coal industry provides another illustration of the vulnerability of a resource economy dependent on export markets—and the near impossibility of devising provincial policies to address the problem. Coal mining revived from near extinction in the late 1960s in response to demand from Japanese steel mills. The recovery began in the southeast, where the local, provincial, and federal governments eagerly provided tax breaks, infrastructure, and other subsidies. Since 1970, the CPR has carried the coal to the specially built loading dock at Roberts Bank, south of Vancouver. In the Crow's Nest Pass, government money replaced the grimy mining towns of Michel and Natal with the shiny 'instant towns' of Sparwood and Elkford. The Balmer open-pit mine near Sparwood, owned by US-based Kaiser Resources, Mitsubishi Corporation, and Japanese steel firms earned an average profit of 16 per cent; in 1981 BCRIC bought Kaiser's share and renamed the operation Westar Mining. As in previous resource booms, projections of virtually limitless demand had nothing to do with economic reality. In 1981 Bill Bennett's Socred government announced a coal mining megaproject in the northeast. Provincial subsidies built the transportation infrastructure, including a branch line

*Facing above.* Gitxsan dancers perform in front of the Supreme Court of Canada building in Ottawa, while their leaders and lawyers present their BC land claims case to the Supreme Court, 16 June 1997, by Fred Chartrand. CP Archives PLS Image 354694.

*Facing below.* In the summer of 1970 an uncredited BC government photographer made a series of photos showing the new 'instant town' of Sparwood to its best advantage. Although it looked more attractive than Anyox did in 1923 (p. 109), as a single-industry town Sparwood was no less a hostage to international market forces. BCA, I-08038.

*Overleaf above.* Betty Krawczyk, a 72-year-old great-grandmother, camps out on the lawn of the BC legislature, demanding to meet with Premier Ujjal Dosanjh; photo by John McKay. A few days later Ms Krawczyk entered the Burnaby Correctional Centre for Women to serve four months of a one-year sentence for contempt of court in connection with a peaceful protest against the logging of old-growth forests. NDP premiers faced protesting environmentalists abroad as well as at home. In Europe Mike Harcourt had to answer accusations that rainforest logging made BC 'the Brazil of the North', and Dosanjh was greeted with Greenpeace pickets on the same issue while on a trade mission to Hong Kong. CP Archives PLS Image 1807771.

*Overleaf below.* Fishermen and their families protested in May 2000, when Prime Minister Jean Chrétien and Premier Ujjal Dosanjh unveiled a plaque designating Clayoquot Sound a UNESCO Biosphere Reserve; photo by Chuck Stoody. Unable to bridge the green–blue divide, the NDP government also faced *anti*-environmentalist protests. CP Archives PLS Image 1544626.

of the British Columbia Railway, and laid out the 'instant town' of Tumbler Ridge for the workers and their families; federal subsidies double-tracked the railway to Prince Rupert and built the new Ridley Island terminal to ship the coal to Japan. By the time the coal started moving to market, recession and excess capacity had reduced coal prices, and the Japanese buyers had renegotiated their long-term contracts at lower prices. 'It would have been cheaper,' observed a journalist, 'to have told the Japanese that if they did the digging themselves they could have the coal free.' In 1992 Westar declared bankruptcy. Small investors still around from the brighter days of BCRIC lost their money. Miners and their families lost their livelihood and left Elkford, Sparwood, and Tumbler Ridge, selling their homes at a loss—if they could sell them at all. The isolated communities that they left behind are still struggling to find new economic bases in tourism or the retirement industry.[39] The story has been repeated on Vancouver Island, where the early instant town of Gold River lost its pulp

mill in 1999; and in Kimberley, where COMINCO shut down the famed Sullivan Mine in 2001 and townspeople, recognizing the recreational potential of the region for skiers and golfers, created a Bavarian-style village to attract tourists.

The remarkable thing about the NDP government first elected in 1991 was that it was able to navigate the turbulent waters of modern BC politics to a second victory in 1996. Not only did it face extra-parliamentary opposition from business, and hostility from much of the provincial media, but it stood on a political base that was inherently unstable. Like social democratic leaders everywhere, Mike Harcourt had to deal with intra-party tensions between the moderate majority and the radicals who, as he put it in his autobiography, 'often got their ideological rocks off by deliberately stirring debate within the party'. Harcourt also had to deal with the NDP's 'green caucus', part of the significant BC representation within the environmental movement. He could not give in to the environmentalists' demands because, as journalist Barbara McClin-

---

*Facing.* Queen Elizabeth II with federal Minister of Natural Resources Herb Dhaliwal and Premier Gordon Campbell at a multicultural performance held at the University of British Columbia, 7 October 2002, photo by Richard Lam. Census findings that 'British' Columbia had become Canada's most ethnically diverse province were effectively confirmed by the formal photo ops during for Her Majesty's 2002 tour. CP Archives PLS Image 3788632.

*Overleaf above.* Premier Glen Clark with Vancouver Grizzlies GM Stu Jackson (left) and players Ivano Newbill and Pete Chilcutt at the launch of an environmental program in a Vancouver school, October 1997, photo by Chuck Stoody. The Grizzlies (1995–2001) lasted only a little longer than Premier Clark. CP Archives PLS Image ID 447932.

*Overleaf below.* Ujjal Dosanjh, then Attorney General of BC, at a rally in Vancouver with NDP MP Svend Robinson in February 2000, shortly before he won the leadership of the provincial New Democrats; *Maclean's* photo by Bayne Stanley. Dosanjh became BC's first 'visible minority' premier, but lost power and his own seat in the 2001 provincial election. Robinson held a Greater Vancouver seat for the federal NDP for 25 years, until a bizarre shoplifting incident forced his resignation in 2004. In the same year Dosanjh ran successfully for the federal Liberal party in Vancouver South, and was appointed Minister of Health in the federal cabinet. CP Archives PLS Image 1384225.

David Malmo-Levine of the BC Marijuana Party, after the Supreme Court of Canada ruled 6–3 that possession of marijuana remains a criminal offence, 23 Dec. 2003, photo by Richard Lam. The BC Marijuana Party won 51,206 votes (3.22 per cent of the total cast) in the 2001 provincial election. Whether it is grown outdoors or indoors (in hydroponic 'grow ops'), 'BC bud' is estimated to be the province's single largest agricultural crop. The Canadian Press did not comment on what sort of cigarette Malmo-Levine was smoking. CP Archives PLS Image 5298540.

tock quipped, the NDP had to 'love loggers and tree-huggers equally'. A telling example of the unbridgeable 'green' / 'blue collar' divide within the NDP's constituency came when the government cancelled the Kemano II hydroelectric pro-

ject because its dams threatened the salmon fishery. Environmentalists were happy but labour was divided; the angry crowd of six hundred at Kitimat that booed Harcourt when he explained the decision cared more about jobs than fish. For all the genuine accomplishments of its first term in office, the NDP government seemed to please no one. Faced with a large deficit left behind by the Vander Zalm Socreds, Finance Minister Glen Clark followed a fiscally responsible policy that succeeded in raising the province's bond rating, but his caution won little praise from voters tired of 'restraint'. A reworked labour code was not enough to counterbalance trade unions' outrage when the NDP legislated striking teachers back to work. The Commission on Resources and Environment (CORE) set up regional committees that brought together resource industries, Aboriginal people, and environmentalists to plan land use; but none of the participants seemed content with the results. Battered by the contradictory demands, and criticized for his handling of a party fund-raising scandal that journalists dubbed 'Bingogate', Mike Harcourt announced his resignation in November 1995, almost exactly four years after he was sworn in as premier.[40]

Delegates to the NDP convention of February 1996 chose Glen Clark to succeed Harcourt on the first ballot. Younger, tougher, and more partisan than Harcourt, Clark promised a government that would deliver social programs more effectively and stimulate the economy to create employment.[41] The irony of the May 1996 election was that for once the NDP, so long disadvantaged by the skewed distribution of legislative seats, benefited from it to win a second term and a narrow majority with 39 of 75 seats and less than 40 per cent of the popular vote. The opposition Liberals, now led by former Vancouver mayor Gordon Campbell, won a larger proportion of the popular vote (almost 42 per cent) but only 33 seats. As in 1972 and 1991, the presence on the ballot of a second 'free enterprise' party allowed the NDP to eke out a victory. Social Credit virtually disappeared, though five Socred MLAs who had survived the party's 1991 rout ran for the BC Reform Party, which won two seats and slightly more than 9 per cent of the vote.

Clark's fall from political grace was even more surprising than his victory. Before he could name a cabinet, scandal struck in the form of a conflict-of-interest problem involving prominent New Democrats and BC Hydro. Then—to the delight of cartoonists—there were Clark's own toys: three expensive and technologically challenged catamaran 'fast ferries' that never operated as they were supposed to and were mothballed shortly after they were launched. The fiscal prudence of the Harcourt years gave way to large deficits, created in part by the 'Asian flu'—an economic crisis among BC's trading partners on the Pacific Rim. And when Clark tried to intervene in a US–Canada salmon dispute, hoping to present himself as both a patriot and an environmental champion, the federal government simply ignored him and he wound up looking foolish; a cartoon cover on *Maclean's* showed him pathetically struggling with Uncle Sam over a wriggling salmon. The coup de grâce, though, came when he was charged with using his influence to obtain a casino licence for a friend; it was then that a *Globe and Mail* editorial suggested that he 'rechristen himself . . . Amor de Chaos'.[42] Clark resigned in August 1999. The Nisga'a Treaty, passed five months earlier, was undoubtedly his most significant achievement, but it had won the NDP few friends among non-Native British Columbians. Shamelessly exploiting prejudices against First

Cartoon by Graham Harrop, *Vancouver Sun*, 5 July 2000. Because processing can create more jobs than logging, the export of logs has long been controversial. Born in England in 1944, Graham Harrop moved to British Columbia as a teenager. He draws regularly for both the *Vancouver Sun* and the *Globe and Mail*. Simon Fraser University Library, Special Collections, Harrop Collection, MsC 25.HAR.6.20

Nations, Liberal opposition leader Gordon Campbell predicted 'certain defeat in the next election for every NDP member who voted for the treaty'.[43] When the time came, in May 2001, Campbell's prediction proved to be almost exactly correct—all but two NDP members went down to defeat, including Clark's successor as premier and party leader, Ujjal Dosanjh—although the reasons had less to do with the NDP's Aboriginal policy than with its bad management, as epitomized by the 'fast ferries'.

The Campbell Liberals swept to power with 75 of the 77 seats and the votes of almost six in every ten British Columbians. Like Bill Bennett's

Socreds before them, they had the 'free enterprise' vote all to themselves. The NDP lost a considerable part of what had once been its core vote to the environmentalist Green Party of BC. Yet despite winning 12 per cent of the popular vote, the Greens were unable to capture a seat.

Campbell made it clear that he would use his huge mandate to govern from the right while doing his best to turn back the clock on negotiations with Native peoples, natural resource extraction, and the environment. Unlike many of his predecessors, however, Campbell has said that he sees no value in trying 'to score cheap political points when going after Ottawa'.[44] His friendliness towards the federal government has nothing to do with party politics, for there is little connection between the provincial and federal Liberal parties. Rather, it reflects the fact that in 2001 British Columbia qualified as a 'have not' province and received additional federal subsidies. Will Campbell be able to dominate politics as McBride and the two Bennetts once did? As of 2004, it is impossible to tell, though it may be worth noting that Campbell had an easier ride from the media than his Socred and NDP predecessors did, even when he was arrested for drunk driving while on a vacation in Hawaii.

In September 2003 the Victoria *Times–Colonist* published an 11-part series about the BC interior by reporter Jody Paterson. The series' title was 'Heartland Road'—'heartland' being the Campbell Liberals' preferred name for a region that in fact remains a hinterland to world markets and the Lower Mainland alike. Each stop on Paterson's tour yielded depressing accounts of jobs losses and community erosion. 'We don't call this the Heartland,' she was told in Prince George; 'We call it the Hurtland.' Yet despite the discouraging stories, Patterson 'got the feeling that none of them will be giving up until they find what they are looking for'. More than four million British Columbians, together with countless others who dream of becoming British Columbians in the future, believe that, as the last headline on Paterson's series put it, 'Despite a ragged couple of years, BC is still the place to be'. No doubt they would agree with the 'town booster' from Nelson quoted in the final sentence of that article, who echoed BC boosters more than a century earlier: 'All you have to do is wake up in BC to realize how lucky you are.'[45]

# NOTES

## Intro: Land of Promises

1. Four others have been published to date: William R. Morrison, *True North: The Yukon and the Northwest Territories* (1998), John Herd Thompson, *Forging the Prairie West* (1998), Margaret Conrad and James K. Hiller, *Atlantic Canada: A Region in the Making* (2001), and Peter A. Baskerville, *Ontario: Image, Identity, and Power* (2002).

2. G.R. Cook, 'Canadian Centennial Celebrations', *International Journal* XIII (Autumn 1967), 663, as quoted in J.M.S. Careless, '"Limited Identities" in Canada', *Canadian Historical Review* [hereafter *CHR*] L, 1 (1969), 1–10.

3. Patricia Nelson Limerick, *The Legacy of Conquest: The Unbroken Past of the American West* (New York: Norton, 1987).

4. Benedict Anderson, *Imagined Communities: Reflections on the Origins and Spread of Nationalism* (London and New York: Verso, 1983 and 1991).

5. (Toronto: UTP, 1991 and 1996).

6. Joan M. Schwartz, 'The Past in Focus: Photography and British Columbia, 1858–1914', *BC Studies* 52 (Winter 1981–2), 14.

7. Between the time that Schwartz made her comment in 1981 and December 2003, 'Recent Publications Relating to Canada' in the *CHR* has listed 34 'illustrated' or 'pictorial' histories on BC topics. The best of these are cited in our notes or listed in the Suggestions for Further Reading. In addition to these illustrated histories, another 326 books on BC historical topics were described as 'illus' (i.e., illustrated).

8. In the interest of harmonious relations with other historians, we offer only our own earlier work as examples of shabby treatment of images by academic historians. Patricia Roy, *Vancouver: An Illustrated History* (Toronto: James Lorimer, 1980), and John Herd Thompson with Allen Seager, *Canada 1922–1939: Decades of Discord* (Toronto: McClelland and Stewart, 1985), identify images only by the name of the repository.

9. Two female BC photographers have been the subjects of books, however: Claire Weissman Wilks, *The Magic Box: the Eccentric Genius of Hannah Maynard* (Toronto: Exile Editions, 1980), and Henri Robideau, *Flapjacks & Photographs: The History of the Famous Camp Cook and Photographer Mattie Gunterman* (Vancouver: Polestar Publishers, 1995).

10. This is not to argue that no photographer took pride in the artistic presentation of his or her work—simply that commercial reality more often constrained photographic art.

11. The work of Lilly Koltun is particularly useful to explain this in a Canadian context. See 'Pre-Confederation Photography in Toronto', *History of Photography* 2, 3 (July 1978), 249–63, and

'Not the World of William Notman', *Journal of Canadian Studies* 30, 1 (1995), 125–33.

12. Bryan D. Palmer, review of Elaine Bernard et al., *Working Lives: Vancouver, 1886–1986*, in *BC Studies* 73 (1987), 52–67.

13. This is especially true, for obvious reasons, of war photographs; see Jim Burant, 'The Military Archivist and the Documentary Record', *Archivaria* 26 (1988), 33–51.

14. Jerry Thompson, *Truth and Photography* (Chicago: Ivan R. Dee, 2003), 3–49.

15. T.D. Pattullo to R.B. Bennett, 18 December 1933, BCA, T.D. Pattullo Papers, vol. 69 quoted in Robin Fisher, *Duff Pattullo of British Columbia* (Toronto: UTP, 1991), 256.

16. Michael P. Robinson, *Sea Otter Chiefs* (Calgary: Boyeaux Arts, 1996); Pattullo quoted in Margaret Ormsby, *BC: A History* (Toronto: Macmillan, 1958), 458.

17. W.A. Baillie-Grohman, *Fifteen Years' Sport and Life in the Hunting-grounds of western America and British Columbia* (London: Horace Cox, 1900), 320. The notion is not unique to BC. David E. Smith makes this argument for the West as a whole in 'Western Politics and National Unity', in David Jay Bercuson, ed., *Canada and the Burden of Unity* (Toronto: Macmillan, 1977), 143.

18. Pettipiece quoted in Ross A. Johnson, 'No compromise—no political trading: the Marxian socialist tradition in British Columbia', University of British Columbia, Ph.D. dissertation (1975), 193.

**1: Contesting Empires: Prehistory to 1858**

1. Liz Bryan, *British Columbia: This Favoured Land* (Vancouver/Toronto: D&M, 1982), 27; Geoffrey Molyneux, *British Columbia: An Illustrated History* (Vancouver: Raincoast Books, 1992/2002), 1; Margaret Ormsby, *British Columbia: A History* (Toronto: Macmillan, 1958), ch. 1 and 2; Jean Barman, *The West Beyond the West: A History of British Columbia* (Toronto: UTP, 1991), 3–12.

2. Robert Galois, 'Two Views of Land in British Columbia', inset in 'Territorial Evolution', Plate 10 of *The Concise Historical Atlas of Canada* (Toronto: UTP, 1998).

3. Rosemary Neering, *A Traveler's Guide to Historic British Columbia* (North Vancouver: Whitecap, 1992/2002), 289.

4. Fraser from W. Kaye Lamb, ed., *The Letters and Journals of Simon Fraser 1808–1808* (Toronto: Macmillan, 1960), 96. See also Bruce Hutchison's 1950 volume in the *Rivers of America* series (New York/Toronto: Rinehart) and Richard Bocking's *Mighty River: A Portrait of the Fraser* (Vancouver: D&M, and Seattle: University of Washington Press, 1997).

5. A useful introduction and overview is Robert J. Muckle, *The First Nations of British Columbia* (Vancouver: UBCP, 1998).

6. George Woodcock, *Peoples of the Coast: The Indians of the Pacific Northwest* (Bloomington and London: Indiana University Press, 1977), ch. 1; R.L. Carlson, 'The First British Columbians', in Hugh J.M. Johnston, ed., *The Pacific Province: A History of British Columbia* (Vancouver/Toronto: D&M, 1996), 32–3; Cole Harris, *The Resettlement of British Columbia: Essays on Colonization and Geographical Change* (Vancouver: UBCP, 1997), 27–30.

7. This paragraph is based on articles collected in part two, 'Social Organization', in Tom McFeat, ed., *Indians of the North Pacific Coast*, (Toronto: M&S, 1966), 29–71.

8. Helen Codere, *Fighting With Property: A Study of Kwakiutl Potlatching and Warfare, 1792–1930* (New York, J.J. Augustin, 1950); Jay Miller, 'Feasting with the Southern Tsimshian', in Margaret Seguin, ed., *The Tsimshian: Images of the Past, Views for the Present* (Vancouver: UBCP, 1984), 28; H.G. Barnett, 'The Nature of the Potlatch', in McFeat, *Indians of the North Pacific Coast*, 80–91.

9. Robin Fisher, 'The Northwest From the Beginning of Trade With the Europeans to the 1880s', 119 in vol. 1, pt.2 of Bruce G. Trigger and Wilcomb E. Washburn, *The Cambridge History of the Native Peoples of the Americas*

(Cambridge and New York, Cambridge University Press, 1996), 121; Hugh Brody, *Maps and Dreams* (New York: Pantheon Books, 1981) provides extensive discussion of the hunting peoples of northeastern BC.

10. Robin Fisher makes this argument vigorously throughout his work. For a succinct statement see his 'Contact and Trade' chapter in Johnston, ed., *Pacific Province*, 49.

11. Barry Gough, 'The Backside of America', ch. 1 of *The Northwest Coast: British Navigation, Trade, and Discoveries to 1812* (Vancouver: UBCP, 1992); Alan Taylor provides a splendid survey of the 18th-century rivalry for the northwest coast in 'The Pacific, 1760–1820', the final chapter of *American Colonies: The Settling of North America* (New York: Penguin, 2001).

12. Glynn Barratt, *Russia in Pacific Waters, 1715–1825: A Survey of the Origins of Russia's Naval Presence in the North and South Pacific* (Vancouver: UBCP, 1981), 16–112.

13. The Nuu-chah-nulth accounts are from the American trader Joseph Ingraham in 1789 and the Spanish botanist José Mariano Moziño in 1792, both cited in Daniel W. Clayton, *Islands of Truth: The Imperial Fashioning of Vancouver Island* (Vancouver: UBCP, 2000), 22. The 'fateful omission' comment is from Warren L. Cook, *Flood Tide of Empire: Spain and the Pacific Northwest, 1543 to 1819* (New Haven: Yale University Press, 1973), 67; Christon I. Archer discusses these Spanish voyages in 'The Transient Presence: A Re-appraisal of Spanish Attitudes Toward the Northwest Coast in the Eighteenth Century', *BC Studies* 18 (Summer 1973), 3–32.

14. Spanish comment quoted in Gough, *The Northwest Coast*, 121. The tribal council officially adopted the name Nuu-chah-nulth in 1978. Alan D. McMillan, *Since the Time of the Transformers: The Ancient Heritage of the Nuu-chah-nulth, Ditidaht, and Makah* (Vancouver: UBCP, 1999), 6. An excellent recent 'Cook book', Nicholas Thomas's *The Extraordinary Voyages of Captain James Cook* (New York: Walker and Co., 2003) devotes only eight of

more than 400 pages to the 1778 sojourn at Nootka. See Daniel Clayton's discussion in *Islands of Truth*, 3–5, 50–66. The quotations from Cook's journals and this account are drawn from in Robin Fisher, 'Cook and the Nootka', in Fisher and Johnston, eds, *Cook and His Times*, 81–98.

15. For a thorough and colourful account, see Barry Gough, *Distant Dominion: Britain and the Northwest Coast of North America, 1579–1809* (Vancouver: UBCP, 1980) 100–15; Christon I. Archer, 'Transient Presence', 11–19, and 'The Spanish Reaction to Cook's Third Voyage', in Fisher and Johnston, eds, *Cook and His Times*, 99–119; Archer, 'Seduction Before Sovereignty: Spanish Efforts to Manipulate the Natives in Their Claims to the Northwest Coast', in Robin Fisher and Hugh Johnston, eds, *From Maps to Metaphors: the Pacific World of George Vancouver* (Vancouver: UBCP, 1993), 127–59; Taylor, *American Colonies*, 476–7.

16. There is an excellent concise summary of Vancouver's work and of the historical literature in the editors' 'Introduction' to Fisher and Johnston, eds, *From Maps to Metaphors*, 6–18.

17. Barry Gough, *First Across the Continent: Sir Alexander Mackenzie* (Norman, OK, and London: University of Oklahoma Press, 1997), 105–62.

18. Trader quoted in James R. Gibson, *The Lifeline of the Oregon Country: The Fraser Columbia Brigade System, 1811–47* (Vancouver: UBCP, 1997), 1. Richard Somerset Mackie, *Trading Beyond the Mountains: The British Fur Trade on the Pacific 1793–1843* (Vancouver: UBCP, 1996), 3–30.

19. Sylvia Van Kirk, *'Many Tender Ties': Women in Fur-Trade Society, 1670–1870* (Winnipeg: Watson and Dwyer, 1980); Robin Fisher, *Contact and Conflict: Indian–European Relations in British Columbia, 1774–1890* (Vancouver: UBCP, 1977), ch. 1 and 2, direct quotations from 47–8. See also Fisher's 'Preface' to the second edition, published in 1992.

20. Briton C. Busch and Barry M. Gough, eds, *Fur*

*Traders from New England: The Boston Men in the North Pacific, 1787–1800* (Spokane: Arthur H. Clark, 1997), 22–3.

21.  Cole Harris, *Resettlement of British Columbia*, ch. 2, 'Strategies of Power in the Cordilleran Fur Trade'. The best summary of these arguments is Harris's essay 'Social Power and Cultural Change in Pre-colonial British Columbia', *BC Studies* 115 and 116 (Autumn–Winter 1997–8), 45–82; Clayton, *Islands of Truth*; Mary Molloy, *Boston Men on the Northwest Coast: The American Maritime Fur Trade, 1788–1844* (Kingston: Limestone Press, 1998); James Gibson, *Otter Skins, Boston Ships, and China Goods: The Maritime Fur Trade of the Northwest Coast, 1785–1841* (Montreal and Kingston: MQUP, 1992). 'Culture of terror' is Harris's phrase, from 'Social Power and Cultural Change', 65; George MacDonald, 'The Epic of Nekt' in Margaret Seguin, *The Tsimshian: Images of the Past, Views for the Present*, (Vancouver: UBCP, 1984), 78–81.

22.  Alfred W. Crosby introduced this concept in 'Virgin Soil Epidemics as a Factor in the Aboriginal Depopulation in America', *William and Mary Quarterly*, 3 ser. 33 (April 1976), 289–99; all cited in Elizabeth Fenn, *Pox Americana: The Great Smallpox Epidemic of 1775–1782* (New York: Hill and Wang, 2001), 230–31; Harris, 'Voices of Smallpox around the Straight of Georgia', in his *Resettlement of British Columbia*, 3–30; Robert Boyd, *The Coming of the Spirit of Pestilence: Introduced Infectious Diseases and Population Decline among Northwest Coast Indians, 1774–1874* (Seattle: University of Washington Press, 1999), ch.2 and 7, direct quotation from 278.

23.  Simpson to the [London] Governor and Committee of the HBC, March 1825, quoted in Mackie, *Trading Beyond the Mountains*, 50; Simpson to the [London] Governor and Committee of the HBC, 1 March 1829, quoted in Mackie, *Trading Beyond the Mountains*, 58; quoted in ibid., 223. Details on the early days of Fort Langley may be found in Morag

Maclachlan, *The Fort Langley Journals, 1827–30* (Vancouver: UBCP, 1998).

24.  Quoted in Mackie, *Trading Beyond the Mountains*, 123.

25.  Simpson quoted in Daniel Francis, *Battle for the West: Fur Traders and the Birth of Western Canada* (Edmonton: Hurtig, 1982), 145–7.

26.  'Babies' from Hall Kelley, *A Geographical Sketch of that Part of North America Called Oregon* (1830); Frederick Merk, *Manifest Destiny and Mission in American History: A Reinterpretation* (New York, 1963) 28–32.

27.  John S. Galbraith, *The Hudson's Bay Company as an Imperial Factor 1821–1869* (Berkeley, 1957), ch. 14; James Hendrickson, 'Constitutional Development of Colonial Vancouver Island and British Columbia', in Peter Ward and Robert A.J. McDonald, eds, *British Columbia: Historical Readings* (Vancouver: D&M, 1981), 245–52.

28.  Ormsby, *British Columbia*, ch. 4 and 5, Douglas cited at 122.

## 2: A New Colony, A New Province: 1858–1885

1.   Barry Gough, *Gunboat Frontier: British Maritime Authority and the Northwest Coast Indians, 1846–90* (Vancouver: UBCP, 1984), 101–17; Robin Fisher, *Contact and Conflict: Indian-European Relations in British Columbia, 1774–1890* (Vancouver: UBCP, 1977), 69–72.

2.   Susan Lee Johnson, *Roaring Camp: The Social World of the California Gold Rush* (New York: Norton, 2000), chapter 5; Alfred Waddington, *The Fraser Mines Vindicated, or the History of Four Months* (Victoria: P. de Garro, 1858), 17; visitor quoted in Stella Higgins, 'British Columbia in the Confederation Era', in W. George Shelton, ed., *British Columbia and Confederation* (Victoria: University of Victoria, 1967), 17.

3.   *The Globe*, 'The Gold Discoveries', 24 May 1858, and 'News from the British Goldfields', 17 July 1858; Edgar Wickberg, ed., *From China to Canada, A History of the Chinese Communities in Canada* (Toronto: M&S, 1982), 17; Patricia E. Roy, *A White Man's Province: British Columbia*

*Politicians and Chinese and Japanese Immigration, 1858–1914* (Vancouver: UBCP, 1989), ch. 1; Canadian visitor G.M. Grant quoted in H.A. Innis and A.R.M. Lower, *Select Documents in Canadian Economic History 1783–1885* (Toronto: UTP, 1933), 776.

4. Adele Perry, *On the Edge of Empire: Gender, Race, and the Making of British Columbia, 1849–1871* (Toronto: UTP, 2001), 44. The best study of Begbie is David Ricardo Williams, '. . . *The Man for a New Country': Sir Matthew Baillie Begbie* (Sidney, BC: Gray's, 1977). See, for an example, Desmond Morton, 'Cavalry or Police: Keeping the Peace of Two Adjacent Frontiers, 1870–1900, *Journal of Canadian Studies* 12, 2 (1977), 27; Roger McGrath, *Gunfighters, Highwaymen and Vigilantes: Violence on the Frontier* (Berkeley: University of California Press, 1985) argues that the US gold rush West was less 'wild' than once believed.

5. Letter to the San Francisco *Bulletin*, 31 May 1858, cited in Daniel P. Marshall, 'No Border: American Miner-Soldiers at War with the Nlaka'pamux of the Canadian West', in Kenneth Coates and John M. Findlay, eds, *Parallel Destinies: Canadian–American Relations West of the Rockies* (Seattle: University of Washington Press, 2002), 41 and 63; Tom G. Todd to Charlie M. Dewey, 18 Aug. 1858, cited in Marshall, 'No Border', 47.

6. Douglas to Colonial Secretary Labouchere, 29 Dec. 1857, cited in Tina Loo, *Making Law, Order and Authority in British Columbia, 1821–1871* (Toronto: UTP, 1994), 57–8; song quoted in Margaret Ormsby, *British Columbia: A History* (Toronto: MacMillan, 1958), 142; Viscount W.F. Milton and Dr. W.B. Cheadle, *The North West Passage By Land* (London: Cassell, Peter and Galpin, 1865), 352; Barry Gough, *The Royal Navy and the Northwest Coast of North America, 1810–1914* (Vancouver: UBCP, 1971), 134–41.

7. W.N. Sage, *Sir James Douglas and BC* (Toronto: UTP, 1930). A more recent biography that concentrates on Douglas's private life is John Adams, *Old Square-Toes and His Lady: The Life of James and Amelia Douglas* (Victoria: Horsdal and Schubart, 2001). Victoria to Sir Edward Bulwer Lytton, cited in G.P.V. and Helen B. Akrigg, *British Columbia Chronicle, 1847–1871* (Vancouver: Discovery Press, 1977), 137.

8. Robert A.J. McDonald and H. Keith Ralston, 'Amor De Cosmos', *Dictionary of Canadian Biography* XII (Toronto: UTP, 1990), 238.

9. Innis and Lower, *Documents in Canadian Economic History*, 804; J.I. Little, 'The Foundations of Government', in Hugh J.M. Johnston, ed., *The Pacific Province: A History of British Columbia* (Vancouver: D&M, 1996), 75–7.

10. Loo, 'Bute Inlet Stories: Crime, Law, and Colonial Identity', ch. 7 of *Making Law, Order, and Authority*. The direct quotations are from *The British Columbian* [New Westminster], 14 May 1864, 151.

11. Perry (*Edge of Empire*, 110–23) argues that the epidemic launched a campaign to segregate Europeans and Native people in the colony. Lt. H.S. Palmer prospector Joseph Harrison quoted in Akrigg and Akrigg, *Chronicle, 1847–1871*, 255–6. Robin Fisher argues for a much lower death rate in *Contact and Conflict*, 115–16, and repeats this argument in his chapter 'The Northwest From the Beginning of Trade With Europeans to the 1880s', in Bruce G. Trigger and Wilcomb E. Washburn, eds, *The Cambridge History of the Native Peoples of the Americas* (Cambridge and New York: Cambridge University Press, 1996), 142–45. Sproat's trip is described in Cole Harris, *The Resettlement of British Columbia: Essays on Colonialism and Geographic Change* (Vancouver: UBCP, 1997), 118–20.

12. Cole Harris, *Making Native Space: Colonialism, Resistance, and Reserves in British Columbia* (Vancouver: UBCP, 2002), xviii, 56–69. A number of historians make this argument, most notably Fisher in *Contact and Conflict* and Robert E. Cail, *Land, Man, and the Law: The Disposal of Crown Lands in British Columbia, 1871–1913* (Vancouver: UBCP, 1974), ch. 1. In

her foreword to Cail's book, Margaret Ormsby criticizes 'this myopic vision of early legislators', which 'tragically . . . strained the harmonious relations with the native peoples, a relationship which Douglas had fostered'. A handsomely illustrated history of the Songhees Reserve is Grant Keddie, *Songhees Pictorial: A History of the Songhees People as seen by Outsiders, 1790–1912* (Victoria: Royal BC Museum, 2003).

13. Hind letter home, 31 Jan. 1864, cited in Mary Jo Hughes, *Hindsight: William Hind in the Canadian West* (Winnipeg: Winnipeg Art Gallery, 2002), 131.

14. Douglas to Colonial Secretary Lytton, 18 Oct. 1859, cited in Loo, *Making Law, Order, and Authority*, 75; Paul Phillips, 'Confederation and the Economy of British Columbia', in George Shelton, ed., *British Columbia and Confederation* (Victoria: Morriss Printing Co., 1967), 43–65.

15. Seymour to the Duke of Buckingham, 13 July 1867, BCA, British Columbia Governors Seymour and Musgrave, Despatches, 1869–1871, quoted in Ormsby, *British Columbia*, 222.

16. California resolution in Donald Warner, *The Idea of Continental Union: Agitation for the Annexation of Canada to the United States, 1849–1893* (Lexington: University of Kentucky Press, 1960), 135; David Shi, 'Seward's Attempt to Annex British Columbia, 1865–1869', *Pacific Historical Review* 47, 2 (1978), 217–38; Charles John Fedorak, 'The United States Consul in Victoria and the Political Destiny of the Colony of British Columbia, 1862–1870', *BC Studies* 79 (1988), 8–15.

17. 'The Gold Discoveries', *The Globe* [Toronto], 29 May 1858; Henry Youle Hind, *A Sketch of an Overland Route to British Columbia* (Toronto: W.C. Chewett and Co., 1862), 126, emphasis in original.

18. Poem in the *British Colonist*, cited in Walter N. Sage, 'British Columbia Becomes Canadian, 1871–1901', *Queen's Quarterly* LII, 2 (1945), 170; quoted in Gordon Elliott, 'Henry P. Pellew Crease: Confederation or No Confederation', *BC*

*Studies* 12 (Winter 1971–2), 69–70.

19. H. Robert Kendrick, 'Amor De Cosmos and Confederation', in Shelton, *British Columbia and Confederation*, 82–4; Olive Fairholm, 'John Robson and Confederation', in Shelton, *British Columbia and Confederation*, 108–14.

20. Dorothy Blakey Smith, ed., *The Reminiscences of Doctor John Sebastian Helmcken* (Vancouver: UBCP, 1975), 247; Susan Dickinson Scott, 'The Attitude of Colonial Governors and Officials towards Confederation', in Shelton, *British Columbia and Confederation*, 144–8; Margaret A. Ormsby, 'Frederick Seymour', *Dictionary of Canadian Biography* IX (Toronto: UTP, 1976), 716.

21. Kent Haworth and Charles Maier, '"Not a Matter of Regret": Granville's Response to Seymour's Death', *BC Studies* 27 (Autumn 1975), 66.

22. Jean Barman, *The West Beyond the West: A History of British Columbia* (Toronto: UTP, 1996), 379; Smith, *Reminiscences of Doctor John Sebastian Helmcken*, 343–6, 349, 351. The terms of union may be found in James E. Hendrickson, ed., *Journals of the Colonial Legislatures of the Colonies of Vancouver Island and British Columbia, 1851–1871* (Victoria: Provincial Archives of British Columbia, 1980), V, 390—3. Willard Ireland, 'British Columbia's American Heritage', Canadian Historical Association, *Annual Report*, 1948, reprinted in J. Friesen and H.K. Ralston, *Historical Essays on British Columbia* (Toronto: M&S, 1975), 119.

23. As for example in 1967, Canada's centennial year in Robert Collins, 'Consolidation: One Country Sea to Sea', *Imperial Oil Review* (July 1967), 95.

24. Elections British Columbia, *Electoral History of British Columbia, 1871–1986* (Victoria: Elections BC and the Legislative Library, 1988), 9; Hamar Foster, 'George Anthony Walkem', *Dictionary of Canadian Biography* XIII (Toronto: UTP, 1994), 1063.

25. F. Henry Johnson, *A History of Public Education in British Columbia* (Vancouver: Publications Centre, UBC, 1964), ch. 3.

26. This paragraph draws on Daniel P. Marshall, 'An Early Rural Revolt: the Introduction of the Canadian System of Tariffs to British Columbia, 1971–4', in R.W. Sandwell, ed., *Beyond the City Limits: Rural History in British Columbia* (Vancouver: UBCP, 1999), 47–61.

27. F.W. Howay, *British Columbia: From the Earliest Times to the Present* (Vancouver: S.J. Clarke, 1914), II, 354.

28. Canadian Pacific Railway, Sandford Fleming, Engineer in Chief, *Report on Progress of the Explorations and Surveys up to January 1874* (Ottawa: MacLean, Roger and Co., 1874), 23.

29. Howay, *British Columbia*, II, 392.

30. This paragraph draws largely on Foster, 'Walkem', 1063–5.

31. Ormsby, *British Columbia*, ch. 11.

32. A vivid and detailed description of the strike may be found in Lynne Bowen, *Three Dollar Dreams* (Lantzville, BC: Oolichan, 1987), 152–75; John Douglas Belshaw, *Colonization and Community: The Vancouver Island Coalfield and the Making of the British Columbia Working Class* (Montreal and Kingston: MQUP, 2002), 204.

33. Bowen, *Three Dollar Dreams*, 320.

34. Gordon Hak, *Turning Trees Into Dollars: The British Columbia Coastal Lumber Industry, 1858–1913* (Toronto: UTP, 2000), passim.

35. Dianne Newell, ed., *The Development of the Pacific Salmon-Canning Industry* (Montreal and Kingston: MQUP, 1989), 4; Keith Ralston, 'John Sullivan Deas: A Black Entrepreneur in British Columbia Salmon Canning', *BC Studies* 32 (Winter 1976–7), 64–79; David J. Reid, 'Company Mergers in the Fraser River Salmon Canning Industry, 1885–1902', *CHR*, LVI: 3 (September 1975), 282–3.

36. G.W.S. Brooks, 'An Entrepreneur in Early British Columbia', *BC Studies* 31 (Autumn 1976), 23–43.

37. Robin Fisher, 'Joseph Trutch and Indian Land Policy', *BC Studies* 12 (Winter 1971–2), 3–33. The careful work of historians like Sarah Carter and John Tobias makes clear that the record of federal Indian administration in the Prairie West

is a dismal catalogue of ineptitude, blunder, and mismanagement. See Sarah Carter, *Lost Harvests: Prairie Indian Reserve Farmers and Government Policy* (Montreal and Kingston: MQUP, 1990); John L. Tobias, 'Canada's Subjugation of the Plains Cree, 1879–1885', *CHR* LXIV, 4 (1983), 519–48.

38. Harris, *Making Native Space*, 98–166; Fisher, *Contact and Conflict*, 185–99.

39. Fisher, *Contact and Conflict*, 199–206; Harris, *Making Native Space*, 169–215 and *The Resettlement of British Columbia*, 92–102; Douglas C. Harris, *Fish, Law, and Colonialism: The Legal Capture of Salmon in British Columbia* (Toronto: UTP, 2001), 33–78; Rolf Knight, *Indians at Work: An Informal History of Native Indian Labour in British Columbia, 1858–1930* (Vancouver: New Star Books, 1978, 1996); John Lutz, 'Work, Sex, and Death on the Great Thoroughfare: Annual Migrations of 'Canadian Indians' to the American Pacific Northwest', in Coates and Findlay, *Parallel Destinies*, 80–1.

40. Sproat to Macdonald, 27 Oct. 1879, cited in Douglas Cole and Ira Chaikin, *An Iron Hand Upon the People: The Law Against the Potlatch on the Northwest Coast* (Vancouver: D & M, 1990), 15; Jay Miller, 'Feasting with the Southern Tsimshian', in Margaret Seguin, ed., *The Tsimshian: Images of the Past, Views for the Present* (Vancouver: UBCP, 1984), 28–30; Helen Codere, 'Daniel Cranmer's Potlatch', in Tom McFeat, ed., *Indians of the North Pacific Coast* (Toronto: M&S, 1966), 116–17; Tina Loo, 'Dan Cranmer's Potlatch: Law as Coercion, Symbol and Rhetoric', *CHR* LXXIII (June 1992), 125–65; Cole and Chaikin, *An Iron Hand Upon the People*, 2.

41. *Inland Sentinel*, 27 Nov. 1884; Patricia E. Roy, 'A Choice Between Evils: The Chinese and the Construction of the Canadian Pacific Railway in British Columbia', in Hugh A. Dempsey, ed., *The CPR West: The Iron Road and the Making of a Nation* (Vancouver: D&M, 1984), 13–34, quotation from 17; T.D. Regehr, 'Letters from End of Track', in ibid, 47–51.

### 3: Promise and Disappointment: 1885–1914

1. *Illustrated British Columbia* (Victoria: J.B. Ferguson, 1884); *Canada Year Book, 1913* (Ottawa: King's Printer, 1914), 79; W.A. Baillie-Grohman, *Fifteen Years Sport and Life in the Hunting-grounds of Western America and British Columbia* (London: Horace Cox, 1900), 320.

2. R. Byron Johnson, *Very Far West Indeed: A Few Rough Experiences on the North-west Pacific Coast* (London: Sampson Low, 1872). This book was reprinted in several editions.

3. F.W. Howay, *British Columbia: From the Earliest Times to the Present* (Vancouver: S.J. Clarke, 1914), vol. II, 491–2.

4. Gordon Hak, *Turning Trees into Dollars: The British Columbia Coastal Lumber Industry, 1858–1913* (Toronto: UTP, 2000), 28.

5. Stephen Gray, 'The Government Timber Policy: Forest Policy and Administration in British Columbia, 1912–1928', *BC Studies* 81 (Spring 1989), 26; Hak, *Turning Trees into Dollars*, 43–4; J. Castell Hopkins, *Canadian Annual Review, 1909* (Toronto: Annual Review Publishing, 1910), 570; Donald MacKay, *Empire of Wood: The MacMillan Bloedel Story* (Vancouver: D&M, 1982), 18.

6. Richard Rajala, *Clearcutting the Pacific Rain Forest: Production, Science and Regulation* (Vancouver: UBCP, 1998), 89; Hak, *Turning Trees into Dollars*, 114.

7. The complex legal stories are set out in W.F. Bowker, 'The Sproule Case: Bloodshed at Kootenay Lake, 1885', in Louis Knafla, ed., *Law and Justice in a New Land: Essays in Western Canadian Legal History* (Toronto: Carswell, 1986), 233–66.

8. G.M. Dawson, Summary Reports of the Operations of the Geological Survey, 65A, quoted in Jeremy Mouat, *Roaring Days: Rossland's Mines and the History of British Columbia* (Vancouver: UBCP, 1995), 14.

9. Jeremy Mouat, *The Business of Power: Hydro-electricity in Southeastern British Columbia, 1897–1997* (Victoria: Sono Nis, 1997); Mouat, *Roaring Days*, ch. 7.

10. Mouat, *Roaring Days,* 95 and passim. A lively history of Nelson until its incorporation in 1897 is John Norris, *Historic Nelson: The Early Years* (Lantzville, BC: Oolichan, 1999).

11. John A. Eagle, *The Canadian Pacific Railway and the Development of Western Canada* (Montreal and Kingston: MQUP, 1989), 108; Barrie Sanford, *McCulloch's Wonder: The Story of the Kettle Valley Railway* (Vancouver: Whitecap, 1978), 67.

12. Howay, *British Columbia*, II, 500–1.

13. On Vancouver entrepreneurs, see Robert A. J. McDonald, *Making Vancouver, Class, Status and Social Boundaries, 1863–1913* (Vancouver: UBCP, 1996), passim; H. Keith Ralston, 'The 1900 Strike of Fraser River Sockeye Salmon Fishermen' (University of British Columbia, M.A. thesis, 1965), 25 quoted in Patricia Marchak, Neil Guppy and John McMullan, eds, *Uncommon Property; The Fishing and Fish-Processing Industries in British Columbia* (Toronto: Methuen, 1987), 49; Geoff Meggs, *Salmon: The Decline of the British Columbia* Fishery (Vancouver: D&M, 1991), 81.

14. Duncan A. Stacey, *Sockeye & Tinplate: Technological Change in the Fraser River Canning Industry, 1871–1912* (Victoria: Provincial Museum, 1982), 21.

15. This account is based on Stuart Jamieson, *Times of Trouble: Labour Unrest and Industrial Conflict in Canada, 1900–1966* (Ottawa: Information Canada, 1971), 138–40 and Paul A. Phillips, *No Power Greater: A Century of Labour in BC* (Vancouver: BC Federation of Labour, 1967), 34–7. Both draw on Ralston, 'The 1900 Strike'; Dianne Newell, *The Development of the Pacific Salmon-Canning Industry: A Grown Man's Game* (Montreal and Kingston: MQUP, 1989), 23–5.

16. Dianne Newell, 'Dispersal and Concentration: The Slowly Changing Spatial Pattern of the British Columbia Salmon Canning Industry', *Journal of Historical Geography*, 14 (1988), 22–36; Joseph E. Taylor III, 'Burning the Candle at Both Ends: Historicizing Overfishing in Oregon's 19th-Century Salmon Fisheries',

*Environmental History* 4, 1 (January 1999); Matthew Evenden, 'Remaking Hells Gate: Salmon, Science and the Fraser River, 1938–1948', *BC Studies* 127 (Autumn 2000), 47–82.

17. J. C. Hopkins, *Canadian Annual Review, 1905* [hereafter *CAR*] (Toronto: Annual Review Publishing, 1906), 369.

18. E.G. Prior, 1903 quoted in British Columbia, *Sessional Papers*, 1903, K6.; Hopkins, *CAR, 1907* (Toronto: Annual Review Publishing, 1908), 605.

19. Eva MacLean, *The Far Land* (Prince George: Caitlin, 1993), 20; Frank Leonard, *A Thousand Blunders: The Grand Trunk Pacific Railway and Northern British Columbia* (Vancouver: UBCP, 1996), ch. 5.

20. Patricia E. Roy, 'Progress, Prosperity and Politics: The Railway Policies of Richard McBride', *BC Studies* 47 (Autumn 1980), 3–28.

21. *Nelson Daily News,* 18 Nov. 1910; A convenient table is in Jean Barman, *The West Beyond the West: A History of British Columbia* (Toronto: UTP, 1996), 385.

22. F. Henry Johnson, *A History of Public Education in British Columbia* (Vancouver: Publications Centre, University of British Columbia, 1964), 61.

23. Johnson, *History of Public Education,* 81–2; Cole Harris, 'Locating the University of British Columbia', *BC Studies* 32 (1976–7), 106–25.

24. Leonard, *A Thousand Blunders,* ch. 6; *Omineca Herald,* 13 Nov. 1909 and 20 June 1913; Chris Hope, '"Indian Unrest at Hazelton" or "Rumpus at Kispiox"? Newspapers, Racism, and the Clash of Cultures, 1909', History 355 term paper, 1994; Bowser to McBride, 26 May 1910, BCA, GR 441, 37/5; *Colonist,* 16 Nov. 1910; McBride to Laurier, 9 March 1911, NAC, Laurier Papers, #189290 and Charles C. Perry to Laurier, 23 March 1911, ibid., #183737; *Colonist,* 12 March 1911; MacLean, *The Far Land,* 56.

25. This account draws on the fine analysis in Cole Harris, *Making Native Space: Colonialism, Resistance, and Reserves in British Columbia* (Vancouver: UBCP, 2002), ch. 8.

26. Patricia E. Roy, *A White Man's Province: British Columbia Politicians and Chinese and Japanese Immigrants, 1858–1914* (Vancouver: UBCP, 1989), 24–7.

27. David Chuenyan Lai, *Chinatowns: Towns Within Cities in Canada* (Vancouver: UBCP, 1988), 43 and passim; Edgar Wickberg, ed., *From China to Canada: A History of the Chinese Communities in Canada* (Toronto: M&S, 1982), 26, 303.

28. The most comprehensive study of the *Komagata Maru* is Hugh Johnston, *The Voyage of the Komagata Maru: The Sikh Challenge to Canada's Colour Bar* (Delhi: Oxford University Press, 1979).

29. Sandon *Paystreak,* 2 March 1901; quoted in McDonald, *Making Vancouver,* 208; Kelowna *Courier,* 4 Jan. 1906; Mariana Valverde, *The Age of Light, Soap, and Water: Moral Reform in English Canada, 1885–1925* (Toronto: M&S, 1991); Cranbrook *Herald,* 6 Dec. 1900.

30. *Colonist,* 23 Sept. 1898, quoted in K.J. Tarasoff, *In Search of Brotherhood* (Vancouver, 1960 [mimeographed]), 180; Vancouver *Daily World,* 2 Feb. 1899; Nelson *Daily News,* 17 May 1899.

31. British Columbia, Royal Commission on Matters Relating to the Sect of Doukhobors in the Province of British Columbia, *Report* (Victoria: King's Printer, 1911), T 28 and T30; *The Week,* 22 June 1912.

32. George Woodcock and Ivan Avakumovic, *The Doukhobors* (Toronto: M&S, 1977 [reprint]) 245; Royal Commission on Doukhobors, *Report,* T7 and T63–6.

33. Woodcock and Avakumovic, *The Doukhobors,* 249–51.

34. McDonald, *Making Vancouver,* 234–5; Cole Harris, 'Introduction', *Letters from Windermere, 1912–1914* (Vancouver: UBCP, 1984), xviii; Jean Barman, *Growing Up British in British Columbia: Boys in Private Schools* (Vancouver: UBCP, 1984); MacLean, *The Far Land,* 20–1.

35. Harris, *Letters from Windermere, 1912–1914,* passim.

36. This paragraph is based on Nelson Riis, 'The

Walhachin Myth: A Study in Settlement Abandonment', *BC Studies* 17 (Spring 1973), 3–25, and Patricia Badir, '"Our Performance Careless of Praise": Loss, Recollection, and the Production of Space in Walhachin, British Columbia', *BC Studies* 133 (Spring 2002), 31–68.

37.  John Norris, *Strangers Entertained: A History of the Ethnic Groups of British Columbia* (Vancouver: BC Centennial '71 Committee, 1971) 127–8. The early history of Norwegians in British Columbia has been collected by Eric Faa, *Norwegians in the Northwest: Settlement in British Columbia, 1858–1918* (Victoria: Runestad, 1995).

38.  Quoted in Ross Johnson, 'No Compromise—No Political Trading: The Marxian Socialist Tradition in British Columbia' (University of British Columbia, Ph.D. thesis, 1975), 193; for example, A.R. McCormack, 'The Emergence of the Socialist Movement in British Columbia', *BC Studies* 21 (Spring 1974), 6; Walter Young, 'Ideology, Personality and the Origin of the CCF in British Columbia', *BC Studies* 32 (Winter 1976–7), 140; David Akers, 'Rebel or Revolutionary? Jack Kavanagh and the Early Years of the Communist Movement in Vancouver, 1920–1925', *Labour/LeTravail* 30 (Fall 1992), 13; Mark Leier, 'Ethnicity, Urbanism, and the Labour Aristocracy: Rethinking Vancouver Trade Unionism, 1889–1909', *Canadian Historical Review* 74 (December 1993), 510–34; John Douglas Belshaw, *Colonization and Community: The Vancouver Island Coalfields and the Making of the British Columbian Working Class* (Montreal and Kingston: MQUP, 2002); Dorothy Steeves, *The Compassionate Rebel: Ernest E. Winch and His Times* (Vancouver: Boag Foundation, 1960), 13.

39.  A good brief overview of the Royal Commission may be found in Stuart Marshall Jamieson, *Times of Trouble: Labour Unrest and Industrial Conflict in Canada, 1900–66* (Ottawa: Information Canada, 1971), 112–21. In the wake of the 1903 strike, employers in Vancouver organized an Employers' Association to combat organized labour; Andrew Yarmie, 'The Right to Manage: Vancouver Employers' Associations, 1900–1923', *BC Studies* 90 (Summer 1991), 40–74.

40.  R.M. Dawson, *William Lyon Mackenzie King: A Political Biography, 1874–1923* (Toronto: UTP, 1958), 138; this account is mainly based on Jamieson, *Times of Trouble,* 112–21; Hardie quoted in A. Ross McCormack, *Reformers, Rebels, and Revolutionaries: the Western Canadian Radical Movement, 1899–1919* (Toronto: UTP, 1977), 61.

41.  *CAR,* 1913, 602; *Proceedings of the First [IWW] Convention, 1905,* quoted in David Brundage, *The Making of Western Labor Radicalism: Denver's Organized Workers, 1878–1905* (Urbana: University of Illinois, 1994), 3. Mark Leier, *Where the Fraser River Flows: The Industrial Workers of the World in British Columbia* (Vancouver: New Star, 1990), 44 and 49–52; McDonald, *Making Vancouver,* 182; The text and the music, to the tune of 'Where the River Shannon Flows' are in Philip J. Thomas, *Songs of the Pacific Northwest* (Saanichton, BC: Hancock, 1979), 97.

42.  A fine account of the coal mining industry, told mainly from the miners' point of view, is Lynne Bowen, *Boss Whistle: The Coal Miners of Vancouver Island Remember* (Lantzville, BC: Oolichan, 1982).

43.  John R. Hinde, *When Coal Was King: Ladysmith and the Coal-Mining Industry on Vancouver Island* (Vancouver: UBCP, 2003), 12; John R. Hinde, '"Stout Ladies and Amazons": Women in the British Columbia Coal-Mining Community of Ladysmith, 1912–14', *BC Studies* 114 (Summer 1997), 33; Anthony W. Rasporich, *For a Better Life: A History of the Croatians in Canada* (Toronto: M&S, 1982), 70; *Colonist,* 15 Aug. 1913; Bowen, *Boss Whistle,* 188.

44.  Mark Leier, *Red Flags and Red Tape: The Making of a Labour Bureaucracy* (Toronto: UTP, 1995), 92; James Conley, '"Open Shop' Means Closed to Union Men": Carpenters and the 1911 Vancouver Building Trades General Strike', *BC*

*Studies* 91–2 (Autumn–Winter, 1991–2), 126–51; Phillips, *No Power Greater,* 169.

## 4: The Limits of Promise: 1914–1941

1. This account is based on Gilbert N. Tucker, *The Naval Service of Canada,* I (Ottawa: King's Printer, 1952), 283–303.

2. British Columbia, Commissioner of Fisheries, *Annual Report,* 1919, BCSP, N8.

3. *British Columbia: From the Earliest Times to the Present* – Biographical, III (Vancouver: S.J. Clarke, 1914), 1114; Charles Humphries, 'War and Patriotism: The *Lusitania* Riot', *BC Historical News* 3 (November 1971), 15–23; Wayne Norton with Ella Verkerk, 'Communities Divided: The Internment Camps of World War One', in W. Norton and Naomi Miller, *The Forgotten Side of the Border: British Columbia's Elk Valley and Crow's Nest Pass* (Kamloops: Plateau Press, 1998), 66–92.

4. C.P. Stacey, *Canada and the Age of Conflict: A History of Canadian External Policies,* I (Toronto: Macmillan, 1977), 235. The only higher figures were Yukon, 33.0%, and Manitoba, 9.8%; Frank Leonard, *A Thousand Blunders: The Grand Trunk Pacific Railway and Northern British Columbia* (Vancouver: UBCP, 1996), 244.

5. McBride to Donald Mann, 28 Jan. 1915, BCA, McBride Papers, CNR File, 1915; T.D. Regehr, *The Canadian Northern Railway: Pioneer Road of the Northern Prairies, 1895–1918* (Toronto: Macmillan, 1976), 390–1.

6. Board of Health, *Annual Report,* 1919, *BCSP,* 1920, B6; Board of Health, *Annual Report,* 1923, *BCSP,* 1924.

7. Robert A. Campbell, *Demon Rum or Easy Money: Government Control of Liquor in British Columbia from Prohibition to Privatization* (Ottawa: Carleton University Press, 1991), 98–9. According to the Annual Report of the Liquor Control Board, in 1925–6 it sold 31,000 gallons of loganberry wine and could have sold more if it had been available; *BCSP* 1926–7, O7.

8. British Columbia, Minister of Mines, *Annual Report,1914, BCSP, 1915,* K226; Bill Sloan,

'Prosperity and Recession Before the 1930s', in Norton and Miller, *The Forgotten Side of the Border,* 45; Lynne Bowen, *Boss Whistle: The Coal Miners of Vancouver Island Remember* (Lantzville, BC: Oolichan, 1982), 195.

9. British Columbia, Minister of Mines, *Annual Report, 1916, BCSP, 1917,* K15 and *Annual Report, 1918, BCSP, 1919,* K16 and K209; *British Columbia in the Canadian Federation: A Submission presented to the Royal Commission on Dominion Provincial Relations by the Government of the Province of British Columbia* (Victoria: King's Printer, 1938), 49; BC, Minister of Mines, *Annual Report, 1926; BCSP, 1927,* A45.

10. Report of the Managing Director, Consolidated Mining and Smelting Company, reprinted in BC Minister of Mines, *Annual Report,* 1918, K177; Jeremy Mouat, *The Business of Power: Hydro-Electricity in South Eastern British Columbia* (Victoria: Sono Nis, 1997), 74–91; British Columbia, Minister of Mines, *Annual Report, 1926, BCSP, 1927,* A10; Chris Rose, 'Reclaiming the Sullivan', *Vancouver Sun,* 21 Dec. 2001.

11. British Columbia Forest Branch, *Annual Report,* 1916, *BCSP, 1917,* N7; the material on MacMillan draws largely from Ken Drushka, *H.R.: A Biography of H.R. MacMillan* (Madeira Park, BC: Harbour, 1995), 68–119 and 333.

12. *Times,* 9 March 1918 and 2 May 1919.

13. J.H. Hamilton quoted in *A History of Shipbuilding in British Columbia* (Vancouver: Marine Retirees Association, 1977), 11; *CAR, 1918,* 744; Joseph Flavelle to Butchart, 28 May 1917 quoted in Michael Bliss, *A Canadian Millionaire: The Life and Business Times of Sir Joseph Flavelle, Bart, 1858–1939* (Toronto: Macmillan, 1978), 323.

14. Paul Phillips, *No Power Greater: A Century of Labour in British Columbia* (Vancouver: BC Federation of Labour, 1967) 70.

15. Phillips, *No Power Greater,* 74–81; Sloan, 'Prosperity and Recession', 46.

16. O.M. Biggar, Lt.-Col., Judge Advocate-General, Regina, 20 May 1919, NAC, R.L. Borden Papers, #61555; Adjutant-General to General

Officer-Commanding, c. 3 June 1919, Department of National Defence, Directorate of History, 322.09(D806); G.O.C. (Victoria) to Secretary Militia Council, Ottawa, 5 June 1919, Borden Papers, #61809; G.G. McGeer to John Oliver, 23 May 1919, BCA, Premiers' Official Correspondence.

17. Sloan, 'Prosperity and Recession', 46; Bowen, *Boss Whistle,* 234; Phillips, *No Power Greater,* 96.

18. BC Department of Labour, *Annual Report, 1925, BCSP, 1926–27,* G45; Jack Mould, *Stumpfarms and Broadaxes* (Saanichton, B.C.: Hancock House, 1976), 43, 47. On Sumas see Laura Cameron, *Openings: A Mediation on History, Method and Sumas Lake* (Montreal and Kingston: MQUP, 1997).

19. Victor Casorso, *The Casorso Story: A Century of Social History in the Okanagan Valley* (Okanagan Falls, BC: Rima, 1983), 169; Morag Maclachlan, 'The Success of the Fraser Valley Milk Producers Association', *BC Studies* 24 (Winter 1974–5), 52–64.

20. *Province,* 17 July 1920, quoted in Russell Walker, *Politicians of a Pioneering Province* (Vancouver: Mitchell Press, 1969), 6.

21. J.C. Gwillim, *Report of Oil Survey in the Peace River District,* 1919, in *BCSP,* 1920, M5, M12. Reports on the oil surveys of the Peace River district were published in the *BCSP* beginning in 1920.

22. See table on grain shipments in Patricia E. Roy, *Vancouver: An Illustrated History* (Toronto: Lorimer, 1980), 171; R.G. Large, *Skeena: River of Destiny* (Sidney: Gray, 1981), 147.

23. Public Works, *Annual Report, 1921, BCSP* 1922, G5–6

24. R.G. Harvey, *The Coast Connection:* (Lantzville, BC: Oolichan, 1994), 128; Department of Public Works, *Annual Report, 1929–30, BCSP, 1931,* T29.

25. These figures are from the *Census of Canada,* 1931. Barman's *West Beyond the West* has a convenient series of demographic tables drawn from the censuses.

26. Sarjeet Singh Jagpal, *Becoming Canadians: Pioneer Sikhs In Their Own Words* (Madeira Park, BC: Harbour, 1994), 34; Norman Buchignani and Doreen M. Indra, *Continuous Journey: A Social History of South Asians in Canada* (Toronto: M&S, 1985), 73.

27. W.A. Carrothers, 'Oriental Standards of Living' in Charles H. Young and Helen R.Y. Reid, *The Japanese Canadians* (Toronto: UTP, 1938) 213; The previous two paragraphs are based on Patricia E. Roy, *The Oriental Question: Consolidating a White Man's Province, 1914–41* (Vancouver: UBC Press, 2003).

28. G.G. Reiman to Farris, 3 May 1919 and A.E. Skinner to A.L. Jolliffe, 31 Oct. 1919, NAC, Department of Immigration Records, vol. 185, file 65101–10; *Province,* 5 and 19 June 1923.

29. CCUB, Nelson, B.C. to W.L.M. King, 24 April 1925, NAC, Department of External Affairs Records, vol. 427/671.

30. *HCD,* 9 June 1925, 3959; Henry B. Hawthorn, ed. *The Doukhobors of British Columbia* (Vancouver: University of British Columbia and J.M. Dent, 1955).

31. The best account of the impact of the economic collapse of the 1930s remains A.E. Safarian, *The Canadian Economy in the Great Depression* (Toronto: M&S, 1959 and 1970.)

32. *British Columbia in the Canadian Confederation,* 247.

33. Bettina Bradbury, 'The Road to Receivership: Unemployment and Relief in Burnaby, 1929–33' (MA thesis, Simon Fraser University, 1976).

34. Ian D. Parker, 'Simon Fraser Tolmie: The Last Conservative Premier of British Columbia', *BC Studies* 11 (Fall 1971), 21–36.

35. Dorothy Steeves, *The Compassionate Rebel: Ernest E. Winch and His Times* (Vancouver: Boag Foundation, 1960), 89. The CCF did not run a candidate against Tom Uphill, the veteran Labour member from Fernie.

36. On Pattullo, see Robin Fisher, *Duff Pattullo of British Columbia* (Toronto: UTP, 1991); McGeer cited in John Herd Thompson with Allen Seager, *Canada 1922 to 1989: Decades of Discord* (Toronto: M&S, 1985), 243.

37. Thompson, *Canada 1922–1939*, 269–72. The On-To-Ottawa Trek has been well described in Bill Waiser, *All Hell Can't Stop Us: The On-to-Ottawa Trek and Regina Riot* (Calgary: Fifth House, 2003).

38. *CAR, 1937–1938*, 507.

39. *British Columbia in the Canadian Confederation*, 111.

40. Ibid., iii; quoted in Margaret Prang, *Newton W. Rowell: Ontario Nationalist* (Toronto: UTP, 1975), 484.

**5: The Two Sides of Prosperity: 1941–1972**

1. T.D. Pattullo to W.L.M. King, 8 Sept. 1939, BCA, GR 1222, box 157.

2. So worried was the provincial government that it stored vital records in specially constructed vaults or microfilmed them. The latter work was not completed until the danger of attack had passed.

3. Ken Adachi, *The Enemy That Never Was* (Toronto: M&S, 1976), 424.

4. Among the most useful sources on the Japanese in Canada during the Second World War are Adachi, *The Enemy That Never Was;* Patricia E. Roy, J.L. Granatstein, Masako Iino, and Hiroko Takamura, *Mutual Hostages: Canadians and Japanese during the Second World War* (Toronto: UTP, 1990) and Ann Gomer Sunahara, *The Politics of Racism* (Toronto: James Lorimer, 1981).

5. R.H. Roy, *For Most Conspicuous Bravery: A Biography of Major-General George R. Pearkes, V.C. through Two World Wars* (Vancouver: UBCP, 1977), 182, 184; BC, Public Utilities Commission, *Annual Report, 1950, BCSP, 1952,* I11.

6. BC, Dept of Trade and Industry, *Annual Report, 1940, BCSP*, 1940, D5; BC, Forest Branch, *Annual Report, 1940, BCSP, 1941–2,* F5 and *Annual Report, 1941, BCSP, 1943,* G5; Norbert MacDonald, *Distant Neighbors: A Comparative History of Seattle and Vancouver* (Lincoln: University of Nebraska Press, 1987), 141–3; 'Shipbuilding', in Daniel Francis, ed. *Encyclopedia of British Columbia* (Madeira Park,

BC: Harbour, 2000), 644.

7. BC, Dept of Trade and Industry, *Annual Report, 1941,* 1941–42, *BCSP,* G5; BC, Dept of Labour, *Annual Report, 1939, BCSP, 1940,* G7 and G119; *Annual Report, 1940, BCSP, 1941–42,* E177, E180, *Annual Report, 1943,* K110; *Annual Report, 1944, BCSP, 1947,* I81; BC, Dept of Mines, *Annual Report, 1943, BCSP, 1945,* A10 and *Annual Report, 1943, BCSP, 1947,* A15; BC, Provincial Police, *Annual Report, 1943, BCSP, 1945,* W12; BC, Social Assistance Branch, *Annual Report, 1946,* S7.

8. F.H. Leacy, *Historical Statistics of Canada,* 2nd edn (Ottawa: Statistics Canada and Social Science Federation of Canada, 1983), Series E175–177; BC, Dept of Labour, *Annual Report, 1954, BCSP, 1956; Annual Report, 1946, BCSP, 1948,* K105 and *Annual Report, 1952, BCSP, 1953–4,* E9; H111; Paul Phillips, *No Power Greater: A Century of Labour in B.C.* (Vancouver: BC Federation of Labour, 1967), 148; Jerry Lembcke and William M. Tattam, *One Union in Wood: A Political History of the International Woodworkers of America* (Madeira Park, BC: Harbour, 1984, 114; H.A. Logan, *Trade Unions in Canada* (Toronto: Macmillan, 1948), 285.

9. BC, Dept of Trade and Industry, *Annual Report, 1945,* R5; BC, Forest Service, *Annual Report, 1947, BCSP, 1948,* 31; Donald McKay, *Empire of Wood: The MacMillan Bloedel Story* (Vancouver: D&M, 1982), ch. 10.

10. Ken Drushka, 'Pulp and Paper', *Encyclopedia of British Columbia*, 580–3.

11. John Douglas Belshaw and David J. Mitchell, 'The Economy Since the Great War', in Hugh M. Johnston, ed., *The Pacific Province: a History of British Columbia* (Vancouver: D&M, 1996), 325–7.

12. BC, Dept of Agriculture, *Annual Report, 1949, BCSP, 1951,* W13; John McMullan, 'The Organization of the Fisheries: An Introduction', in Patricia Marchak, Neil Guppy, and John McMullan, eds, *Uncommon Property: The Fishing and Fish-Processing Industries in British Columbia* (Toronto: Methuen, 1987), 42–3; Marchak,

'Uncommon Property', in Marchak et al., *Uncommon Property*, 17.

13. T.D. Regehr, *Mennonites in Canada, 1939-1970* (Toronto: UTP, 1996), 111–12.

14. Department of Social Welfare, *Annual Report*, 1950, *BCSP*, 1951, R14, R20; Public Utilities Commission, *Annual Report*, 1945, *BCSP*, N8.

15. Jack Fossum, *Mancatcher: An Immigrant's Story of Logging, Policing and Pioneering in the Canadian West* (Comox, BC: Lindsay Press, 1989), 148, 179. A critical study of the Kemano project is Bev Christensen, *Too Good to be True: Alcan's Kemano Completion Project* (Vancouver: Talonbooks, 1995).

16. BC, Dept of Social Welfare, *Annual Report, 1952, BCSP*, 1953, p. BB54; Dept of Social Welfare, *Annual Report, 1952, BCSP*, 1953, W21; BC, Dept of Lands, *Annual Report, 1951, BCSP, 1952*, BB46–48.

17. BC, Dept of Trade and Industry, *Annual Report, 1953, BCSP*, 1953–4, LL5; Trade and Industry, *Report*, 1952, *BCSP*, 1953, FF9.

18. BC, Dept of Education, *Annual Report, 1949–50, BCSP, 1951*, O31.

19. Gordon Wismer to Louis St. Laurent, 18 June 1949, NAC, St. Laurent Papers, vol. 66.

20. 'Stale eggs' quoted in Donald Alper, 'From Rule to Ruin: the Conservative Party of British Columbia, 1928–1954', (PhD thesis, University of British Columbia, 1975), 334; 'CCF Only Pink Reds, Says Socred', *Vancouver Sun*, 4 June 1952.

21. Gordon Hak, 'Populism and the 1952 Social Credit Breakthrough in British Columbia', *CHR*, 85 (June 2004), 277–96.

22. Patricia Marchak, *Green Gold: The Forest Industry in British Columbia* (Vancouver: UBCP, 1983), 305.

23. R.G. Harvey, *The Coast Connection* (Lantzville, BC: Oolichan, 1994), 135, 141; David J. Mitchell, *W.A.C Bennett and the Rise of British Columbia* (Vancouver: D &M, 1983), 350.

24. Eileen Williston and Betty Keller, *Forests, Power and Policy: the Legacy of Ray Williston* (Prince George: Caitlin, 1997), 174–6; Mitchell, *W.A.C.*

*Bennett*, 298. For recollections of Peace River residents see Earl K. Pollon and Shirlee Smith Matheson, *This Was Our Valley* (Calgary: Detselig, 1989).

25. Gordon Wismer to Stuart Garson, 1 May 1950, NAC, Records of Parliament, vol. 192. A government study that is very sympathetic to the children's plight is *Righting the Wrong: The Confinement of the Sons of Freedom Doukhobor Children* (Victoria: Ombudsman, Province of British Columbia, 1999).

26. Wilson Duff, *The Indian History of British Columbia* (Victoria: BC Provincial Museum, 1969), 45–6; For example, Victoria *Times*, 6 November 1940; *Fraser Valley Record*, 20 May 1941; Vernon *News*, 4 January 1945; Vancouver *Province*, 26 February 1945; Vancouver *Sun*, 16 May 1946; Provincial Advisory Committee on Indian Affairs, 1955, *BCSP*, 1957, F144.

27. *Province*, 28 January 1947 and 24 December 1951; Paul Tennant, *Aboriginal Politics and Peoples: The Indian Land Question in British Columbia, 1849–1949* (Vancouver: UBCP, 1990), 121; Provincial Advisory Committee on Indian Affairs, 1952, *BCSP*, 1953–54, E155. See also Robert A. Campbell, 'A "Fantastic Rigmarole": Deregulating Aboriginal Drinking in British Columbia, 1945-62', *BC Studies* 141 (Spring 2004), 81–104.

28. Patricia K. Wood, *Nationalism from the Margins: Italians in Alberta and British Columbia* (Montreal and Kingston: MQUP, 2002), 58–65; *Province*, 3 Oct. 1960; David Chuenyan Lai, *Chinatowns: Towns Within Cities in Canada* (Vancouver: UBCP, 1988), 123; Wing Chung Ng, *The Chinese in Vancouver, 1945–80: The Pursuit of Identity and Power* (Vancouver: UBCP, 1999), 23; Dept of Social Welfare, *Annual Report*, 1952, *BCSP*, 1953–54, U24.

29. For Vancouver's housing problems see Jill Wade, *Houses for All: The Struggle for Social Housing in Vancouver, 1919–50* (Vancouver: UBCP, 1994); Peter A. Baskerville, *Beyond the Island: An Illustrated History of Victoria* (Burlington, ON: Windsor, 1986), 108.

30. BC, Royal Commission on Education, *Report* (Victoria: Queen's Printer, 1960), 28; 38; BC, Dept of Education, *Annual Report, 1940–1, BCSP, 1943,* D4; Vital Statistics, *Annual Report, BCSP* 1957, R13 and *Annual Report*, 1951, *BCSP,* 1953–54, C13; Dept of Social Welfare, *Annual Report*, 1954, *BCSP, 1955,* 311; Dept of Social Welfare, *Annual Report*, 1954, *BCSP,* 1955, 311 and *Annual Report*, 1955, *BCSP,* 1956, O9, O27.

31. BC, Public Schools, *Annual Report, 1944–45, BCSP,* 1946, Y42.

32. Dept of Social Welfare, *Annual Report, 1969*, 46; Dept of Rehabilitation and Social Improvement, *Annual Report*, 1971, N9–10.

## 6: A New British Columbia? 1972–2004

1. Dave Barrett interview with John Herd Thompson, 7 April 1988; Donald E. Blake, R.K Carty, and Lynda Erickson, *Grassroots Politicians: Party Activists in British Columbia* (Vancouver: UBCP, 1991) 6; Stan Persky, *Son of Socred* (Vancouver: New Star, 1979), 27; Rosemary Brown, *Being Brown: A Very Public Life* (Toronto: Ballantine, 1989), 129–30.

2. R. Jeremy Wilson, 'The Legislature' in T.J. Morley et al., *The Reins of Power* (Vancouver: D&M, 1983), 35–6.

3. Barrett interview with JHT, 7 April 1987; Philip Resnick, 'Social Democracy in Power: The Case of British Columbia', *BC Studies* 34 (Summer 1977), 9–18, provides a critical summary of NDP legislation from a Marxist perspective.

4. Resnick, 'Social Democracy in Power', 10–11; Barrett interview, 1988; quoted in Neil Swainson, 'British Columbia', *Canadian Annual Review of Politics and Public Affairs [CAR]*, 1972, ed. John Saywell (Toronto: UTP, 1974), 202.

5. Barrett interview, 1988; Swainson, *CAR*, 1972, 202; Patricia Roy, 'British Columbia', *CAR, 1975,* 185; Norman Ruff, 'British Columbia and Canadian Federalism', in Morley, *The Reins of Power,* 300.

6. Persky, *Son of Socred*, 26.

7. Quoted in Roy, 'British Columbia', *CAR, 1975,* 196.

8. Barrett claims that he 'expected to lose' but chose the early election 'because we would have been down to five or six seats' had he waited until 1976 or 1977 (Barrett interview). Calder, a Nisga'a leader and CCF–NDP member for Atlin since 1949, claimed that he defected because the Barrett government was 'anti-Indian, anti-labour and anti-North', and had failed to negotiate Aboriginal rights. But Barrett had dismissed him from the cabinet after Calder was arrested for being drunk in a public place (Persky, *Son of Socred*, 32, 58).

9. Allen Garr, *Tough Guy: Bill Bennett and the Taking of British Columbia* (Toronto: Key Porter, 1985), 26–7; Blake et al., *Grassroots Politicians*, 6–7.

10. David Mitchell, *Succession: The Political Reshaping of British Columbia* (Vancouver: D&M, 1987), 30–2; Gary Mason and Keith Baldrey, *Fantasyland: Inside the Reign of Bill Vander Zalm* (Toronto: McGraw-Hill Ryerson, 1989), 37; Persky, *Son of Socred,* 21; Ruff, 'Managing the Public Service', in *The Reins of Power,* 177; Alan F.J. Artibise and Peter A. Baskerville, 'British Columbia', *CAR*, 1980, ed. R.B. Byers, 300–1; ibid. (1981), 413; 'British Columbia Resources and Investment Corporation', *Encyclopedia of British Columbia*, ed. Daniel Francis (Madeira Park, BC: Harbour Publishing, 2000), 63.

11. Mitchell, *Succession,* 34–5; Donald E. Blake, *Two Political Worlds: Parties and Voting in British Columbia* (Vancouver: UBCP, 1985), 23.

12. Mitchell, *Succession,* 47.

13. John Scholefield, 'Recovery through Restraint?', in Warren Magnusson et al., *The New Reality: The Politics of Restraint in British Columbia* (Vancouver: New Star, 1984), 43–4; Garr, *Tough Guy,* 51–2; John Malcolmson, 'The Hidden Agenda of Restraint', in Magnusson et al., *The New Reality,* 77–80. Quoted in Alan Twigg, *Vander Zalm: From Immigrant to Premier* (Madeira Park, BC: Harbour Publishing, 1986), 94-107. Garr, *Tough Guy,* 78 suggests the premier dropped Vander Zalm; quoted in Garr, *Tough Guy,* 68.

14. Stan Persky, *Fantasy Government: Bill Vander*

*Zalm and the Future of Social Credit* (Vancouver: New Star, 1989), 63; Garr, *Tough Guy,* 50 and 83.

15.   Marilyn Callahan, 'The Human Costs of Restraint', in Magnusson, *The New Reality,* 227. Appendix A to this book provides a descriptive list of the 'The 'Restraint" Package', 281–5; Persky, *Fantasy Government,* 10.

16.   Mitchell, *Succession,* 65; Garr, *Tough Guy,* 124, 110; Malcolmson in Magnusson et al., *New Reality,* 103; Alex Macdonald, *'My Dear Legs...',* *Letters to a Young Social Democrat* (Vancouver: New Star, 1985), 75; William K. Carroll, 'The Solidarity Coalition', in Magnusson et al., *New Reality,* 94–113.

17.   Jeremy Wilson, 'The Legislature Under Siege,' in Magnusson et al., *The New Reality,* 114–27.

18.   Cliff Andstein of the BCGEU and Mike Kramer of the BC Federation of Labour also participated. Art Kube, the president of the BC Federation, had to retire from the negotiations because of illness, exhaustion, and conflicts with Operation Solidarity; Jack Munro and Jane O'Hara, *Union Jack: Labour Leader Jack Munro* (Vancouver: D&M, 1988), 6–17.

19.   Persky, *Fantasy Government,* 15; Stan Persky and Lanny Beckman, 'Downsizing the Unemployment Problem', in Magnusson et al., *The New Reality,* 196; Garr, *Tough Guy,* 169.

20.   Kim Campbell, *Time and Change: The Political Memoirs of Canada's First Woman Prime Minister* (Toronto: McClelland and Stewart, 1997), 59; Mitchell, *Succession,* 45; Garr, *Tough Guy,* 53, 55, 177.

21.   Geoffrey Molyneux, *British Columbia: An Illustrated History* (Vancouver: Raincoast Books, 2002), chapter 5.

22.   Blake et al., *Grassroots Politicians,* 93, 99–102; Campbell, *Time and Chance,* 65.

23.   Resnick, *The Politics of Resentment,* 16, 49; according to Andrew Cohen, in *A Deal Undone: The Making and Breaking of the Meech Lake Accord* (Vancouver: D&M, 1990), 84-5, Vander Zalm's main constitutional advisor, Mel Smith, did not like the idea of talking only about

Quebec (16). Other reporters joked that Vander Zalm was only at the meetings 'to explain the hard parts' to Premier Don Getty of Alberta (Susan Delacourt, *United We Fall: The Crisis of Democracy in Canada* [Toronto: Viking, 1993], 189); Gary Mason and Keith Baldrey, *Fantasyland: Inside the Reign of Bill Vander Zalm* (Toronto: McGraw-Hill Ryerson, 1989), 137–49; Resnick, *The Politics of Resentment,* 41, 107; *Sun,* 13 June 1988.

24.   John Cruickshank, 'Vander Zalm's Vitriol', *Globe and Mail,* 5 March 1988.

25.   Persky, *Fantasy Government,* ii; G.L. Kristianson, 'British Columbia', in *CAR, 1991,,* 218–19.

26.   Delacourt, *United We Fall,* 188, 195; Mike Harcourt, *Mike Harcourt: A Measure of Defiance* (Vancouver: D&M, 1996), 83

27.   Delacourt, *United We Fall,* 214; Pat Carney, *Trade Secrets: A Memoir* (Toronto: Key Porter, 2000), 350; Barbara Yaffe, 'Quebecers no more "A People" than are British Columbians', *Sun,* 4 Dec. 1997. Viewpoints Research Limited took the poll.

28.   Paul Tennant, 'British Columbia: A Place for Aboriginal Peoples?' *BC Studies* 57 (Spring 1983), 5; Paul Tennant, *Aboriginal Peoples and Politics: The Indian Land Question in British Columbia, 1849–1989* (Vancouver: UBCP, 1990), 152–5.

29.   There is an excellent summary of the first cen-tury of 'The Political Struggle in British Columbia' in Arthur J. Ray, *I Have Lived Here Since the World Began: An Illustrated History of Canada's Native People* (Toronto: Lester/Key Porter, 1996), 319–37. *Calder v. Attorney-General of BC* (1973), *Supreme Court Reports* [1973], 328, is quoted in Tennant, *Aboriginal Peoples and Politics,* 221.

30.   Tennant, *Native Peoples and Politics,* 227–35; 'West stalls deal on native self-rule', Montreal *Gazette* 27 March 1987; Rudy Platiel and Graham Fraser, 'Native self-government talks stall over question of "inherent" right', *Globe and Mail,* 27 March 1987; Dara Culhane, *The Pleasure of the Crown: Anthropology, Law, and*

*First Nations* (Burnaby, BC: Talon Books, 1998), 229–30. See also Stan Persky, 'Commentary', in *Delgamuukw: the Supreme Court of Canada Decision on Aboriginal Title* (Vancouver: D&M, 1998), 8, and 'Anthropology and History in the Courts', *BC Studies* 95 (Autumn 1992).

31. Rudy Platiel, 'Status Indians number half a million', *Globe and Mail*, 30 Aug. 1990; 'Ottawa seeks settlements in native standoffs', *Maclean's*, 25 Sept. 1995; *Maclean's*, 11 Aug. 1997.

32. *Sun*, 2 Feb. 1998, and First Nations statement are both cited in Persky, 'Commentary', 4.

33. Dan Schrier and Frank Ip, 'British Columbia's Changing Ethnic Mosaic'; http:www/bcstats.gov.bc/data/pop/pop/ethnic.pdf (accessed 30 June 2004); Ian Haysom, 'The making of a polyglot patriot', *Times-Colonist* (Victoria), 28 June 2003.

34. http://www.bcstats.gov.bc.ca/data/pop/pop/project/bctab1.htm

35. The information in this paragraph is drawn from Herbert C. Northcott and P. Jane Milliken, *Aging in British Columbia: Burden or Benefit* (Calgary: Detselig, 1998), 15, 21, 27–37, 77.

36. 'Aboriginal Demographics', BC Statistics, Census 91 Fast Facts, Issue 21; Schrier and Ip, 'British Columbia's Changing Ethnic Mosaic', 1-8; *Vancouver Sun*, 7 Feb. 2003.

37. Statistics Canada, 1996 Census, *Immigration and Citizenship*, catalogue # 11–001E. Wing Chung Ng, *The Chinese in Vancouver, 1945–80: The Pursuit of Identity in Power* (Vancouver: UBCP, 1999), 4; *Vancouver Sun*, 7 Feb. 2003.

38. www.bcstats.gov.bc.ca/data/qf.pdf

39. Paul Ciccantell, 'Globalization, Restructuring, and Hard Times in Three Raw Materials-dependent Communities', paper presented to the Association for Canadian Studies in the US, November 2003; unnamed journalist quoted in Geoffrey Molyneux, *British Columbia: An Illustrated History*, 2nd edn (Vancouver: Raincoast, 2002), 109; Brent McGillivray, *Geography of British Columbia: People and Landscapes in Transition* (Vancouver: UBCP, 2000), 17–18, 93, 155–6, 205–6, 221–2.

40. On the 'Harcourt Regime', see Richard Sigurdson, 'The British Columbia New Democratic Party', in Carty, ed., *Politics, Policy, and Government*, 325–35.

41. Ibid., 335–8.

42. Jennifer Hunter, 'Glen Clark Stands Firm', *Maclean's*, 2 Aug. 1999, 20–2; 'Amor de Chaos', *Globe and Mail*, 24 Aug. 1999.

43. 'Nisga'a treaty passes', CBC News, 13 April 1999, http://www.cbc.ca/cgi-bin/templates/view.cgi?/news/1999/04/22.

44. Quoted in Barbara Yaffe, *Vancouver Sun*, 10 July 2003.

45. *Times–Colonist* (Victoria), 2–21 Sept. 2003.

# SUGGESTIONS FOR FURTHER READING

The historical resources available on British Columbia are as varied as the province itself. Space limitations mean that this essay can offer no more than a sampling, so we have concentrated on recent works. Many notes, however, provide 'leads' to other material. A reliable source of bibliographical information is the quarterly journal *BC Studies* (1968–). In addition to articles reflecting new research, most issues have comprehensive listings of new publications and reviews of recent books. The list of 'Recent Publications Relating to Canada' in the *Canadian Historical Review* (1920–) has a BC section.

From 1958, when it was published as a centennial project, until the early 1990s, the classic work was *British Columbia: A History* (Toronto: Macmillan, 1958 and 1971) by Margaret A. Ormsby. It remains the best source for general political history from colonial times to the 1940s. Today's standard, Jean Barman's *The West Beyond the West* (Toronto: UTP, 1991, 1996), focuses on social history. Many essays in *The Pacific Province: A History of British Columbia*, ed. Hugh M. Johnston (Vancouver: D&M, 1996) complement Barman.

Older histories began with European explorers, the earliest of whom arrived from the sea. For the Spaniards see Warren L. Cook, *Flood Tide of Empire: Spain and the Pacific Northwest, 1543–1819* (New Haven: Yale University Press, 1973). Bicentennials inspired essays on the major British navigators: Robin Fisher and Hugh Johnston, eds, *Captain James Cook and His Times* (Vancouver: D&M, 1979) and Robin Fisher, ed., *From Maps to Metaphors: The Pacific World of George Vancouver* (Vancouver: UBCP, 1993). The overland explorers may be studied through their journals. W. Kaye Lamb edited *The Letters and Journals of Simon Fraser, 1806–1808* (Toronto: Macmillan,1960) and *The Journals and Letters of Sir Alexander Mackenzie* (Cambridge, UK: for the Hakluyt Society at the University Press, 1970) while Victor G. Hopwood did the same for David Thompson in *Travels in Western North America, 1784–1812* (Toronto: Macmillan, 1971). Communication between BC and Canada was scarcely any easier half a century later: for an evocative account of an 1862 expedition, see *Overland from Canada to British Columbia by Mr. Thomas McMicking of Queenston, Canada West*, ed. Joanne Leduc (Vancouver: UBCP, 1981), a volume in the UBCP series The Pioneers of British Columbia, which publishes edited memoirs, letters, and journals.

As Cole Harris, a historical geographer, reminds us in *The Resettlement of British Columbia* (Vancouver: UBCP, 1997), Europeans were not the first to settle in what is now BC. Inspired by the growing strength of the First Nations' presence in the province and their demands for land and other Aboriginal rights, historians and geographers have joined the anthropologists to produce a small library. Harris has made another major contribution with: *Making Native Space: Colonialism, Resistance, and Reserves in British Columbia*

(Vancouver: UBCP, 2002). It offers a thoughtful analysis of how and why Aboriginal people were consigned to reserves and how they responded. Paul Tennant, *Aboriginal Peoples and Politics: The Indian Land Question in British Columbia, 1849–1989* (Vancouver: UBCP, 1990) focuses on Aboriginal people's political responses. Daniel Clayton's *Islands of Truth: The Imperial Fashioning of Vancouver Island* (Vancouver: UBCP, 2000), a volume that is informed by colonial and postcolonial studies, is an important new contribution. In addition, students of early contact must still consult Robin Fisher, *Contact and Conflict: Indian–European Relations in British Columbia, 1774–1890* (Vancouver: UBCP, 1977 and 1992), although the newer histories challenge some of Fisher's arguments.

Several collections of traditional First Nations stories have been published. Wendy Wickwire has presented the stories of the Okanagan storyteller Harry Robinson in two volumes: *Write It on Your Heart* (Vancouver: Talonbooks, 1989) and *Nature Power: In the Spirit of an Okanagan Storyteller* (Vancouver: D&M, 1992). Stories from the Nunne-za (Beaver) people of northeastern BC are the basis of Robin Ridington, *Trail to Heaven: Knowledge and Narrative in a Northern Native Community* (Vancouver: D&M, 1988) and *Little Bit Know Something: Stories in a Language of Anthropology* (Vancouver: D&M, 1990). Andrea Laforet worked with Annie York, a Nlaka'pamux elder, to relate the history of York's people in *Spuzzum: Fraser Canyon Histories, 1808–1939* (Vancouver: UBCP, 1998).

First Nations people have also produced their own histories. An outstanding example is *A Stó:lō–Coast Salish Historical Atlas* (Vancouver: D&M, 2001), a handsome volume edited by Keith Thor Carlson and sponsored by the Stó:lō Heritage Trust. Several special issues of *BC Studies* have essays by First Nations activists, artists, and scholars. A recent work is Shirley Louis, *Q'Sapi: A History of the Okanagan People as Told by Okanagan Families* (Penticton: Theytus Books, 2003).

The pioneer work on the role of Aboriginal people in the provincial economy is Rolf Knight, *Indians at Work: An Informal History of Native Labour in British Columbia, 1958–1930* (Vancouver: New Star, 1978 and 1996). Douglas C. Harris, in *Fish, Law, and Colonialism: The Legal Capture of Salmon in British Columbia* (Toronto:

UTP, 2001), shows how the First Nations managed the fishery before the Canadian state 'legally captured' it. Dianne Newell's *Tangled Webs of History: Indians and the Law in Canada's Pacific Coast Fisheries* (Toronto: UTP, 1993) complements Harris's work. The potlatch is the subject of Douglas Cole and Ira Chaikin, *An Iron Hand Upon the People: The Law Against the Potlatch on the Northwest Coast* (Vancouver: D&M, 1990). Finally, for a new approach to Aboriginal studies see Paige Raibmon's *Authentic Indians: Episodes of Encounter from the Late-Nineteenth-Century Northwest Coast* (Durham, NC: Duke University Press, 2005). Combining cultural and labour history, Raibmon examines both the constraints and the room to manoeuvre that Aboriginal people found within the colonizers' definitions of 'real Indians'.

People of British and Canadian origin have been the most numerous and influential settlers in the province, but no one has yet attempted a systematic overview of either group. A sample of what such a study might do is the analysis of ethnic and class relations in Robert A. J. McDonald, *Making Vancouver: Class, Status and Social Boundaries, 1863–1913* (Vancouver: UBCP, 1996).

Because of immigration patterns, women were a small minority in the early years, accounting for less than 40 per cent of the population until the 1920s. Adele Perry looks at gender issues in *On the Edge of Empire: Gender, Race and the Making of British Columbia, 1849–1871* (Toronto: UTP, 2001). Jean Barman's *Sojourning Sisters: The Lives and Letters of Jessie and Annie McQueen* (Toronto: UTP, 2003) traces the lives of two teachers who from Nova Scotia who settled in the Nicola Valley in the 1890s. The most recent anthology on women's history, *British Columbia Reconsidered: Essays on Women*, edited by Gillian Creese and Veronica Strong-Boag (Vancouver: Press Gang, 1992), has an extensive bibliography. An informative biography of a social and political activist in the first half of the twentieth century is Irene Howard, *The Struggle for Social Justice in British Columbia: Helena Gutteridge, the Unknown Reformer* (Vancouver: UBCP, 1992).

Among the first 'minority' immigrants were the Chinese. For a useful overview see Edward Wickberg, ed., *From China to Canada: A History of the Chinese Communities in Canada* (Toronto: M&S, 1982).

Another nation-wide study, *Chinatowns: Towns within Cities in Canada* by David Chuenyan Lai (Vancouver: UBCP, 1988), includes a detailed study of Victoria's Chinatown. Kay Anderson's *Vancouver's Chinatown: Racial Discourse in Canada, 1875–1980* (Montreal and Kingston: MQUP, 1991) is an outsider's view; Wing Chung Ng in *The Chinese in Vancouver, 1945–80* (Vancouver: UBCP, 1999) looks at what it has meant to be Chinese in Canada.

The best introduction to Japanese-Canadian history is Ken Adachi, *The Enemy That Never Was* (Toronto: M&S, 1976). The volume on South Asians in the Generations series (sponsored by the federal department of the secretary of state) is Norman Buchignani and Doreen M. Indra with Ram Srivastava, *Continuous Journey: A Social History of South Asians in Canada* (Toronto: M&S, 1985). *The Voyage of the Komagata Maru: The Sikh Challenge to Canada's Colour Bar* (Bombay: Oxford University Press, 1979; repr. Vancouver: UBCP, 1989) by Hugh Johnston is a detailed study of that event and its wide repercussions. Johnston also assisted Tara Singh Bains, a Punjabi who came to BC in the early 1950s, in writing his recollections, published as *The Four Quarters of the Night: The Life-Journey of an Emigrant Sikh* (Montreal and Kingston: MQUP, 1995). Many Chinese and Japanese have told their own stories. For a guide, see Patricia E. Roy, 'Active Voices: A Third Generation of Studies of the Chinese and Japanese in British Columbia', *BC Studies* 117 (Spring 1998).

Several works analyze the reactions of the white majority to Asian immigrants. They include W. Peter Ward, *White Canada Forever: Popular Attitudes and Public Policy Toward Orientals in British Columbia* (Montreal and Kingston: MQUP, 1978; 3rd edn, 2002) and Patricia E. Roy, *A White Man's Province: British Columbia Politicians and Chinese and Japanese Immigrants, 1858–1914* (Vancouver: UBCP, 1989) and *'The Oriental Menace:' Consolidating a White Man's Province, 1914–1941* (Vancouver: UBCP, 2003).

Asians were not the only immigrants to encounter hostility. In *Nationalism from the Margins: Italians in Alberta and British Columbia* (Montreal and Kingston: MQUP, 2002), Patricia K. Wood examines how Italians negotiated new Canadian and Italian identities.

Among the Doukhobors, only the Sons of Freedom blatantly challenged the law, and yet all suffered from the animosity they provoked. The literature on the Doukhobors is extensive, but the best introduction is George Woodcock and Ivan Avakumovic, *The Doukhobors* (Toronto: Oxford University Press, 1968; reprinted Toronto: M&S, 1977).

Canadians and the British made their first permanent imprint in British Columbia through the fur traders of the North West and Hudson's Bay companies. Richard Mackie, *Trading Beyond the Mountains: the British Fur Trade on the Pacific, 1793–1843* (Vancouver: UBCP, 1997) examines the multi-faceted economic activities of the Hudson's Bay Company. Three volumes by Barry Gough, all published by UBCP, record the exploits of the other major imperial force, the Royal Navy: *Distant Dominion: Britain and the Northwest Coast of North America, 1759–1809* (1980); *The Royal Navy on the Northwest Coast of North America, 1810–1914* (1971); and *Gunboat Frontier: British Maritime Authority and Northwest Coast Indians, 1846–1890* (1984).

The coal fields of Vancouver Island closed long ago, but historians continue to mine them. Lynne Bowen has written two popular histories based on sound scholarship: *Three Dollar Dreams* (Lantzville, BC: Oolichan, 1987) and *Boss Whistle: The Coal Miners of Vancouver Island Remember* (Lantzville, BC: Oolichan, 1982). The latter draws on interviews with miners and their families. John Douglas Belshaw, *Colonization and Community: The Vancouver Island Coal Field and the Making of the British Columbian Working Class* (Montreal and Kingston: MQUP, 2002) focuses on British miners before 1900; John Hinde, *When Coal Was King: Ladysmith and the Coal-Mining Industry on Vancouver Island* (Vancouver: UBCP, 2003) studies a community in the early twentieth century and provides new insight into the strike of 1912–14. The interior's hard-rock miners have been less frequently studied, but Jeremy Mouat, *Roaring Days: Rossland's Mines and the History of British Columbia* (Vancouver: UBCP, 1995) gives the flavour of mining-town society and the speculative fever that financed much of the early industry.

As the last of the mining booms faded, forestry became the province's main industry. Its modern beginnings are traced by Gordon Hak in *Trees Into Dollars: The British Columbia Coastal Lumber Industry, 1858–1913* (Toronto: UTP, 2000), while Richard Rajala examines the relationships between technology and conservation in *Clear Cutting the Pacific Rain Forest: Production, Science, and Regulation* (Vancouver: UBCP, 1998). Richard Mackie's *Island Timber: A Social History of the Comox Logging Company, Vancouver Island* (Victoria: Sono Nis, 2000) focuses on a single company and, with copious photographs, clearly describes the nature of the work. The major corporations have had their historians too: E.G. Perrault, *Wood & Water: The Story of Seaboard Lumber and Shipping* (Vancouver: D&M, 1985); Donald MacKay, *Empire of Wood: The MacMillan Bloedel Story* (Vancouver: D&M, 1982); and Ken Drushka, *H.R.: A Biography of H.R. MacMillan* (Madeira Park, BC: Harbour, 1995). In *Green Gold: The Forest Industry in British Columbia* (Vancouver: UBCP, 1983) Patricia Marchak, a sociologist, suggests that capital and the state together created a vulnerable economy, with significant consequences for workers in the hinterland. Jeremy Wilson examines the politics of the 'wars in the woods' between environmentalists and the forest industry in *Talk and Log: Wilderness Politics in British Columbia, 1965–96* (Vancouver: UBCP, 1998).

A popular overview of the salmon fishery is Geoff Meggs, *Salmon: The Decline of the British Columbia Fishery* (Vancouver: D&M, 1991). More specialized studies include Dianne Newell, ed., *The Development of the Pacific Salmon-Canning Industry: A Grown Man's Game* (Montreal and Kingston: MQUP, 1989), which documents the industry in the early twentieth century, and Alicja Muszynski, *Cheap Wage Labour: Race and Gender in the Fisheries of British Columbia* (Montreal and Kingston: MQUP, 1996), which examines the industry's labour force. A team of sociologists led by Patricia Marchak, Neil Guppy, and John McMullan reported on the industry and its contemporary problems in *Uncommon Property: The Fishing and Fish-Processing Industries in British Columbia* (Toronto: Methuen, 1987).

Agriculture has never been a major industry, and no comprehensive history has been written of it. *Beyond the City Limits: Rural History in British Columbia*, edited by Ruth Sandwell (Vancouver: UBCP, 1999), includes valuable papers on First Nations peoples as well as gender issues, but only four essays deal with agriculture. Footnotes in David DeMerritt's 'Visions of Agriculture in British Columbia', *BC Studies* 108 (Winter 1995–6) offer leads to the scattered literature.

Transportation has been a key consideration in economic development. The major railways have been documented in nation-wide studies; Frank Leonard in *A Thousand Blunders: The Grand Trunk Pacific Railway and Northern British Columbia* (Vancouver: UBCP, 1996) focuses on the troubled history of that transcontinental line within BC. John A. Eagle, *The Canadian Pacific Railway and the Development of Western Canada, 1896–1914* (Montreal and Kingston: MQUP, 1989) has a considerable amount of BC material. Robert D. Turner, who also writes on coastal shipping, has published several well-researched and handsomely illustrated histories of interior railways. No one has really tackled the history of roads in British Columbia—a subject that might yield something like a history of the province.

Two collections on legal issues offer insight into social history: *Essays in the History of Canadian Law: British Columbia and the Yukon*, ed. Hamar Foster and John McLaren (Toronto: The Osgoode Society, 1995) and *Regulating Lives: Historical Essays on the State, Society, The Individual and the Law*, ed. John McLaren, Robert Menzies, and Dorothy Chunn (Vancouver: UBCP, 2002). Tina Loo, *Making Law, Order and Authority in British Columbia, 1821–1871* (Toronto: UTP, 1994) deals with the colonial period. Robert A. Campbell has written on liquor control in *Demon Rum or Easy Money: Government Control of Liquor in British Columbia from Prohibition to Privatization* (Ottawa: Carleton University Press, 1991) and *Sit Down and Drink Your Beer: Regulating Vancouver's Beer Parlours, 1925–1954* (Toronto: UTP, 2001). Megan J. Davis, in *Into the House of Old: A History of Residential Care in British Columbia* (Montreal and Kingston: MQUP, 2003), examines the institutional care of the elderly.

Studies of education also contribute to social history. Several recent anthologies cover aspects of educational history: Jean Barman, Neil Sutherland and J. Donald Wilson, eds, *Children, Teachers & School* (Calgary: Detselig, 1995); a revision edited by Barman and Mona Gleason, *Children, Teachers and Schools in the History of British Columbia* (Calgary: Detselig, 2003); and Thomas Fleming, ed., *School Leadership: Essays on the British Columbia Experience, 1872–1995* (Mill Bay, BC: Bendall, 2001) cover aspects of educational history. *Alex Lord's British Columbia: Recollections of a Rural School Inspector, 1915–36*, edited by John Callam (Vancouver: UBCP, 1991) is a delightful account of rural schooling. Jean Barman's *Growing Up British in British Columbia: Boys in Public Schools* (Vancouver: UBCP, 1984) shows the persistence of British traditions. Apart from celebratory volumes and a few specialized works or biographies, there are no histories of the province's institutions of higher education.

The education of First Nations children in residential schools is a controversial subject. Celia Haig-Brown's study of the Kamloops School, *Resistance and Renewal: Surviving the Indian Residential School* (Vancouver: Arsenal Pulp, 1988 and 1991), is highly critical. A thinly disguised memoir, Shirley Stirling's novel *My Name is Seepeetza* (Vancouver: D&M, 1992), offers a student's point of view. A work that is sympathetic to teachers and administrators while noting their failings is Margaret Whitehead, *The Cariboo Mission: A History of the Oblates* (Victoria: Sono Nis, 1981). The thesis of Elizabeth Furniss, *Victims of Benevolence: The Dark Legacy of the Williams Lake Residential School* (Vancouver: Arsenal Pulp, 1992 and 1995), is clear in its title. In *Colonizing Bodies: Aboriginal Health and Healing in British Columbia, 1900–1950* (Vancouver: UBCP, 1998) Mary Ellen Kelm examines health care, or rather its lack, in residential schools and for Aboriginal people generally; she also discusses traditional healing.

In the early period, the first Euro-Canadians (other than traders) that most Aboriginal people met were Christian missionaries. Missionary biographies include Clarence Bolt, *Thomas Crosby and the Tsimshian: Small Shoes for Feet Too Large* (Vancouver: UBCP, 1992); Brett Christophers, *Positioning the Missionary: John Booth Good and the Confluence of Cultures in Nineteenth Century British Columbia* (Vancouver: UBCP, 1998); and David Mulhall, *Will to Power: The Missionary Career of Father [A.G]. Morice* (Vancouver: UBCP, 1986). Margaret Whitehead edited

*They Call Me Father: Memoirs of Father Nicolas Coccola* (Vancouver: UBCP, 1988); Coccola was a peripatetic Roman Catholic missionary who served both First Nations residents and white settlers. Myra Rutherdale looks at female missionaries in *Women and the White Man's God: Gender and Race in the Canadian Mission Field* (Vancouver: UBCP, 2002). In *The Heavens Are Changing: Nineteenth-Century Protestant Missions and Tsimshian Christianity* (Montreal and Kingston: MQUP, 2003), Susan Neylan focuses on Native responses to Christianization. The churches themselves have not been a popular subject, but there are two recent exceptions: Robert K. Burkinshaw, in *Pilgrims in Lotus Land: Conservative Protestantism in British Columbia, 1917–1981* (Montreal and Kingston: MQUP, 1995), focuses on the evangelical tradition, while Vincent J. McNally examines aspects of Roman Catholic history in *The Lord's Distant Vineyard: A History of the Oblates and the Catholic Community in British Columbia* (Edmonton: University of Alberta Press, 2000).

Despite the liveliness of British Columbia politics, there are no comprehensive overviews. Martin Robin's two volumes, *The Rush for Spoils: The Company Province, 1871–1933* and *Pillars of Profit: The Company Province* (Toronto: M&S, 1972 and 1973) have a plausible thesis, but sloppiness detracts from what could have been a major contribution to provincial historiography. Most early premiers have entries in the *Dictionary of Canadian Biography*, and several politicians who were prominent in the 1930s have been the subjects of biographies: *Duff Pattullo of British Columbia* (Toronto: UTP, 1991) by Robin Fisher, *Mayor Gerry: The Remarkable Gerald Grattan McGeer* (Vancouver: D&M, 1986) by David Ricardo Williams, and *The Compassionate Rebel: E.E. Winch and His Times* (Vancouver: Boag Foundation, 1960; repr. Vancouver: J.J. Douglas, 1977) by Dorothy Steeves. Otherwise, the political history of the province before the 1950s has been almost untouched. W.A.C. Bennett (premier 1952–72) has attracted several biographers; the best is David Mitchell, *W.A.C.: Bennett and the Rise of British Columbia* (Vancouver: D&M, 1983).

The expansion of university political science departments, beginning in the 1960s, was eventually reflected in several interpretive studies. J. Terence Morley et al., *The Reins of Power: Governing British Columbia* (Vancouver: D&M, 1983) is a collection focusing on the short-lived NDP government of the early 1970s and the first years of its Social Credit successor. The grassroots supporters of both parties are the subjects of Donald E. Blake, R.K. Carty, and Lynda Erickson, *Grassroots Politicians: Party Activists in British Columbia* (Vancouver: UBCP, 1991). In *2 Political Worlds: Parties and Voting in British Columbia* (Vancouver: UBCP, 1985) Blake examines a survey of voters in the 1979 federal and provincial elections, but also broadly sketches the province's political history. Most of the essays in R.K. Carty, *Politics, Policy, and Government in British Columbia* (Vancouver: UBCP, 1996) focus on contemporary issues, but many also provide some background. Philip Resnick, in *The Politics of Resentment: British Columbia Regionalism and Canadian Unity* (Vancouver: UBCP, 2000), sets the discussion of the 1997 BC Unity Panel in historical context.

Despite the importance of labour relations, the historiography is spotty. No book has yet replaced Paul Phillips, *No Power Greater: A Century of Labour in British Columbia* (Vancouver: B.C. Federation of Labour, 1967) as a broad survey. The essays in *Workers, Capital and the State in British Columbia: Selected Papers*, ed. Rennie Warburton and David Coburn (Vancouver: UBCP, 1988), include both case studies and some broader works. Mark Leier's *Where the Fraser River Flows: The Industrial Workers of the World in British Columbia* (Vancouver: New Star, 1990) will be an important source for any new overview, as will his *Red Flags & Red Tape: The Making of a Labour Bureaucracy* (Toronto: UTP, 1995), an analysis of the Vancouver Trades and Labour Council from its founding in 1889 to 1913.

Maps, documentary art, and photographs have been essential to this book. Readers will find in our captions and notes many references to important works that present and discuss these forms of historical evidence. Three very important resources merit special mention. Derek Hayes' *Historical Atlas of British Columbia and the Pacific Northwest* (Delta, BC: Cavendish Books, 1999) reprints and provides context for more than 300 maps drawn between the late sixteenth and late nineteenth centuries. John Frazier Henry introduces the major artists of Russian, British, French, Spanish, and American expeditions in *Early Maritime Artists of the Northwest Pacific Coast, 1741–1841* (Seattle: University of Washington Press, 1984). Finally, all who work with photo sources are indebted to the painstaking research on individual photographers done by David Mattison and presented both in his book *Camera Workers: The British Columbia Photographers Directory, 1858–1900* (Victoria: Camera Workers Press, 1985) and on his remarkable website: <http://collection.nlc-bnc.ca/100/200/300/david_mattison/camera_workers/2001-09/>

British Columbia has a rich historiography, but it is by no means complete. We hope that this volume will whet readers' appetites for further knowledge of the province's complex history; perhaps it will even encourage some of them to help fill in the picture.

# INDEX